Astronomical observations :
520 AST

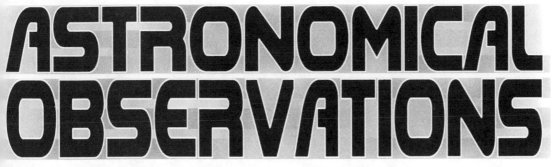

ASTRONOMICAL OBSERVATIONS

ASTRONOMY AND THE STUDY OF DEEP SPACE

AN EXPLORER'S GUIDE TO THE UNIVERSE

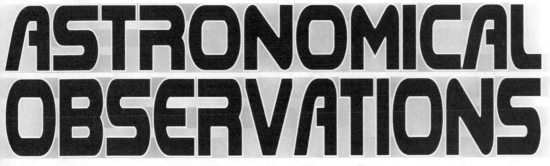

ASTRONOMICAL OBSERVATIONS

ASTRONOMY AND THE STUDY OF DEEP SPACE

EDITED BY ERIK GREGERSEN, ASSOCIATE EDITOR, ASTRONOMY AND SPACE EXPLORATION

Britannica®
Educational Publishing

IN ASSOCIATION WITH

ROSEN
EDUCATIONAL SERVICES

Published in 2010 by Britannica Educational Publishing
(a trademark of Encyclopædia Britannica, Inc.)
in association with Rosen Educational Services, LLC
29 East 21st Street, New York, NY 10010.

Distributed exclusively by Rosen Educational Services.
For a listing of additional Britannica Educational Publishing titles, call toll free (800) 237-9932.

First Edition

Britannica Educational Publishing
Michael I. Levy: Executive Editor
Marilyn L. Barton: Senior Coordinator, Production Control
Steven Bosco: Director, Editorial Technologies
Lisa S. Braucher: Senior Producer and Data Editor
Yvette Charboneau: Senior Copy Editor
Kathy Nakamura: Manager, Media Acquisition
Erik Gregersen: Associate Editor, Astronomy and Space Exploration

Rosen Educational Services
Jeanne Nagle: Senior Editor
Nelson Sá: Art Director
Matthew Cauli: Designer
Introduction by Stephanie Watson

Library of Congress Cataloging-in-Publication Data

Astronomical observations: astronomy and the study of deep space / edited by Erik
Gregersen.—1st ed.
      p. cm.—(An explorer's guide to the universe)
"In association with Britannica Educational Publishing, Rosen Educational Services."
Includes bibliographical references and index.
ISBN 978-1-61530-025-9 (lib. bdg.: alk. paper)
1. Astronomy—Popular works. 2. Astronomical instruments—Popular works.
3. Astronomy—Observations—Popular works. I. Gregersen, Erik.
QB44.3.A88 2010
520—dc22

                                                                          2009036102

Manufactured in the United States of America

On the cover: Nestled high on a dormant volcano in Hawaii, the Keck I observatory, one of
the most advanced telescopes in the world, prepares to scan the night skies. *Joe McNally/
Getty Images*

CONTENTS

28

35

42

106

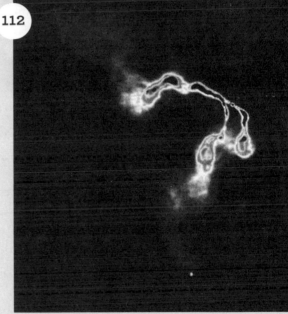

112

124

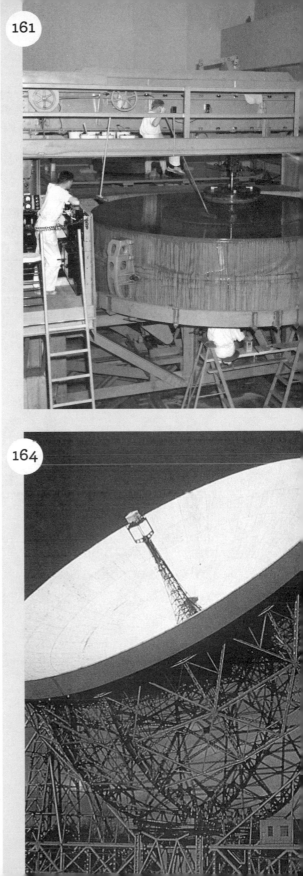

161

164

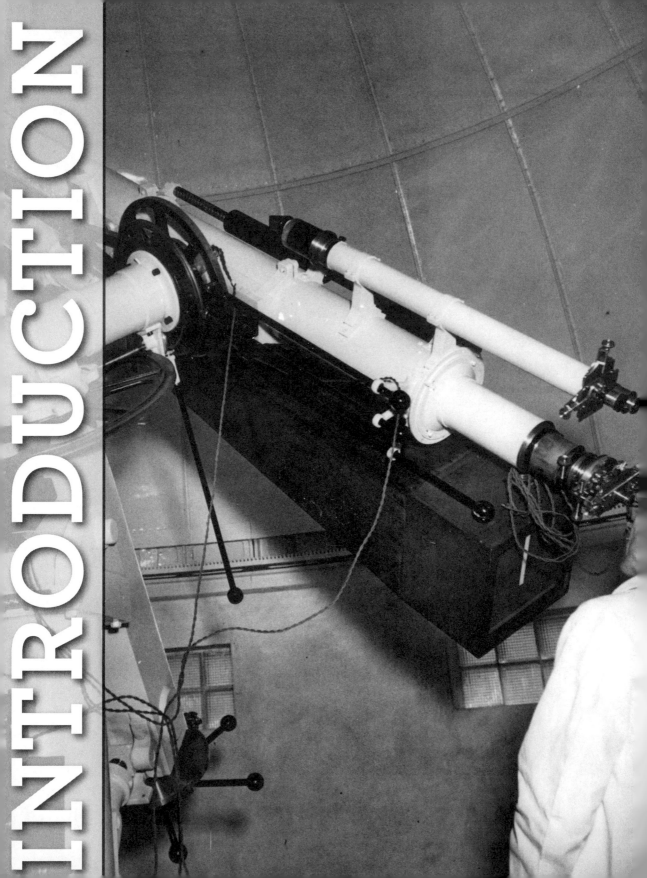

INTRODUCTION

Everyone at one time or another has looked up at the night sky and wondered about the stars, planets, and other celestial bodies that lie beyond the Earth's atmosphere. One doesn't have to be a professional astronomer to marvel at the enormity and complexity of the universe. All that's needed is the power of observation, perhaps aided by some type of magnification device such as a telescope, and a willingness to learn about the heavens.

This book, which details the tools and purposes of astronomy, could prove useful as well. *Astronomical Observations* chronicles the many accomplishments that have moved the field of astronomy forward—from the earliest theories about planetary motion to the development of modern telescopes. In its pages readers will also meet the people whose innovations made it possible to see farther and deeper into the skies, as well as those who meticulously charted the stars, planets, and constellations they found there.

Everyday citizens who lived thousands of years ago similarly gazed in wonder at that same night sky as people today, also trying to discern their place in the universe. To ancient peoples, the sky was a mystical place ruled by deities like the Egyptian Sun god Ra, who was thought to ride his great boat across the heavens every day. They believed the skies were responsible for events on Earth, and they looked to the heavens to predict the future. Today's astrological horoscopes are direct descendants of this practice.

Without modern telescopic tools for visualizing the farthest reaches of space, the ancient astronomers' understanding of the universe was based primarily on direct observation and calculation. They meticulously watched and recorded what they saw in the skies, and their observations were often surprisingly sophisticated. After charting the movements of the stars over time, the Egyptians eventually learned that the star Sirius's rise in the eastern sky coincided with the Nile River's annual floods. The Egyptians were also the first to develop a solar calendar, more than 4,000 years ago, that looked very similar to what people use today.

Still, people were unable to visualize what lies beyond the sky surrounding Earth. At that time, they understandably assumed that the only world they knew sat at the centre of the universe, and that the Sun and all of the planets revolved around it. Early astronomers devised crude celestial spheres and globes to document their observations. However, later astronomical research led to the realization that the Earth actually occupies an infinitesimally small

The advent of telescopes brought astronomical observations into the modern age. Observing the night skies, however, is an ancient practice. Central Press/Hulton Archive/Getty Images

part of an almost incomprehensibly huge universe. There are one hundred billion stars in the Milky Way Galaxy alone.

Mapping the sky is not the only goal of astronomical discovery. Measuring how far planets and stars are from one another is another important application of astronomy. Distances in space can be difficult to determine when dealing with such enormous numbers—trillions of miles, billions of years, and millions of billions of stars. Calculations are even more difficult when you consider that the universe has been continually expanding since the big bang nearly 14 billion years ago. Because the universe is expanding, the light that reaches Earth from distant galaxies will have taken billions of years to get here. That is why looking deep into space through a powerful telescope is somewhat like looking into a time machine. Astronomers are seeing the universe not as it is today, but rather as it looked billions of years ago.

The oldest means of determining astronomical distances involves triangulation, based on Earth's diameter. Triangulation is still used by modern astronomers when gauging outer solar system distances, but the measurement of closer objects has benefited greatly from technological advances. These days it is also possible to measure distances of heavenly objects using radar reflection and laser ranging.

As technology has evolved, so has the study of deep space. In the 17th century, astronomy entered a new era with the introduction of the telescope, which magnified the skies and brought the universe into much sharper focus. The invention was credited to a Dutch spectacle maker named Hans Lippershey (1570–1619). According to one story, the origins of this highly influential tool were surprisingly humble. Two children in Lippershey's shop were reportedly playing with lenses, when they put two lenses together. As the children peered through the double lenses, they noticed that a weathervane on a distant church appeared much closer. Lippershey supposedly seized on the concept and began making telescopes.

The basic telescope design has been improved many times over the years. Lens diameters grew in size, increasing the distance astronomers could see out into space. Lens quality also greatly improved, providing clearer images. Chester Moor Hall (1703–1771) and John Dolland (1706–1761) invented the achromatic refracting telescope to remove the colour distortions that once blurred the edges of telescopic images (chromatic aberrations). Scottish optician James Short (1710–1768) perfected the use of parabolic mirror systems to provide greater accuracy in reflecting telescopes.

Little by little, with ever more sophisticated viewing systems, astronomers broadened their view and understanding of the universe. In the 1660s, Italian optician and astronomer Giuseppe Campani (1635–1715) capitalized on his invention, the lens-grinding lathe, to create stronger lenses. Combining these improved

Located high atop Mt. Hamilton in San Jose, Calif., the Lick Observatory currently serves as a multicampus research unit of the University of California. Shutterstock.com

optics with a refined telescope tube of his own devising, Campani was able to observe Jupiter's moons and Saturn's rings. More than 200 years later an American astronomer, Asaph Hall (1829–1907), discovered and calculated the diameters of the Martian moons. Nineteenth-century German astronomer Karl Ludwig Harding (1765–1834) is credited with discovering three comets and cataloging more than 120,000 stars.

Observatories were built to house each new generation of telescope. Just as

one groundbreaking observatory was built, a larger and more sophisticated one would come along to supersede it. In the 1890s, the Lick Observatory in California held the world's largest telescope. Through its 91-cm (36-inch) lens, astronomers were able to view several of Jupiter's moons. The Lick telescope is dwarfed by modern observatories such as Mauna Kea in Hawaii. The two Keck telescopes housed at the observatory each measure 10 metres (33 feet) in diameter and are comprised of 36 individual pieces of glass that work in unison, continually adjusting to stay aligned with gravity.

Today, computer-controlled guidance systems enable telescopes to track objects across the sky. Cameras capture celestial images, and computers record data for analysis. Yet even the most sophisticated telescopes face one great challenge—revealing a complete picture of the skies. Earth's atmosphere blocks certain wavelengths of radiation (such as ultraviolet and X-rays) before they can reach the ground. Because many celestial bodies emit different wavelengths of radiation, this atmospheric blockade vastly limits astronomers' ability to view the skies. A modern solution to this problem has been to bypass the Earth's atmosphere by sending telescopes into space.

Endeavours to observe planets and other objects directly from space began in earnest in the early 1960s, when the United States and the Soviet Union, in an effort to further their fledgling space programs and learn more about the solar system, launched a multitude of unmanned deep-space probes. These probes carried television cameras, detectors, and an assortment of other instruments, sending back scientific data and close-up pictures that would have been harder, or impossible, to attain from Earth-bound observation.

Telescopic devices designed specifically to be launched into orbit, such as the Hubble Space Telescope (1990), have given astronomers an unprecedented view of the universe. During its mission, the Hubble has enabled scientists to catch a glimpse of cosmic collisions, watch as stars are born and die, and learn more about the infinite darkness and mysteries of black holes. Another space mission, the NASA Wilkinson Microwave Anisotropy Probe (WMAP), has traveled 1.5 million kilometres (900,000 miles) from Earth to measure the properties of microwave radiation released nearly 13.7 billion years ago. The aim of WMAP is to reveal a picture of the universe as it appeared shortly after its birth.

Beyond observation and the revelation of galactic origins, astronomy is also a potent means by which humans may discover whether or not they are the only intelligent life source in the universe. Astrobiology involves the search for habitable worlds. Using astronomical methods and tools, scientists look for biologic and geologic factors, such as sources or remnants of water, which might indicate the presence of life on distant planets. Astronomers anticipate that single-cell organisms are the most likely life forms to be revealed by such studies, but they remain open to the discovery

The Huygens space probe (artist's conception, below) was able to capture fascinating images of Titan's surface (above) as it descended onto Saturn's largest moon in 2005. ESA/NASA/ JPL/University of Arizona, (above) ESA (below)

Aerial View of Titan Around the Huygens Landing Site from 10 km Altitude

South West North East South

of sentient "alien" beings with whom humans can communicate and interact.

Astronomers have learned a tremendous amount about the universe, and they continue to learn more every day. They are developing new instruments here on Earth and sending more advanced probes out into space. Yet there is still so much of the universe that has not been explored.

Beyond revealing what objects adorn the universe at present, astronomical observations have the power to help scientists predict the future. People generally want to know not only where they came from, but where they are going. What will the distant future hold for planet Earth and its solar system? Astronomers know that nearly all stars ultimately meet the same fate. They become white dwarfs, cooling and growing dimmer over billions of years until they eventually vanish away into nothingness. In a few billion years, the Sun will become a white dwarf,

too. Its outer layers will gradually peel away, stripping away its warmth until Earth and the other planets of the solar system are left in utter darkness and unimaginable cold.

And what about the universe as a whole? One of the biggest questions for astronomers is whether it will continue to expand indefinitely or will eventually retreat back from where it came. If the universe is above a certain density, gravity will eventually force it to stop expanding. On the other hand, if the universe's density is below a certain level, it will expand forever. Astronomical observations have revealed that the density of the universe is poised between the two such that it will expand without collapsing.

As it has in the past, astronomy should provide some tantalizing clues as to what lies ahead, as well as what lies beyond.

CHAPTER 1

An Overview

Astronomy is the science that encompasses the study of all extraterrestrial objects and phenomena. Until the invention of the telescope and the discovery of the laws of motion and gravity in the 17th century, astronomy was primarily concerned with noting and predicting the positions of the Sun, Moon, and planets, originally for calendrical and astrological purposes and later for navigational uses and scientific interest. The catalog of objects now studied is much broader and includes, in order of increasing distance, the solar system, the stars that make up the Milky Way Galaxy, and other, more distant galaxies. With the advent of scientific space probes, Earth has also come to be studied as one of the planets, though its more detailed investigation remains the domain of the geologic sciences.

THE SCOPE OF ASTRONOMY

Since the late 19th century astronomy has expanded to include astrophysics, the application of physical and chemical knowledge to an understanding of the nature of celestial objects and the physical processes that control their formation, evolution, and emission of radiation. In addition, the gases and dust particles around and between the stars have become the subjects of much research. Study of the nuclear reactions that provide the energy radiated by stars has shown how the diversity of atoms found in nature can be derived

Hubble Space Telescope, photographed by the space shuttle Discovery. NASA

Almost all measurements must be performed at great distances from the objects of interest, with no control over such quantities as their temperature, pressure, or chemical composition. There are a few exceptions to this limitation—namely, meteorites, rock and soil samples brought back from the Moon, samples of comet dust returned by robotic spacecraft, and interplanetary dust particles collected in or above the stratosphere. These can be examined with laboratory techniques to provide information that cannot be obtained in any other way. In the future, space missions may return surface materials from Mars, asteroids, or other objects, but much of astronomy appears otherwise confined to Earth-based observations augmented by observations from orbiting satellites and long-range space probes and supplemented by theory.

MAPPING THE SKY

One of the first endeavours of astronomers was to map what they saw in the heavens, to make a cartographic representation of the stars, galaxies, or surfaces of the planets and the Moon. Modern maps of this kind are based on a coordinate system analogous to geographic latitude and longitude. In most cases, modern maps are compiled from

from a universe that, following the first few minutes of its existence, consisted only of hydrogen, helium, and a trace of lithium. Concerned with phenomena on the largest scale is cosmology, the study of the evolution of the universe. Astrophysics has transformed cosmology from a purely speculative activity to a modern science capable of predictions that can be tested.

Its great advances notwithstanding, astronomy is still subject to a major constraint: it is inherently an observational rather than an experimental science.

photographic observations made either with Earth-based equipment or with instruments carried aboard spacecraft.

NATURE AND SIGNIFICANCE

Brighter stars and star groupings are easily recognized by a practiced observer. The much more numerous fainter celestial bodies can be located and identified only with the help of astronomical maps, catalogs, and in some cases almanacs.

The first astronomical charts, globes, and drawings, often decorated with fantastic figures, depicted the constellations, recognizable groupings of bright stars known by imaginatively chosen names that have been for many centuries both a delight to man and a dependable aid to navigation. Several royal Egyptian tombs of the 2nd millennium BCE include paintings of constellation figures, but these cannot be considered accurate maps. Classical Greek astronomers used maps and globes; unfortunately, no examples survive. Numerous small metal celestial globes from Islamic makers of the 11th century onward remain. The first printed planispheres (representations of the celestial sphere on a flat surface) were produced in 1515, and printed celestial globes appeared at about the same time.

Telescopic astronomy began in 1609, and by the end of the 17th century the telescope was applied in mapping the stars. In the latter part of the 19th century, photography gave a powerful impetus to precise chart making, culminating in the 1950s in the publication of *National Geographic Society–Palomar Observatory Sky Survey*, a portrayal of the part of the sky visible from Palomar Observatory in California.

Many modern maps used by amateur and professional observers of the sky show stars, dark nebulas of obscuring dust, and bright nebulas (masses of tenuous, glowing matter). Specialized maps show sources of radio radiation, sources of infrared radiation, and quasi-stellar objects having very large redshifts (the spectral lines are displaced toward longer wavelengths) and very small images. Astronomers of the 20th century have divided the entire sky into 88 areas, or constellations; this international system codifies the naming of stars

THE RUDOLPHINE TABLES

The Rudolphine Tables (Latin: Tabulae Rudolphinae) were planetary tables and a star catalog published in 1627 by Johannes Kepler, based principally on the observations of fellow astronomer Tycho Brahe. The best of the pretelescopic catalogs, it is accurate to a few minutes of arc and contains positions for 1,005 stars (increased by Kepler from Tycho's 777), as well as tables and directions for locating the planets. It is the first catalog to include corrective factors for atmospheric refraction and logarithmic tables. It was named for Rudolf II, Holy Roman emperor and patron of Kepler and Tycho.

and star patterns that began in prehistoric times. Originally only the brightest stars and most conspicuous patterns were given names, probably based on the actual appearance of the configurations. Beginning in the 16th century, navigators and astronomers have progressively filled in all the areas left undesignated by the ancients.

THE CELESTIAL SPHERE

To any observer, ancient or modern, the night sky appears as a hemisphere resting on the horizon. Consequently, the simplest descriptions of the star patterns and of the motions of heavenly bodies are those presented on the surface of a sphere.

The daily eastward rotation of Earth on its axis produces an apparent diurnal westward rotation of the starry sphere. Thus, the stars seem to rotate about a northern or southern celestial pole, the projection into space of Earth's own poles. Equidistant from the two poles is the celestial equator; this great circle is the projection into space of Earth's Equator.

Part of the sky adjacent to a celestial pole is always visible, and an equal area about the opposite pole is always invisible below the horizon. The rest of the celestial sphere appears to rise and set each day. For any other latitude, the particular part of sky visible or invisible will be different. An observer situated at Earth's North Pole could observe only the stars of the northern celestial hemisphere. An observer at the Equator, however, would be able to see the entire celestial sphere as the daily motion of Earth carried him around.

In addition to their apparent daily motion around Earth, the Sun, Moon, and planets of the solar system have their own motions with respect to the starry sphere. Since the Sun's brilliance obscures the background stars from view, it took many centuries before observers discovered the precise path of the Sun through the constellations that are now called the signs of the zodiac. The great circle of the zodiac traced out by the Sun on its annual circuit is the ecliptic (so called because eclipses can occur when the Moon crosses it).

As viewed from space, Earth slowly revolves about the Sun in a fixed plane, the ecliptic plane. A line perpendicular to this plane defines the ecliptic pole, and it makes no difference whether this line is projected into space from Earth or from the Sun. All that is important is the direction because the sky is so far away that the ecliptic pole must fall on a unique point on the celestial sphere.

The principal planets in the solar system revolve about the Sun in nearly the same plane as Earth's orbit, and their movements are therefore projected onto the celestial sphere nearly, but seldom exactly, on the ecliptic. The Moon's orbit is tilted by about five degrees from this plane, and hence its position in the sky deviates from the ecliptic more than those of the other planets.

Because the blinding sunlight blocks some stars from view, the particular constellations that can be seen depend on the position of Earth in its orbit—i.e., on the apparent place of the Sun. The stars visible at midnight will shift westward by about one degree each successive midnight as the Sun progresses in its apparent eastward motion. Stars visible at midnight in September will be concealed by the dazzling noontime Sun 180 days later in March.

Why the ecliptic and celestial equator meet at an angle of 23° 26.6' is an unexplained mystery originating in Earth's past. The angle gradually varies by small amounts as a result of Moon- and planet-caused gravitational perturbations on Earth. The ecliptic plane is comparatively stable, but the equatorial plane is continually shifting as Earth's axis of rotation changes its direction in space. The successive positions of the celestial poles trace out large circles on the sky within a period of about 26,000 years. This phenomenon, known as precession of the equinoxes, causes a series of different stars to become pole stars in turn. Polaris, the present pole star, will come nearest to the north celestial pole around the year 2100 CE. At the time the pyramids were built, Thuban in the constellation Draco served as the pole star, and in about 12,000 years the first-magnitude star Vega will be near the north celestial pole. Precession also makes the coordinate systems on precise star maps applicable only for a specific epoch.

CELESTIAL COORDINATE SYSTEMS

On Earth, locations are designated by latitude and longitude. Yet there are several coordinate systems that work in much the same way as the longitude-latitude system.

THE HORIZON SYSTEM

The simple altazimuth system, which depends on a particular place, specifies positions by altitude (the angular elevation from the horizon plane) and azimuth (the angle clockwise around the horizon, usually starting from the north). Lines of equal altitude around the sky are called almucantars. The horizon system is fundamental in navigation, as well as in terrestrial surveying. For mapping the stars, however, coordinates fixed with respect to the celestial sphere itself (such as the ecliptic or equatorial systems) are far more suitable.

THE ECLIPTIC SYSTEM

Celestial longitude and latitude are defined with respect to the ecliptic and ecliptic poles. Celestial longitude is measured eastward from the ascending intersection of the ecliptic with the equator, a position known as the "first point of Aries," and the place of the Sun at the time of the vernal equinox around March 21. The first point of Aries is symbolized by the ram's horns (Υ).

Unlike the celestial equator, the ecliptic is fixed among the stars. However, the ecliptic longitude of a given star increases by 1.396° per century owing to the precessional movement of the equator—similar to the precessional movement of a child's top—which shifts the first point of Aries.

The first 30 degrees along the ecliptic is nominally designated as the sign Aries, although this part of the ecliptic has now moved forward into the constellation Pisces. Ecliptic coordinates predominated in Western astronomy until the Renaissance. (In contrast, Chinese astronomers always used an equatorial system.) With the advent of national nautical almanacs, the equatorial system, which is better suited to observation and navigation, gained ascendancy.

THE EQUATORIAL SYSTEM

Based on the celestial equator and poles, the equatorial coordinates, right ascension and declination, are directly analogous to terrestrial longitude and latitude. Right ascension, measured eastward from the first point of Aries, is customarily divided into 24 hours rather than 360°, thus emphasizing the clocklike behaviour of the sphere. Precise equatorial positions must be specified for a particular year, since the precessional motion continually changes the measured coordinates.

THE GALACTIC SYSTEM

In the galactic system the two coordinates, galactic latitude and longitude, constitute a useful means of locating the relative positions and motions of components of the Milky Way. Galactic latitude (denoted by the symbol b) is measured in degrees north or south of the galaxy's fundamental plane of symmetry. This plane is defined by the galactic equator, the great circle in the sky best fitting the plane of the Milky Way, as determined by a combination of optical and radio measurements. The galactic equator is inclined at about 62°36' to the celestial equator, which is the projection of Earth's Equator into the sky.

Galactic longitude (denoted by the symbol l) is measured in degrees eastward of an imaginary line running across the plane of the galaxy and connecting Earth (assumed to be on that plane) with a point near the galactic centre in the constellation Sagittarius. Before 1958, galactic longitude was measured from an arbitrarily chosen point, an intersection of the galactic and celestial equators in the constellation Aquila. The development of radio astronomy and rediscussion of optical results led to a more accurate determination of the position of the galactic centre and its adoption in 1958 as the new zero point of longitude. (Subsequent observations have identified the radio source Sagittarius A*, which is offset from the longitude zero point, as the true centre of the Milky Way Galaxy.)

At the same time, the positions of the galactic poles and equator were redefined, with a change of less than 2° in the positions of the poles. The north galactic pole is now considered to be in the constellation Coma Berenices, at +90° galactic latitude, and with equatorial (Earth-based) coordinates of 12 hours 49 minutes right ascension, 27°24' north declination.

THE CONSTELLATIONS AND OTHER SKY DIVISIONS

Recognition of the constellations can be traced to early civilization. The oldest astronomical cuneiform texts, from the second half of the second millennium BCE, record the Sumerian names of the constellations still known as the lion, the bull, and the scorpion. Drawings of these astronomical animals appear on Babylonian boundary stones of the same period, and the earlier occurrence of these motifs on prehistoric seals, Sumerian vases, and gaming boards suggests that they may have originated as early as 4000 BCE. In China a handful of configurations show similarity to those of the West, including the scorpion, lion, hunter (Orion), and northern dipper, suggesting the possibility of a very old common tradition for a few groups, but, otherwise, almost complete independence.

Greek literature reflects the impact of the stars on the life of an agricultural and seafaring people. Homer (c. 9th century BCE) records several constellations by the names used today, and the first mention of circumpolar stars is in the *Odyssey*:

> *Odysseus is*
> *Gazing with fixed eye on the*
> *Pleiades,*
> *Boötes setting late and the*
> *Great Bear,*
> *By others called the Wain, which*
> *wheeling round,*
> *Looks ever toward Orion and alone*

> *Dips not into the waters of*
> *the deep.*
> —*Odyssey*, V

In England the Great Bear (Ursa Major), also known as the Big Dipper, was still called Charles's Wain (or Wagon) in Shakespeare's day:

> *An't be not four by*
> *The day I'll be hanged; Charles'*
> *Wain is over*
> *The new chimney and yet our*
> *horse not pack'd.*
> —*King Henry IV*, Part I, Act ii,
> Scene 1

This form derives from Charlemagne, and according to *The Oxford English Dictionary*, apparently from a verbal association of the name of the bright nearby Arcturus with Arturus, or Arthur, and the legendary association of Arthur and Charlemagne.

The earliest systematic account of the constellations is contained in the *Phaenomena* of Aratus, a poet of the 3rd century BCE, who described 43 constellations and named five individual stars. Cicero recorded that

> *The first Hellenic globe of the sky*
> *was made by Thales of Miletus,*
> *having fallen into a ditch or well*
> *while star-gazing. Afterwards*
> *Eudoxos of Cnidus traced on its*
> *surface the stars that appear in*
> *the sky; and . . . many years after,*

borrowing from Eudoxos this beautiful design and representation, Aratos had illustrated it in his verses, not by any science of astronomy, but by the ornament of poetical description.
—*De republica,* I, 14

By far the most important list of stars and constellations still extant from antiquity appears in the *Almagest* of Ptolemy (flourished 2nd century CE). It contains ecliptic coordinates and magnitudes (measures of brightness) for 1,022 stars, grouped into 48 constellations. Numerous writers have stated that Ptolemy simply borrowed his material from a now-lost catalog of Hipparchus compiled in 129 BCE. A critical analysis of the Hipparchian fragments still extant, including his commentary on the *Phaenomena* of Aratus, indicates that (1) the catalog of Hipparchus did not include more than 850 stars and (2) Ptolemy most likely obtained new coordinates for even those 850 stars. The evidence suggests that Ptolemy, who for

Youngsters investigate the granite constellation sphere while touring the Kennedy Space Center Visitor Complex in Florida. Constellations identified as early as 450 BCE still serve as a map of the sky today. Chip Somodevilla/Getty Images

more than a century has been considered a mere compilator, should be placed among the first-rank astronomical observers of all ages.

Nevertheless, Ptolemy's star list presents a curious puzzle. The southernmost heavens, invisible at the latitude of Alexandria, naturally went unobserved. On one side of the sky near this southern horizon, he tabulated the bright stars of the Southern Cross (although not as a separate constellation) and of Centaurus, but on the opposite side a large area including the first-magnitude star Achernar had been left unrecorded. Because of precession, before 2000 BCE this region would have been invisible from Mesopotamia. Perhaps neither Hipparchus nor Ptolemy considered that part of the heavens unnamed by their ancient predecessors. Ptolemy's catalog of 1,022 stars remained authoritative until the Renaissance.

Ptolemy divided his stars into six brightness, or magnitude, classes. He listed 15 bright stars of the first magnitude but comparatively few of the faint, much more numerous but barely visible sixth magnitude at the other limit of his list. Aṣ-Ṣūfī, a 10th-century Islamic astronomer, carried out the principal revision made to these magnitudes during the Middle Ages. Ulūgh Beg, grandson of the Mongol conqueror Tamerlane, is the only known Oriental astronomer to reobserve the positions of Ptolemy's stars. His catalog, put together in 1420–37, was not printed until 1665, by which time it had already been surpassed by European observations.

CONSTELLATIONS OF THE ZODIAC

The Mesopotamian arrangement of constellations has survived to the present day because it became the basis of a numerical reference scheme—the ecliptic, or zodiacal, system. This occurred around 450 BCE, when the ecliptic was clearly recognized and divided into 12 equal signs of the zodiac. Most modern scholars take the zodiac as a Babylonian invention; the oldest record of the zodiacal signs as such is a cuneiform horoscope from 419 BCE. However, as Greek sources attribute the discovery of the ecliptic to Oenopides in the latter part of the 5th century BCE, a parallel development in both Greece and Babylon should not be excluded.

At the time the zodiac was established, it was probably necessary to invent at least one new constellation, Libra. Centuries later Ptolemy's *Almagest* still described the stars of Libra with respect to the ancient figure of the scorpion.

NEW CONSTELLATIONS: 16TH–20TH CENTURIES

Star charts contained only the 48 constellations tabulated by Ptolemy until the end of the 16th century. Then Pieter Dircksz Keyser, a navigator who joined the first Dutch expedition to the East Indies in 1595, added 12 new constellations in the southern skies, named in part after exotic birds such as the toucan, peacock, and phoenix.

The southern constellations were introduced in 1601 on a celestial globe by

J. Hondius and, in 1603, on the globe of Willem Blaeu and a single plate in the *Uranometria* of Johann Bayer. The *Uranometria*, the first serious star atlas, has a plate for each of the 48 traditional figures. Its scientific integrity rested on Tycho Brahe's then newly determined stellar positions and magnitudes.

In his *Uranographia* of 1687, the German astronomer Johannes Hevelius devised seven new constellations visible from mid-northern latitudes that are still accepted, including Sextans (the sextant), named for one of his own astronomical instruments. Fourteen additional southern constellations were formed by Nicolas Louis de Lacaille after his visit to the Cape of Good Hope in 1750. They appeared in the *Memoires* of the Académie Royale des Sciences for 1752 (published in 1756). All other attempts to invent constellations have failed to win acceptance.

The classic atlases of Bayer and Hevelius, as well as John Flamsteed's *Atlas Coelestis* (1729), showed only the brighter naked-eye stars. Johann Elert Bode's *Uranographia* of 1801 was the first reasonably complete depiction of the stars visible to the unaided eye. It included an early use of constellation boundaries, a concept accepted and refined by 19th-century cartographers. Friedrich W.A. Argelander's *Uranometria Nova* (1843) and Benjamin A. Gould's *Uranometria Argentina* (1877–79) standardized the list of constellations as they are known today. They divided Ptolemy's largest constellation, Argo Navis (the ship), into four parts: Vela (the sail), Pyxis (the compass), Puppis (the stern), and Carina (the keel).

The definitive list of 88 constellations was established in 1930 under the authority of the International Astronomical Union. Its rectilinear constellation boundaries preserve the traditional arrangements of the naked-eye stars. The smallest of the constellations, Equuleus ("the Little Horse") and Crux ("the [Southern] Cross"), nestle against constellations that are more than 10 times larger, Pegasus and Centaurus, respectively. The standard boundaries define an unambiguous constellation for each star. (See Appendix C: Constellations on page 196.)

THE DECANS AND LUNAR MANSIONS

Two other astronomical reference systems developed independently in early antiquity, the Egyptian decans and the lunar mansions. The decans are 36 star configurations circling the sky somewhat to the south of the ecliptic. They make their appearance in drawings and texts inside coffin lids of the 10th dynasty (around 2100 BCE) and are shown on the tomb ceilings of Seti I (1318–04 BCE) and of some of the Rameses in Thebes. The decans appear to have provided the basis for the division of the day into 24 hours.

Besides representing star configurations as decans, the Egyptians marked out about 25 constellations, such as crocodile, hippopotamus, lion, and a falcon-headed god. Their constellations can be divided

PLANETARIUMS

The planetarium is a theatre devoted to popular education and entertainment in astronomy and related fields, especially space science, and traditionally constructed with a hemispheric domed ceiling that is used as a screen onto which images of stars, planets, and other celestial objects are projected. The term planetarium *may also refer to an institution in which such a theatre functions as the principal teaching arrangement or to the specialized projector employed. Planetarium is applied in yet another sense to describe computer software or Internet sites that allow the user to simulate views of the night sky and various celestial phenomena.*

Permanent planetarium installations vary greatly. Those within a large supporting institution may coexist with extensive exhibit space and museum collections and have sizable professional and support staffs. Their projection theatres can be 25 metres (82 feet) or more in diameter and have capacities in excess of 600 persons. On the other hand, community or local college planetariums may accommodate only small groups of people. In a separate class are portable planetariums comprising inflatable domes and lightweight projectors that can be set up at schools and can hold several dozen students at a time.

At the heart of every planetarium theatre is the projection instrument. The first modern electromechanical planetarium projector was built by the German optical firm Carl Zeiss in 1923 for the new Deutsches Museum in Munich. Current descendants of these instruments are technically complex, computer-controlled combinations of lamps, lenses, fibre optics, and motor drives designed to place the planets, Sun, and Moon in their correct locations among the stars for thousands of years past and future and to reproduce their motions through the sky, typically as seen from a selected latitude on Earth. The instruments can also add such details as horizon scenes, the Milky Way, nebulae, comets, meteors, and various reference lines and scales used for teaching descriptive astronomy and celestial navigation.

Increasingly, institution-based planetariums are complementing or replacing electromechanical projectors with other technologies, including all-digital projector systems equipped with fish-eye lenses and laser projection systems that scan their images on the screen with colour-controlled laser beams. Digital and laser systems allow a seamless blending of sky images, photos, artwork, video, and computer-generated animations. They can also simulate

Today's computer-controlled planetarium projectors, such as the one employed by the American Museum of Natural History's Rose Center in New York City, are light years ahead of the electromechanical units first developed in the 1920s. Chris Hondros/Getty Images

accurate views from any perspective in space and take viewers on virtual flights through and beyond the solar system and into interstellar and intergalactic space. Variations in screen configuration and seating arrangements are also becoming common, ranging from the traditional horizontal domed screen and concentric seating around a central projector to tilted or distorted domes or giant wraparound screens and auditorium-style seating.

In a typical planetarium theatre, programs—commonly called sky shows—are offered to the public on a regular schedule. Show themes may focus on straightforward astronomical and space topics or take up related issues such as the cosmologies of ancient cultures, the extinction of the dinosaurs, or the future of life on Earth. The trend, especially for large audiences and multiple daily shows, is toward total computer automation of the program, combining visual display, cued music and sound effects, and prerecorded narration. Large planetariums with technologically advanced multimedia installations often supplement their science programs with shows featuring pure entertainment based on light, video, and music. In significant ways, in both technology and public program content, the distinction has lessened between planetarium theatres and other giant-screen "total immersion" entertainment centres.

When the Deutsches Museum's planetarium, featuring the Zeiss projector, was publicly unveiled in 1923 (two years before the museum's formal opening), it was described as a "schoolroom under the vault of the heavens." Special educational sky shows for schoolchildren remain an essential part of the program in most installations. The facilities are commonly used for courses or lectures in adult continuing-education programs, as well as astronomy lectures that are given to college students.

into northern and southern groups, but the various representations are so discordant that only three constellations have been identified with certainty: Orion (depicted as Osiris), Sirius (a recumbent cow), and Ursa Major (foreleg or front part of a bull). The most famous Egyptian star map is a 1st-century-BCE stone chart found in the temple at Dandarah and now in the Louvre. The Zodiac of Dandarah illustrates the Egyptian decans and constellations, but since it incorporates the Babylonian zodiac as well, many stars must be doubly represented, and the stone can hardly be considered an accurate mapping of the heavens.

Called *hsiu* in China and *nakṣhatra* in India, the lunar mansions are 28 divisions of the sky presumably selected as approximate "Moon stations" on successive nights. At least four quadrantal *hsiu* that divided the sky into quarters or quadrants were known in China in the 14th century BCE, and 23 are mentioned in the *Yüeh Ling*, which may go back to 850 BCE. In India a complete list of *nakṣhatra* are found in the Atharvaveda, providing evidence that the system was organized before 800 BCE. The system of lunar mansions, however, may have a common origin even earlier in Mesopotamia.

STAR NAMES AND DESIGNATIONS

Of approximately 5,000 stars visible to the unaided eye, only a few hundred have proper names, and less than 60 are commonly used by navigators or astronomers. A few names come almost directly from the Greek, such as Procyon, Canopus, and Antares—the latter derived from "anti-Ares" or "rival of Mars" because of its conspicuous red colour. The stars Sirius ("Scorcher") and Arcturus ("Bear Watcher") are mentioned both by Homer and Hesiod (8th century BCE?). Aratus names those two as well as Procyon ("Forerunner of the Dog"), Stachys ("Ear of Corn"?, now Spica), and Protrugater ("Herald of the Vintage," now Latinized to Vindemiatrix).

The *Al* that begins numerous star names indicates their Arabic origin, *al* being the Arabic definite article "the": Aldebaran ("the Follower"), Algenib ("the Side"), Alhague ("the Serpent Bearer"), and Algol ("the Demon"). A conspicuous exception is Albireo in Cygnus, possibly a corruption of the words *ab ireo* in the first Latin edition of the *Almagest* in 1515. Most star names are in fact Arabic and are frequently derived from translations of the Greek descriptions. The stars of Orion illustrate the various derivations: Rigel, from *rijl al-Jawzah*, "Leg of Orion," Mintaka, the "Belt," and Saiph, the "Sword," all follow the Ptolemaic figure; Betelgeuse, from *yad al-Jawzah*, is an alternative non-Ptolemaic description meaning "hand of Orion"; and Bellatrix, meaning "Female Warrior," is either a free Latin translation of an independent Arabic title, *an-najid*, "the conqueror," or is a modification of an alternative name for Orion himself. Only a handful of names have recent origins—for example, Cor Caroli, the brightest star in Canes Venatici, named in 1725 by Edmond Halley.

Bayer's *Uranometria* of 1603 introduced a system of Greek letters for designating the principal naked-eye stars. In this scheme, the Greek letter is followed by the genitive form of the constellation name, so that alpha (α) of Canes Venatici is Alpha Canum Venaticorum. Bayer's letters and their extension to newer constellations apply to about 1,300 stars. In *Historia Coelestis Britannica* (published posthumously in 1725), Flamsteed numbered the stars within each of 54 constellations consecutively according to right ascension, and the Flamsteed numbers are customarily used for the fainter naked-eye stars such as 61 Cygni.

An astronomer wishing to specify an even fainter star will usually take recourse to a more extensive or more specialized catalog. Such catalogs generally ignore constellations and list all stars by right ascension. Thus, astronomers learn to recognize that BD +38°3238 refers to a star in the *Bonner Durchmusterung* and that HD 172167 designates one in the *Henry Draper Catalogue* of spectral classifications; in this case, both numbers refer to the same bright star, Vega (Alpha Lyrae). Vega can also be specified as GC 25466, from Benjamin Boss's *General Catalogue of 33,342 Stars* (1937), or as ADS 11510, from Robert Grant Aitken's *New General Catalogue of Double Stars* (1932). These are the most widely used numbering systems. For more obscure names, such as Ross 614 or Lalande 21185, most astronomers would have to consult a bibliographical aid to discover the original listing.

Variable stars have their own nomenclature, which takes precedence over designations from more specialized catalogs. Variable stars are named in order of discovery within each constellation by the letter R to Z (providing they do not already have a Greek letter). After Z the double from RR to RZ, SS to SZ, ... is used; after ZZ come the letters AA to AZ, BB to BZ, and so on, the letter J being omitted. After the letters QX, QY, and QZ, the names V335, V336, and so on are assigned. Hence, the first lettered variable in Cygnus is R Cygni, and the list reached V1761 by the end of 1981. The names were assigned by the Soviet authors of the *General Catalogue of Variable Stars* (3rd edition, 1969), with the approval of the Commission on Variable Stars of the International Astronomical Union.

ANCIENT STAR MAPS

Ancient peoples sometimes named individual bright stars rather than groups. Sometimes the name of the group and its brightest star were synonymous—as in the case of the constellation Aquila and the star Altair (Alpha Aquilae), both names meaning "flying eagles"—or were used interchangeably, as in the case of both the star Arcturus (Alpha Boötis, "bear watcher") and the constellation Boötes ("plowman"). In the star list of the *Almagest*, Ptolemy cites only about a dozen stars by name, describing the others by their positions within the constellation figures. Most star names in current use have Arabic forms, but these are usually simply translations of Ptolemy's descriptions; for example, Deneb, the name of the brightest star in the constellation Cygnus (Swan), means literally "tail" of the bird. Ptolemy's placement of the stars within apparently well-known figures indicates the earlier existence of star maps, probably globes.

A unique hemispherical celestial map, which furnishes a remarkable connecting link between the classical representation of the constellations and the later Islamic forms, is painted in the dome of a bath house at Quṣayr 'Amra, an Arab palace built in Jordan around 715 CE. The surviving fragments of the fresco show parts of 37 constellations and about 400 stars.

Circumstantial evidence suggests that a flat representation of the sky, in the form of a planisphere using a stereographic projection, had come into use by the beginning of the present era. This provided the basis for the astrolabe, the earliest remaining examples of which date from the 9th century CE. The open metalwork of the top moving plate (called

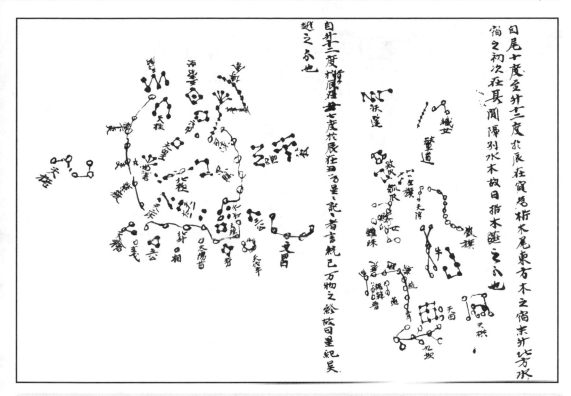

Chinese Tunhuang manuscript, the oldest existing portable star map, excluding astrolabes (c. 940 CE). In the British Museum (MS. Stein 3326). Actual width of portion shown, about 32 centimetres (12.75 inches). Courtesy of the trustees of the British Museum

a spider or rete) of an astrolabe is essentially a star map, and these instruments together with associated manuscript lists provide the basic documentation for Arabic star names.

If astrolabes are excluded, the oldest existing portable star map from any civilization is the Chinese Tunhuang manuscript in the British Museum, dating from about 940 CE. A Latin document of about the same age, also in the British Museum, shows a planisphere to illustrate the *Phaenomena* of Aratus, without,

however, indicating individual stars. The oldest illuminated Islamic astronomical manuscript, a 1009–10 CE copy of Aṣ-Ṣūfī's book on the fixed stars, shows individual constellations, including stars.

The earliest known western maps of the skies of the Northern and Southern Hemispheres with both stars and constellation figures date from 1440; preserved in Vienna, they may have been based on two now-lost charts from 1425 once owned by the German astronomer and mathematician Regiomontanus. In 1515 the noted

THE FARNESE GLOBE

The celestial globe is a representation of stars and constellations as they are located on the apparent sphere of the sky. Celestial globes are used for some astronomical or astrological calculations or as ornaments.

Probably the oldest celestial globe in existence is the Farnese Globe, the most famous astronomical artifact of antiquity. It is estimated to be from the 3rd century BCE and is now in the Museo Archeologico Nazionale at Naples. This huge marble globe, supported by a statue of Atlas, is generally considered to be a Roman copy of an earlier Greek original. It shows constellation figures but not individual stars, although the stars may have been painted on the stone. It would have been of little practical astronomical use.

German painter Albrecht Dürer drew the first printed star maps, a pair of beautiful planispheres closely patterned on the Vienna manuscripts. Dürer and his collaborators numbered the stars on the charts according to the order in Ptolemy's list, a nomenclature that gained limited currency in the 16th century. The first book of printed star charts, *De le stelle fisse* (1540) of the Italian Alessandro Piccolomini, introduced a lettering system for the stars; although frequently reprinted, application of its nomenclature did not spread.

MODERN STAR MAPS AND CATALOGS

Near the end of the 16th century, Tycho Brahe of Denmark resolved to provide an observational basis for the renovation of astronomy. With his large and sturdy (but pre-telescopic) quadrants and sextants, he carefully measured the positions of 777 stars, to which he later added enough hastily observed stars to bring the catalog up to exactly 1,000. A comparable catalog of southern stars was not available until 1678, when the young Edmond Halley published positions of 350 stars measured during a British expedition to St. Helena, an island in the South Pacific.

The first Astronomer Royal, John Flamsteed, pioneered the use of telescopic sights for measuring stars' positions. His aforementioned *Historia Coelestis Britannica* listed 3,000 stars, exceeding all former catalogs in number and accuracy. These observations provided the basis for his great *Atlas Coelestis*. Measurements of the third Astronomer Royal, James Bradley, achieved a precision within a few seconds of arc; as reduced by the German astronomer Friedrich W. Bessel in 1818, his positions are the oldest still considered useful in modern astronomy.

SURVEY AND ZONE MAPS, AND CATALOGS

In the 1850s, Friedrich Argelander undertook to list all the stars visible using an

8-centimetre (3-inch) Bonn refractor. Keeping the telescope fixed, he recorded the stars, zone by zone, as Earth's rotation carried the stars past the field of view. The resulting *Bonner Durchmusterung* (literally a "scanning through"), or *BD* catalog, contains 324,189 stars to about the ninth magnitude between declinations +90° and -2°. The accompanying charts, published in 1863, far surpassed all former maps in completeness and reliability. These maps are still of great value. The Bonn survey was extended to -23° in 1886, and at Córdoba, Arg., it was carried to the parallel of -62° by 1908, and to the South Pole by 1930. Because observing conditions changed over the many years required, the resulting *Córdoba Durchmusterung*, or *CD*, lacks the homogeneity of its northern counterpart.

In 1867 Argelander proposed to the Astronomische Gesellschaft (German Astronomical Society) a massive project to document stellar positions with far greater precision. Although the observing of selected star positions with meridian circle telescopes had become well established by observers during the 18th and early 19th centuries, the new plan called for meridian observations of all stars down to the ninth magnitude. A score of observatories on four continents, each responsible for a specific zone of declination, cooperated to complete the catalog and its southern supplements. The northern sections, known as the *AGK1*, were published by zones; not until 1912 was the *AGK1* complete to -18°.

Meanwhile, in quite another way, the Dutch astronomer Jacobus Cornelius Kapteyn completed an inventory of the southern sky by the measurement of the positions and magnitudes of about 454,000 stars from a set of photographic plates taken in Cape Town. Known as the *Cape Photographic Durchmusterung* (1896–1900), or *CPD*, the result covers the sky from declination -19° to the South Pole, down to the 11th magnitude.

Beginning in 1924, the Astronomische Gesellschaft catalog was repeated photographically by the Bonn and Hamburg-Bergedorf observatories. Published in 1951–58, the new catalog is called the *AGK2*. Neither the *AGK1* nor the *AGK2* provided information on proper motions, that is, the movement of a star through space. Therefore, another set of photographic plates was obtained in Hamburg during the 1950s in order to obtain the motions; the resulting *AGK3* was distributed on magnetic tape in 1969.

In 1966 the Smithsonian Astrophysical Observatory in Cambridge, Mass., issued a reference star catalog for use in finding artificial satellites from photographs. Although the *SAO Star Catalog* of 258,997 stars contains no new basic data, it does present the information in a particularly useful form. An accompanying computer-plotted atlas (1968), which includes more than 260,000 stars in addition to galaxies and nebulas, achieves an unprecedented accuracy for celestial cartography.

The European Space Agency's Hipparcos satellite was launched in 1989. Two star catalogs have been generated from the enormous amount of data on stellar positions it obtained. The Hipparcos catalog has positions for 118,218 stars that are accurate to 1 to 3 milliarcseconds. The Tycho-2 catalog is less accurate (10 to 100 milliarcseconds) but has positions for 2,539,913 stars.

FUNDAMENTAL CATALOGS

The measurements of accurate places for vast numbers of stars rests on painstakingly and independently determined positions of a few selected stars. A list of positions and proper motions for such selected stars well distributed over the sky is called a fundamental catalog, and its coordinate system is a close approximation to a fixed frame of reference. When the German astronomers began the *AGK2* in the 1920s, they first required a fundamental reference system that by the following decade was defined in the *Dritter Fundamental-katalog des Berliner Astronomischen Jahrbuchs*, or *FK3*. The *Fourth Fundamental Catalogue* (1963), or *FK4*, published by the Astronomisches Rechen-Institut in Heidelberg, contains data for 1,535 stars and has now superseded the *FK3*.

PHOTOMETRIC CATALOGS

A complete mapping of the sky includes magnitudes (and colours) as well as positions and motions. The great survey catalogs furnished magnitude estimates, but since photometric procedures are quite different from astrometric ones, a separate family of photometric catalogs has developed. Visual observations provided the basis for major tabulations published at Oxford, Harvard, and Potsdam around the turn of the century, but these were soon superseded by photographic work. Studies of galactic structure, which required accurate magnitudes for at least some very faint stars as well as the bright ones, led to the establishment of the plan of 206 selected areas. These were well-defined areas of sky with stars of many representative kinds that could be used as standards of comparison, and the *Mount Wilson Catalogue of Photographic Magnitudes in Selected Areas* (1930), made about 20 years later, was for many years a leading reference for celestial photometry. Today several catalogs of photoelectric measurements in three or more colours set the standards for precision magnitudes.

Another important quantity that can be measured is a star's spectral type. One of the greatest collections of astronomical data is the *Henry Draper Catalogue* (1918–24), formed at Harvard by Annie Jump Cannon and Edward Charles Pickering. The *HD* lists spectra of 225,300 stars distributed over the entire sky, and the *Henry Draper Extension* (1925–36, 1949) records 133,782 additional spectra.

PHOTOGRAPHIC STAR ATLASES

Astronomical photography was scarcely past its infancy when an international

THE MESSIER AND NGC CATALOGS

The Messier catalog (M) is a list of 110 star clusters, nebulae, and galaxies compiled by Charles Messier, who discovered many of them. The catalog is still a valuable guide to amateur astronomers, although it has been superceded by the New General Catalogue (NGC); both NGC numbers and Messier numbers remain in common use. The Messier catalog includes such diverse objects as the Crab Nebula supernova remnant (M1), the Pleiades star cluster (M45), and the great spiral galaxy in Andromeda (M31).

Messier's purpose was to make comet hunting easier by tabulating permanent deep-sky objects that could be mistaken for comets. He published a preliminary list of 45 such objects in 1771 and compiled the bulk of his catalog 10 years later. By 1784 he had listed 103 objects; in 1783 his friend and collaborator Pierre Mechain added six more. In 1966 British amateur astronomer Kenneth Glyn Jones added a satellite galaxy of M31 that Messier had discovered but not included in his catalog.

The New General Catalogue of Nebulae and Clusters of Stars (NGC) is a basic reference list of star clusters, nebulas, and galaxies. It was compiled in 1888 by Danish astronomer Johan Ludvig Emil Dreyer, who based his work on earlier lists made by the Herschel family of British astronomers. Dreyer included some 8,000 celestial objects, a total raised to about 13,000 by his first and second Index Catalogues (IC), published in 1895 and 1908, respectively. With these supplements the NGC covers the entire sky, although many objects visible with modern instruments are not listed.

An object may be known by several designations; e.g., the Crab Nebula is also called NGC 1952, as well as M1.

French astronomer Charles Messier was the first to compile a systematic catalog of nebulae and star clusters. Begun in 1760, the Messier catalog is still in use today. Private Collection/Archives Charmet/The Bridgeman Art Library

conference in Paris in 1887 all too hastily resolved to construct a photographic atlas of the entire sky down to the 14th magnitude, the so-called *Carte du Ciel*, and an associated *Astrographic Catalogue*, with measured star places down to the 12th magnitude. The original stimulus had come in 1882 with the construction of a 33-cm (13-inch) astrographic objective lens at Paris. For decades the immense *Carte du Ciel* enterprise sapped the energies of observatories around the world, especially in France, and even now is incomplete in the form originally planned. Nowadays such a program could be speedily completed with the use of computerized measuring instruments.

The first photographic atlas of the entire sky (if a set of 55 glass plates offered by Harvard in 1903 be excepted) was initiated by an energetic British amateur. Issued in 1914, the (John) *Franklin-Adams Charts* comprise 206 prints with a limiting magnitude of 15.

The monumental *National Geographic Society–Palomar Observatory Sky Survey*, released in 1954–58, reaches a limiting photographic magnitude of 21, far fainter than any other atlas. (The southernmost band has a slightly brighter limiting magnitude of 20.) Each field was photographed twice with a 124-cm (4.9 inch) Schmidt telescope at Mount Palomar to produce an atlas consisting of 935 pairs of prints made from the original blue-sensitive and red-sensitive plates, each about 6° square. The atlas proper extends to a declination of -33°, but 100 additional prints from red-sensitive plates now carry the coverage to -45°. Photographic mapping of the southern skies by the United Kingdom's 124-cm Schmidt telescope at Siding Spring Observatory in Australia and by the European Southern Observatory's 100-cm (39-inch) Schmidt at La Silla in Chile has penetrated to stars fainter than magnitude 22. In the 1980s improvements in astronomical technology led to the *Second Palomar Observatory Sky Survey* (POSS II).

ATLASES FOR STARGAZING

Three modern atlases have gained special popularity among amateur and professional observers alike. *Norton's Star Atlas*, perfected through numerous editions, plots all naked-eye stars on eight convenient charts measuring 25 by 43 cm (10 by 17 inches). The *Tirion Sky Atlas 2000.0* (1981) includes some 43,000 stars to magnitude eight and is based primarily on the *SAO Star Catalog*. Its 26 charts, measuring 47 by 33 cm (18.5 by 13 inches), include bright star names, boundaries of the Milky Way, and about 2,500 star clusters, nebulas, and galaxies. The companion to the *Tirion Atlas—Sky Catalogue 2000.0* (1982, 1985)—summarizes the essential characteristics of 45,269 stars. The second volume of this work catalogs double stars, variable stars, and various kinds of nonstellar objects, including radio and X-ray sources. The German astronomer Hans Vehrenberg's *Photographischer Stern-Atlas* (1962–64), covering the entire sky in 464 sheets, each 12° square, has probably reached wider use than any other photographic atlas because of its quality and comparatively modest cost.

There are several handbooks that serve as useful supplements to such atlases. *Burnham's Celestial Handbook* (1978) contains comprehensive descriptions of thousands of astronomical objects. *The Observer's Handbook*, published annually by the Royal Astronomical Society of Canada, lists valuable information for locating and observing a wide range of astronomical phenomena.

CHAPTER 2

ASTRONOMICAL TECHNIQUES AND APPLICATIONS

Techniques employed in the astronomical study of the heavens include observation, testing of samples taken from space, and scientific conjecture, or theory, based on the other techniques. Using these methods, astronomers have been able to determine distance, as well as study the stars and our universe.

OBSERVATIONS

Astronomical observations involve a sequence of stages, each of which may impose constraints on the type of information attainable. Radiant energy is collected with telescopes and brought to a focus on a detector, which is calibrated so that its sensitivity and spectral response are known. Accurate pointing and timing are required to permit the correlation of observations made with different instrument systems working in different wavelength intervals and located at places far apart. The radiation must be spectrally analyzed so that the processes responsible for radiation emission can be identified.

Before Galileo Galilei's use of telescopes for astronomy in 1609, all observations were made by naked eye, with corresponding limits on the faintness and degree of detail that could be seen. Since that time, telescopes have become central to astronomy. Having apertures much larger than the pupil of the human eye, telescopes permit the study of faint and distant objects. In addition, sufficient radiant energy can be collected in short time intervals to permit rapid fluctuations in intensity to be detected. Further, with more energy collected, a spectrum can be greatly dispersed and examined in much greater detail.

Optical telescopes are either refractors or reflectors that use lenses or mirrors, respectively, for their main light-collecting elements (objectives). Refractors are effectively limited to apertures of about 100 cm (approximately 40 inches) or less because of problems inherent in the use of large glass lenses. These distort under their own weight

Refractor telescopes have come a long way since Galileo discovered the moons of Jupiter with his self-built 20X refractor, pictured here. Mansell/Time & Life Pictures/Getty Images

and can be supported only around the perimeter; an appreciable amount of light is lost due to absorption in the glass. Large-aperture refractors are very long and require large and expensive domes. The largest modern telescopes are all reflectors, the very largest composed of many segmented components and having overall diameters of about 10 metres (33 feet). Reflectors are not subject to the chromatic problems of refractors, can be better supported mechanically, and can be housed in smaller domes because they are more compact than the long-tube refractors.

The angular resolving power (or resolution) of a telescope is the smallest angle between close objects that can be seen clearly to be separate. Resolution is limited by the wave nature of light. For a telescope having an objective lens or mirror with diameter D and operating at wavelength λ, the angular resolution (in radians) can be approximately described by the ratio λ/D.

Optical telescopes can have very high intrinsic resolving powers. In practice, however, these are not attained for telescopes located on Earth's surface, because atmospheric effects limit the practical resolution to about one arc second. Sophisticated computing programs can allow much-improved resolution, and the performance of telescopes on Earth can be improved through the use of adaptive optics, in which the surface of the mirror is adjusted rapidly to compensate for atmospheric turbulence that would otherwise distort the image. In addition, image data from several telescopes focused on the same object can be merged optically and through computer processing to produce images having angular resolutions much greater than that from any single component.

The atmosphere does not transmit radiation of all wavelengths equally well. This restricts astronomy on Earth's surface to the near ultraviolet, visible, and radio regions of the electromagnetic spectrum, with some relatively narrow "windows" in the nearer infrared. Longer infrared wavelengths are strongly absorbed by atmospheric water vapour and carbon dioxide. Atmospheric effects can be reduced by careful site selection and by carrying out observations at high altitudes. Most major optical observatories are located on high mountains, well away from cities and their reflected lights. Infrared telescopes have been located atop Mauna Kea in Hawaii and in the Canary Islands where atmospheric humidity is very low. Airborne telescopes designed mainly for infrared observations—such as (until 1995) on the Kuiper Airborne Observatory, a jet aircraft fitted with astronomical instruments—operate at an altitude of about 12 km (40,000 feet) with flight durations limited to a few hours. Telescopes for infrared, X-ray, and gamma-ray observations have been carried to altitudes of more than 30 km (100,000 feet) by balloons. Higher altitudes can be attained during short-duration rocket flights for ultraviolet observations. Telescopes for all wavelengths from infrared to gamma rays have been carried by robotic spacecraft observatories such as the Hubble Space Telescope and the Wilkinson Microwave Anisotropy Probe, while cosmic rays have been studied from space by the Advanced Composition Explorer.

Angular resolution better than one milliarcsecond has been achieved at radio wavelengths by the use of several radio telescopes in an array. In such an arrangement, the effective aperture then becomes the greatest distance between component telescopes. For example, in the Very Large Array (VLA), operated near Socorro, N.M., by the National Radio Astronomy Observatory, 27 movable radio dishes are set out along tracks that extend for nearly 21 km (13 miles). In another technique, called very long baseline interferometry (VLBI), simultaneous observations are made with radio telescopes thousands of kilometres apart; this technique requires very precise timing.

Earth is a moving platform for astronomical observations. It is important that the specification of precise celestial coordinates be made in ways that correct for telescope location, the position of Earth in its orbit around the Sun, and the epoch of observation, since Earth's axis of rotation moves slowly over the years. Time measurements are now based on atomic clocks rather than on Earth's rotation, and telescopes can be driven continuously to compensate for the planet's rotation, so as to permit tracking of a given astronomical object.

SOLID COSMIC SAMPLES

As a departure from the traditional astronomical approach of remote observing, certain more recent lines of research involve the analysis of actual samples under laboratory conditions. These include studies of meteorites, rock samples returned from the Moon, cometary dust samples returned by space probes, and interplanetary dust particles collected by aircraft in the stratosphere or by spacecraft. In all such cases, a wide range of highly sensitive laboratory techniques can be adapted for the often microscopic samples. Chemical analysis can be supplemented with mass spectroscopy, allowing isotopic composition to be determined. Radioactivity and the impacts of cosmic-ray particles can produce minute quantities of gas, which then remain trapped in crystals within the samples. Carefully controlled heating of the crystals (or of dust grains containing the crystals) under laboratory conditions releases this gas, which then is analyzed in a mass spectrometer. X-ray spectrometers, electron microscopes, and microprobes are employed to determine crystal structure and composition, from which temperature and pressure conditions at the time of formation can be inferred.

THEORETICAL APPROACHES

Theory is just as important as observation in astronomy. It is required for the interpretation of observational data; for the construction of models of celestial objects and physical processes, their properties, and their changes over time; and for guiding further observations. Theoretical astrophysics is based on laws of physics that have been validated with great precision through controlled experiments. Application of these laws to specific astrophysical problems, however, may yield equations too complex for direct solution. Two general approaches are then available. In the traditional method, a simplified description of the problem is formulated, incorporating only the major physical components, to provide equations that can be either solved directly or used to create a numerical model that can be evaluated. Successively more-complex models can then be investigated. Alternatively, a computer program can be devised that will explore the problem numerically in all its complexity. Computational science is taking its place as a major division alongside theory and experiment. The test of any theory is its ability to incorporate the known facts and to make predictions that can be compared with additional observations.

DETERMINING ASTRONOMICAL DISTANCES

A central undertaking in astronomy is the determination of distances. Without a knowledge of its distance, the size of an observed object in space would remain nothing more than an angular diameter, and the brightness of a star could not be converted into its true radiated power, or luminosity. Astronomical distance measurement began with a knowledge of Earth's diameter, which provided a base for triangulation. Within the inner solar system, some distances can now be better determined through the timing of radar reflections or, in the case of the Moon, through laser ranging. For the outer planets, triangulation is still used. Beyond the solar system, distances to the closest stars are determined through triangulation, with the diameter of Earth's orbit serving as the baseline and shifts in stellar parallax being the measured quantities.

PARALLAX

Parallax is the difference in direction of a celestial object as seen by an observer from two widely separated points. The measurement of parallax is used directly to find the distance of the body from Earth (geocentric parallax) and from the Sun (heliocentric parallax). The two positions of the observer and the position of the object form a triangle; if the base line between the two observing points is known and the direction of the object as seen from each has been measured, the apex angle (the parallax) and the distance of the object from the observer can be found simply.

In the determination of a celestial distance by parallax measurement, the base line is taken as long as possible in order to obtain the greatest precision of measurement. For the Sun and Moon, the base line used is the distance between two widely separated points on Earth; for all bodies outside the solar system, the base line is the diameter of Earth's orbit. The largest measured stellar parallax is

0.76", for the nearest star, Alpha Centauri; the smallest that can be directly measured is about 5,000 times smaller, but indirect methods discussed below permit calculation of the parallax, inversely proportional to the distance, for more and more distant objects but also with more and more uncertainty.

The parallax of the Sun or Moon is defined as the difference in direction as seen from the observer and from Earth's centre. The parallax varies with the altitude of the Moon for an observer on the surface of Earth. If the Moon is directly overhead, the parallax is zero, and parallax is greatest when the body is on the horizon. For all bodies except the Moon, the parallax p is so small that it does not differ appreciably from sin p, and it is usually expressed in angular measure. The definitions of lunar and solar parallax must be further refined because of the spheroidal figure of Earth. The numerical values generally given are those of the equatorial horizontal parallax. The solar parallax is usually derived from measurements of the positions of other bodies of the solar system.

LUNAR PARALLAX

The first parallax determination was for the Moon, by far the nearest celestial body. Hipparchus (150 BCE) determined the Moon's parallax to be 58' for a distance of approximately 59 times Earth's equatorial radius as compared with the modern value of 57' 02.6"; that is, a mean value of 60.2 times. Lunar parallax is directly determined from observations made at two places, such as Greenwich, Eng., and the Cape of Good Hope, that are nearly on the same meridian. Angles are observed, and other data are obtained from the latitudes of the observatories and the known size and shape of Earth. In practice, stars near the Moon are observed also to eliminate errors of refraction and instruments.

Another method rests on a comparison of the force of gravity at Earth's surface with its value at the Moon. If M and m are the masses of Earth and the Moon, r the mean distance, P the sidereal period of revolution of the Moon about Earth, and k the constant of gravitation,

$$k(M + m) = 4\pi^2 r^3 / P^2$$

where $\pi = 3.14$. Also, g, the value of gravity at Earth's surface, determined from pendulum observations, is equal to kM/a^2. Hence

$$\left(\frac{a}{r}\right)^3 = 4\pi^2 \frac{M}{M+m} \cdot \frac{a}{gP^2}$$

As the quantities on the right-hand side are known with great accuracy, a/r is accurately determined as 57' 2.7".

Radar measures of the distance from Earth to the Moon have provided a recent value of the lunar parallax. Radar ranges have the advantage of being a direct distance measure, although the ranges are affected by variations in the surface topography of the Moon and require assumptions about the lunar radius and the centre of mass.

The International Astronomical Union in 1964 adopted a value of 57' 02.608" for the lunar parallax corresponding to a mean distance of 384,400 kilometres (238,855 miles).

SOLAR PARALLAX

The basic method used for determining solar parallax is the determination of trigonometric parallax. In accordance with the law of gravitation, the relative distances of the planets from the Sun are known, and the distance of the Sun from Earth can be taken as the unit of length. The measurement of the distance or parallax of any planet will determine the value of this unit. The smaller the distance of the planet from Earth, the larger will be the parallactic displacements to be measured, with a corresponding increase in accuracy of the determined parallax. The most favourable conditions are therefore provided by the observation, near the time of opposition, of planets approaching close to Earth. The determination can be based either on simultaneous or nearly simultaneous observations from two different places on Earth's surface, or on observations made after sunset and before sunrise at the same place, when the displacement of the place of observation produced by the rotation of Earth provides the base line for the measurements.

The first reasonably accurate determination of the Sun's parallax was made in 1672 from observations of Mars at Cayenne, Fr. Guia., and Paris, from which a value of 9.5" was obtained.

Methods depending on velocity of light are also employed to ascertain solar parallax. The value of the velocity of light has been determined with very high precision and may be utilized in several different ways. A direct method is the converse of the procedure of Ole Rømer in the discovery of the velocity of light; i.e., to use the light equation, or time taken by the light to reach us at the varying distances of Jupiter, but great accuracy is hardly obtainable in this way. A second method is by means of the constant of aberration, which gives the ratio of the velocity of Earth in its orbit to the velocity of light. As aberration produces an annual term of amplitude 20.496" in the positions of all stars, its amount has been determined in numerous ways. Observations made at Greenwich in the years 1911 to 1936 gave the value 20.489" ± 0.003" leading to the value 8.797" ± 0.013" for solar parallax. This method is not free from the suspicion of systematic error.

The velocities of stars toward or away from Earth are determined from spectroscopic observations. By choosing times when the orbital motion of Earth is carrying it toward or from a star, astronomers are able to determine mathematically the velocity of Earth in its orbit. In this way the solar parallax was found from observations at the Cape of Good Hope to be 8.802" ± 0.004".

Radar measures of the distance from Earth to Venus have provided the best determination of the solar parallax. By measuring the flight time of a radar pulse to Venus, the distance between the two planets can be obtained, allowing the determination of the unit distance between Earth and the Sun.

The present value for the radar astronomical unit is 149,598,000 km ± 200 km, corresponding to a solar parallax of 8.79414" ± 0.00004". The principal limitations of the method are its dependence on knowledge of the planetary orbits, the uncertainty in the value of the velocity of light, and the possibility of electromagnetic effects in the Earth–Venus plasma delaying the radar pulse.

Gravitational methods are still another means of determining solar parallax. In lunar theory there is a term of period one month known as the parallactic inequality. The coefficient of the term contains the ratio of the parallaxes of the Sun and Moon as a factor. The coefficient's large size makes it of value.

The ratio of the combined mass of Earth and the Moon to that of the Sun may be determined from the disturbing action of Earth and the Moon on the elliptic motion of the planets. The ratio of the Moon's mass to that of Earth is 1/81.30, and thus the ratio of Earth's mass to that of the Sun is found. In a manner similar to that described above for the Moon's parallax, the solar parallax is then derived.

At the General Assembly of the International Astronomical Union in 1964 the value

8.79405" (8.794") for the solar parallax was adopted, corresponding to an astronomical unit of 149,600,000 km (92,957,130 miles).

STELLAR PARALLAX

The stars are too distant for any difference of position to be perceptible from two places on Earth's surface; but, as Earth revolves at 149,600,000 km from the Sun, stars are seen from widely different viewpoints during the year. The effect on their positions is called annual parallax, defined as the difference in position of a star as seen from Earth and the Sun. Its amount and direction vary with the time of year, and its maximum is a/r, where a is the radius of Earth's orbit and r the distance of the star. The quantity is very small and never reaches 1/206,265 in radians, or 1" in sexagesimal measure.

DIRECT MEASUREMENT

The introduction of the photographic method by F. Schlesinger in 1903 considerably improved the accuracy of stellar parallaxes. In practice a few photographs are taken when the star is on the meridian shortly after sunset at one period (epoch) of the year and shortly before sunrise six months later. Since the star's positions also change because of its motion across the sky (proper motion), a minimum of three such sets of observations is necessary for obtaining the parallax. From approximately 25 photographs taken over five epochs, the parallax of a star usually is determined with an accuracy of about ± 0.001" (probable error), even though the diameter of the photographic disk of the star is rarely less than 2.0".

The unit in which stellar distances are expressed by astronomers, the parsec, is the distance of a star whose parallax is 1". This is equal to 206,265 times Earth's distance from the Sun, or approximately 30,000,000,000,000 km. When p is measured in seconds of arc and the distance d in parsecs, the simple relation $d = 1/p$ holds. One parsec is equal to 3.26 light years.

CONSTANT OF ABERRATION

The constant of aberration is the maximum amount of the apparent yearly aberrational displacement of a star or other celestial body, resulting from Earth's orbital motion around the Sun. The value of the constant, about 20.49" of arc, depends on the ratio of Earth's orbital velocity to the velocity of light. James Bradley, the British astronomer who in 1728 discovered the aberration of starlight, estimated the value of the constant at about 20" and from this calculated the velocity of light at 295,000 kilometres (183,300 miles) per second, within a few thousand kilometres per second of the presently accepted value. The aberrational ellipse described by the image of a star in the course of a year has a major axis equal in angular distance to twice the constant of aberration.

The star with the largest known parallax, 0.76", is Alpha Centauri. Sixty-five separate stars are known within a distance of five parsecs from the Sun. These stars include the bright stars Alpha Centauri, Sirius, Procyon, and Altair, but the majority are faint telescopic objects.

INDIRECT MEASUREMENT

For stars beyond a distance of 1,000 parsecs (parallactic angle 0.001"), the

The fourth-brightest star in the night sky, Alpha Centauri also has the largest measured stellar parallax. STScI Digitized Sky Survey, Anglo-Australian Observatory and NASA

trigonometric method is in general not sufficiently accurate, and other methods must be used to determine their distances.

The parallax can be derived from the apparent magnitude of the star if there are any means of knowing the absolute magnitude of the star—i.e., the magnitude the star would have at the standard distance of 10 parsecs. For many stars a reasonable estimate can be made from their spectral types or their proper motions. The formula connecting the absolute magnitude, M, and the apparent magnitude, m, with parallax, p, is

$$M = m + 5 + 5 \log p$$

expressing the condition that the light received from a star varies inversely as the square of the distance.

Some groups of stars, such as the Hyades cluster in Taurus and the Ursa Major cluster, have proper motions converging toward a definite point on the celestial sphere and are called moving clusters. The apparent convergence is due to the effect of perspective on parallel motions. Once the direction toward the convergent point is known, and the proper and radial motion of a member star is known, the parallax can be determined from the geometry.

One method of indirect measurement involves the determination of mean, or average, stellar parallaxes. The solar system is moving through space with a velocity of 19.5 km (12 miles) per second, carrying it four times Earth's distance from the Sun in one year. This produces a general drift in the angular movement of the stars away from the apex, or point in the sky to which the movement is directed. Were the stars at rest, this would give a ready means of determining their individual distances. As the stars are all moving, the method gives the average distance of a group of stars examined, on the assumption that their peculiar motions are eliminated. In this way the mean parallaxes of stars of successive apparent magnitudes, of different galactic latitudes, and of different spectral types are obtained. Thus the mean parallax of fifth magnitude stars (i.e., of stars just visible to the naked eye) is 0.018", and of the 10th magnitude stars (i.e., of stars each giving about 1/100 of the light of a star of the fifth magnitude) is 0.0027".

Stellar parallaxes are also deduced from spectroscopic observations. The spectra of nearly all stars can be grouped into a small number of classes, which form a continuous sequence depending on the effective (surface) temperatures of the stars. The Henry Draper (HD) classification, which is of this kind, uses the letters O–B–A–F–G–K–M to denote classes with temperatures descending from about 30,000 K for class O to about 2,500 K for class M. The HD system has been generally adopted, usually in combination with a decimal subdivision for refined work.

Empirical studies show that the spectra of the stars also include important clues to their true luminosities. In 1914 Walter Adams and Arnold Kohlschütter established the spectroscopic differences between giant and dwarf stars of the same spectral type and laid the foundation for the determination of spectroscopic parallaxes. These differences, depending upon the intrinsic brightness of the star, allow an estimate of its absolute magnitude, and the parallax can then be deduced by means of the equation (2) given above. This method has been applied to most of the brighter stars in the Northern Hemisphere, using stars of known parallax as standards.

A two-dimensional classification system of stellar spectra, which has been universally adopted, has greatly improved the accuracy of spectroscopic parallaxes. The system, called the MK system, assigns a precise system of Draper classes and five luminosity classes, using the Roman numerals I to V. The system divides the majority of stars into supergiants, bright giants, subgiants, and main sequence (dwarf) stars, depending upon their intrinsic brightness, as determined from the spectral lines most sensitive to this property. The luminosity classes are then calibrated in terms of absolute magnitude.

The colours of the stars can also be used as indicators of their absolute magnitude, as first shown by Ejnar Hertzsprung in 1905 and 1907. A measure of the colour of a star is the difference in brightness, measured in magnitudes, in two selected wavelength bands of its spectrum. Initially the difference between the visual and the photographic magnitude of a star was defined as the colour of its light and called its colour index. A comparison between the colour index and the spectral classification of a star has made it possible to develop a quantitative method of measuring a star's absolute magnitude. Several photometric systems have been developed. The most widely used system is the two-dimensional quantitative classification method based upon photoelectric measurements in three wavelength bands in the ultraviolet, blue, and yellow (or visual) regions of the spectrum, hence called the *UBV* system. The system of the two colour indices *U-B* and *B-V* is calibrated in terms of spectral class and luminosity class on the MK system, based upon a set of standard stars. The relationship between the two indices in the *UBV* system and the absolute magnitudes for the main-sequence stars is of particular interest. By means of this relationship and the inverse square law, it is possible to determine the distances to galactic clusters from photoelectric observations of main-sequence stars in these clusters. In other words, such photometric parallaxes are obtained from a comparison of the observed apparent magnitudes of the stars and the absolute magnitudes inferred from their spectral types.

If the relative orbit of a visual binary system is known, the following relation connects the combined mass, *M*, of the two stars, expressed in the Sun's mass as unit; the orbital period, P, expressed in years, the semimajor axis of the relative orbit; *a*, expressed in seconds of arc; and the parallax *p*:

$$p = a/\sqrt[3]{MP^2}.$$

Both *a* and P are known, but not *M*; it will be noted that an error in the value of *M* gives rise to a much smaller error in *p*. Thus, for instance, increasing *M* by a factor of 8 only halves the value of *p*. The value of *p* obtained by assuming the combined mass to be equal to the mass of the Sun is called the hypothetical parallax.

In many visual pairs the complete orbit has not been observed. If *s* denotes the apparent distance in seconds of arc and *ω* the relative motion in seconds of arc per year, a hypothetical parallax can be derived from the formula

$$p = 0.418 \sqrt[3]{s\omega^2}.$$

By use of the relationship between mass and luminosity of a star, it is possible, knowing the spectral type of the star, to derive a correcting factor that will give a more accurate value of the parallax. Parallaxes so determined are called dynamical parallaxes.

DISTANCES TO GALAXIES

Two general methods for determining galactic distances are described here. In the first, a clearly identifiable type of star is used as a reference standard because its luminosity has been well determined.

This requires observation of such stars that are close enough to Earth that their distances and luminosities have been reliably measured. Such a star is termed a "standard candle." Examples are Cepheid variables, whose brightness varies periodically in well-documented ways, and certain types of supernova explosions that have enormous brilliance and can thus be seen out to very great distances. Once the luminosities of such nearer standard candles have been calibrated, the distance to a farther standard candle can be calculated from its calibrated luminosity and its actual measured intensity. The measured intensity (I) is related to the luminosity (L) and distance (d) by the formula

$$I = L/4\pi d^2.$$

A standard candle can be identified by means of its spectrum or the pattern of regular variations in brightness. (Corrections may have to be made for the absorption of starlight by interstellar gas and dust over great distances.) This method forms the basis of measurements of distances to the closest galaxies.

The second method for galactic distance measurements makes use of the observation that the distances to galaxies generally correlate with the speeds with which those galaxies are receding from Earth (as determined from the Doppler shift in the wavelengths of their emitted light). This correlation is expressed in the Hubble law:

$$\text{velocity} = H \times \text{distance},$$

in which H denotes Hubble's constant, which must be determined from observations of the rate at which the galaxies are receding. There is widespread agreement that H lies between 70 and 76 kilometres per second per megaparsec (km/sec/Mpc), with leading research groups offering estimates that have an average value of about 71 km/sec/Mpc. H has been used to determine distances to remote galaxies in which standard candles have not been found.

KEY ASTRONOMICAL FINDINGS

There are many questions concerning the cosmos at large. How will the universe end? Why did the big bang happen? Is Earth the only planet with life?

Astronomy has solved many of these mysteries, from the motions of the solar system to the age of the universe, from the atmospheres of the planets to the composition of the stars.

Study of the Solar System

The solar system took shape 4.6 billion years ago, when it condensed within a large cloud of gas and dust. Gravitational attraction holds the planets in their elliptical orbits around the Sun. In addition to Earth, five major planets (Mercury, Venus, Mars, Jupiter, and Saturn) have been known from ancient times. Since then only two more have been discovered: Uranus, by accident in 1781, and Neptune, in 1846 after a deliberate search following a theoretical prediction based on observed irregularities in the orbit of Uranus. Pluto, discovered in 1930 after a search for a planet predicted to lie beyond Neptune, was considered a major planet until 2006, when it was redesignated a dwarf planet by the International Astronomical Union.

The average Earth-Sun distance, which originally defined the astronomical unit (AU), provides a convenient measure for distances within the solar system. The AU is now defined dynamically (using Kepler's third law) and has the value $1.49597870691 \times 10^{13}$ cm (about 93 million miles), with an uncertainty of about 2,000 cm. The mean radius of Earth's orbit is $1 + (3.1 \times 10^{-8})$ AU. Mercury, at 0.4 AU, is the closest planet to the Sun, while Neptune, at 30.1 AU, is the farthest. Pluto's orbit, with a mean radius of 39.5 AU, is sufficiently eccentric that at times it is closer to the Sun than is Neptune. The planes of the planetary orbits are all within a few degrees of the ecliptic, the plane that contains Earth's orbit around the Sun. As viewed from far above Earth's North Pole, all planets move in the same (counterclockwise) direction in their orbits.

All of the planets apart from the two closest to the Sun (Mercury and Venus) have natural satellites (moons) that are very diverse in appearance, size, and structure, as revealed in close-up observations from long-range space probes. Pluto has at least three moons, including one fully half the size of Pluto itself. Four planets—Jupiter, Saturn, Uranus, and Neptune—have rings, disklike systems of small rocks and particles that orbit their parent planets.

Most of the mass of the solar system is concentrated in the Sun, with its 1.99×10^{33} grams. Together, all of the planets amount to 2.7×10^{30} grams (i.e., about one-thousandth of the Sun's mass), with Jupiter alone accounting for 71 percent of this amount. The solar system also contains a few known objects of intermediate size classified as dwarf planets and a very large number of much smaller objects collectively called small bodies. The small bodies, roughly in order of decreasing size, are the asteroids, or minor planets; comets, including Kuiper belt and Oort cloud objects; meteoroids; and interplanetary dust particles. Because of their starlike appearance when discovered, the largest of these bodies were termed *asteroids*, and that name is widely used, but, now that the rocky nature of these bodies is understood, their more descriptive name is minor planets.

The four inner, terrestrial planets—Mercury, Venus, Earth, and Mars—along with the Moon, have average densities in the range of 3.9–5.5 grams per cubic cm. Their densities set them apart from the four outer, giant planets—Jupiter, Saturn, Uranus, and Neptune—whose densities are all close to 1 gram per cubic cm, the density of water. The compositions of these two groups of planets must therefore be significantly different. This dissimilarity is thought to be attributable to conditions that prevailed during the early development of the solar system. Planetary temperatures now range from around 170 °C (330 °F, 440 K) on Mercury's surface through the typical 15 °C (60 °F, 290 K) on Earth to -135 °C (-210 °F, 140 K) on Jupiter near its cloud tops and down to -210 °C (-350 °F, 60 K) near Neptune's cloud tops. These are average temperatures; large variations exist between dayside and nightside for planets closest to the Sun, except for Venus with its thick atmosphere.

The surfaces of the terrestrial planets and many satellites show extensive cratering, produced by high-speed impacts. On Earth, with its large quantities of water and an active atmosphere, many of these cosmic footprints have eroded, but remnants of very large craters can be seen in aerial and spacecraft photographs of the terrestrial surface. On Mercury, Mars, and the Moon, the absence of water and any significant atmosphere has left the craters unchanged for billions of years, apart from disturbances produced by infrequent later impacts. Volcanic activity has been an important force in the shaping of the surfaces of the Moon and the terrestrial planets. Seismic activity on the Moon has been monitored by means of seismometers left on its surface by Apollo astronauts and by Lunokhod robotic rovers. Cratering on the largest scale seems to have ceased about three

billion years ago, although on the Moon there is clear evidence for a continued cosmic drizzle of small particles, with the larger objects churning ("gardening") the lunar surface and the smallest producing microscopic impact pits in crystals in the lunar rocks.

Lunar Exploration

During the U.S. Apollo missions a total weight of 381.7 kg (841.5 pounds) of lunar material was collected; an additional 300 grams (0.66 pounds) was brought back by unmanned Soviet Luna vehicles. About 15 percent of the Apollo samples have been distributed for analysis, with the remainder stored at the NASA Johnson Space Center, Houston, Texas. The opportunity to employ a wide range of laboratory techniques on these lunar samples has revolutionized planetary science.

The results of the analyses have enabled investigators to determine the composition and age of the lunar surface. Seismic observations have made it possible to probe the lunar interior. In addition, retroreflectors left on the Moon's surface by Apollo astronauts have allowed high-power laser beams to be sent from Earth to the Moon and back, permitting scientists to monitor Earth-Moon distance to an accuracy of a few centimetres. This experiment, which has provided data used in calculations of the dynamics of the Earth-Moon system, has shown that the separation of the two bodies is increasing by 4.4 cm (1.7 inches) each year.

Apollo 17 geologist-astronaut Harrison Schmitt at the foot of a huge split boulder, Dec. 13, 1972, during the mission's third extravehicular exploration of the Taurus-Littrow Valley landing site. NASA

PLANETARY DISCOVERIES

Mercury is too hot to retain an atmosphere, but Venus's brilliant white appearance is the result of its being completely enveloped in thick clouds of carbon dioxide, impenetrable at visible wavelengths. Below the upper clouds, Venus has a hostile atmosphere containing clouds of sulfuric acid droplets. The cloud cover shields the planet's surface from direct sunlight, but the energy that does filter through warms the surface, which then radiates at infrared wavelengths. The long-wavelength infrared radiation is trapped by the dense clouds such that an efficient greenhouse effect keeps the surface temperature near 465 °C (870 °F, 740 K). Radar, which can penetrate the thick Venusian clouds, has been used to map the planet's surface. In contrast, the atmosphere of Mars is very thin and is composed mostly of carbon dioxide (95 percent), with very little water vapour; the planet's surface pressure is only about 0.006 that of Earth. The outer planets have atmospheres composed largely of light gases, mainly hydrogen and helium.

Each planet rotates on its axis, and nearly all of them rotate in the same direction—counterclockwise as viewed from above the ecliptic. The two exceptions are Venus, which rotates in the clockwise direction beneath its cloud cover, and Uranus, which has its rotation axis very nearly in the plane of the ecliptic.

Some of the planets have magnetic fields. Earth's field extends outward until it is disturbed by the solar wind—an outward flow of protons and electrons from the Sun—which carries a magnetic field along with it. Through processes not yet fully understood, particles from the solar wind and galactic cosmic rays (high-speed particles from outside the solar system) populate two doughnut-shaped regions called the Van Allen radiation belts. The inner belt extends from about 1,000 to 5,000 km (600 to 3,000 miles) above Earth's surface, and the outer from roughly 15,000 to 25,000 km (9,300 to 15,500 miles). In these belts, trapped particles spiral along paths that take them around Earth while bouncing back and forth between the Northern and Southern Hemispheres, with their orbits controlled by Earth's magnetic field. During periods of increased solar activity, these regions of trapped particles are disturbed, and some of the particles move down into Earth's atmosphere, where they collide with atoms and molecules to produce auroras.

Jupiter has a magnetic field far stronger than Earth's and many more trapped electrons, whose synchrotron radiation (electromagnetic radiation emitted by high-speed charged particles that are forced to move in curved paths, as under the influence of a magnetic field) is detectable from Earth. Bursts of increased radio emission are correlated with the

Photo mosaic of Mercury, taken by the Mariner 10 spacecraft, 1974. NASA/JPL

position of Io, the innermost of the four Galilean moons of Jupiter. Saturn has a magnetic field that is much weaker than Jupiter's, but it too has a region of trapped particles. Mercury has a weak magnetic field that is only about 1 percent as strong as Earth's and shows no evidence of trapped particles. Uranus and Neptune have fields that are less than one-tenth the strength of Saturn's and appear much more complex than that of Earth. No field has been detected around Venus or Mars.

INVESTIGATIONS OF THE SMALLER BODIES

More than 200,000 asteroids with well-established orbits are known, and several hundred additional objects are discovered each year. Hundreds of thousands more have been seen, but their orbits have not been as well-determined. It is estimated that several million asteroids exist, but most are small, and their combined mass is estimated to be less than a thousandth that of Earth. Most of the asteroids have orbits close to the ecliptic and move in the asteroid belt, between 2.3 and 3.3 AU from the Sun. Because some asteroids travel in orbits that can bring them close to Earth, there is a possibility of a collision that could have devastating results.

Comets are considered to come from a vast reservoir, the Oort cloud, orbiting the Sun at distances of 20,000–50,000 AU or more and containing trillions of icy objects—latent comet nuclei—with the potential to become active comets. Many comets have been observed over the centuries. Most make only a single pass through the inner solar system, but some are deflected by Jupiter or Saturn into orbits that allow them to return at predictable times. Halley's Comet is the best-known of these periodic comets, with its next return into the inner solar system predicted for 2061 CE. Many short-period comets are thought to come from the Kuiper belt, a region lying mainly between 30 AU and 50 AU from the Sun—beyond Neptune's orbit but including part of Pluto's—and housing perhaps hundreds of millions of comet nuclei. Comet masses have not been well determined, but most are probably less than 10^{18} grams, one billionth the mass of Earth.

Since the 1990s, more than a thousand comet nuclei in the Kuiper belt have been observed with large telescopes; a few are about half the size of Pluto, and at least one, Eris, is estimated to be slightly larger. Pluto's orbital and physical characteristics had long caused it to be regarded as an anomaly among the planets, and, after the discovery of numerous other Pluto-like objects beyond Neptune, Pluto was seen to be no longer unique in its "neighbourhood" but rather a giant member of the local population. Consequently, in 2006 astronomers at the general assembly of the International Astronomical Union elected to create the new category of dwarf planets for objects with such qualifications. Pluto, Eris, and Ceres, the latter being the largest member of the asteroid belt, were given this distinction. Two other Kuiper belt objects, Makemake and Haumea, were also designated as dwarf planets.

Smaller than the observed asteroids and comets are the meteoroids, lumps of stony or metallic material believed to be mostly fragments of asteroids and comets. Meteoroids vary from small rocks to boulders weighing a ton or more. A relative few have orbits that bring them into Earth's atmosphere and down to the surface as meteorites. Most if not all meteorites that have been collected on Earth are probably from asteroids. Meteorites are classified into three broad groups: stony (chondrites and achondrites; about 94 percent), iron (5 percent), and stony-iron (1 percent).

Most meteoroids that enter the atmosphere heat up sufficiently to glow and appear as meteors, and the great majority of these vaporize completely or break up before they reach the surface. Many, perhaps most, meteors occur in showers and follow orbits that seem to be identical with those of certain comets, thus pointing to a cometary origin. For example, each May, when Earth crosses the orbit of Halley's Comet, the Eta Aquarid meteor shower occurs.

Micrometeorites (interplanetary dust particles), the smallest meteoroidal particles, can be detected from Earth-orbiting satellites or collected by specially equipped aircraft flying in the stratosphere and returned for laboratory inspection. Since the late 1960s, numerous meteorites have been found in the Antarctic on the surface of stranded ice

flows. Detailed analyses have shown that some of these meteorites have come from the Moon and others from Mars. Yet others contain microscopic crystals whose isotopic proportions are unique and appear to be dust grains that formed in the atmospheres of different stars.

SOLAR SYSTEM AGE AND CHEMICAL COMPOSITION

The age of the solar system, taken to be close to 4.6 billion years, has been derived from measurements of radioactivity in meteorites, lunar samples, and Earth's crust. Abundances of isotopes of uranium, thorium, and rubidium and their decay products, lead and strontium, are the measured quantities.

Assessment of the chemical composition of the solar system is based on data from Earth, the Moon, and meteorites as well as on the spectral analysis of light from the Sun and planets. In broad outline, the solar system abundances of the chemical elements decrease with increasing atomic weight. Hydrogen atoms are by far the most abundant, constituting 91 percent; helium is next, with 8.9 percent; and all other types of atoms together amount to only 0.1 percent.

THEORIES OF ORIGIN

After the early 1990s, astronomers confirmed that stars other than the Sun have one or more planets revolving around them. Studies of the properties of these solar systems have both supported and challenged astronomers' theoretical models of how Earth's solar system formed.

The origin of Earth, the Moon, and the solar system as a whole is a problem that has not yet been settled in detail. The Sun probably formed by condensation of the central region of a large cloud of gas and dust, with the planets and other bodies of the solar system forming soon after, their composition strongly influenced by the temperature and pressure gradients in the evolving solar nebula. Less-volatile materials could condense into solids relatively close to the Sun to form the terrestrial planets. The abundant, volatile lighter elements could condense only at much greater distances to form the giant gas planets.

The origin of the planetary satellites has not been entirely settled, either. As to the origin of the Moon, the opinion of astronomers had long oscillated between theories that saw its origin and condensation simultaneous with formation of Earth and those that posited a separate origin for the Moon and its later capture by Earth's gravitational field. Similarities and differences in abundances of the chemical elements and their isotopes on Earth and the Moon had challenged each group of theories. Finally, in the 1980s a model emerged that has gained the support of most lunar scientists—that of a large impact on Earth with the expulsion of material that subsequently formed the Moon.

As for the outer planets with their multiple satellites, many very small and quite unlike one another, the picture is less clear. Some of these moons have relatively smooth icy surfaces, whereas others are heavily cratered; at least one, Jupiter's Io, is volcanic. Some of the moons may have formed along with their parent planets, and others may have formed elsewhere and been captured.

STUDY OF THE STARS

The study of the stars forms the backbone of astronomy. Over the thousands of years that humanity has observed them, the stars have gone from points in the vault of heaven to extremely hot balls of gas burning with the fires of nuclear fusion.

MEASURING OBSERVABLE STELLAR PROPERTIES

The measurable quantities in stellar astrophysics include the externally observable features of the stars: distance, temperature, radiation spectrum and luminosity, composition (of the outer layers), diameter, mass, and variability in any of these. Theoretical astrophysicists use these observations to model the structure of stars and to devise theories for their formation and evolution. Positional information can be used for dynamical analysis, which yields estimates of stellar masses.

There are several methods for measuring a star's diameter. From the brightness and distance the luminosity (L) can be calculated, and from observations of the brightness at different

Bright nebulosity in the Pleiades (M45, NGC 1432), distance 430 light-years.Cluster stars provide the light, and surrounding clouds of dust reflect and scatter the rays from the stars. Hale Observatories ©1961

wavelengths the temperature (T) can be calculated. Because the radiation from many stars can be well approximated by a Planck blackbody spectrum, these measured quantities can be related through the expression

$$L = 4\pi R^2 \sigma T^4$$

thus providing a means of calculating R, the star's radius. In this expression, σ is the Stefan-Boltzmann constant, 5.67×10^{-5} ergs/cm^{2}K^{4}sec, in which K is the temperature in kelvins. (The radius R refers to the star's photosphere, the region where the star becomes effectively opaque to outside observation.) Stellar angular diameters can be measured through interference effects. Alternatively, the intensity of the starlight can be monitored during occultation by the Moon, which produces diffraction fringes whose pattern depends on the angular diameter of the star. Stellar angular diameters of several milliarcseconds can be measured, but so far only for relatively bright and close stars.

Many stars occur in binary systems, with the two partners in orbits around their mutual centre of mass. Such a system provides the best measurement of stellar masses. The period (P) of a binary system is related to the masses of the two stars (m_1 and m_2) and the orbital semimajor axis (mean radius; a) via Kepler's third law:

$$P^2 = 4\pi^2 a^3 / G(m_1 + m_2).$$

(G is the universal gravitational constant.) From diameters and masses, average values of the stellar density can be calculated and thence the central pressure. With the assumption of an equation of state, the central temperature can then be calculated.

MAGNITUDE

In a system dating back at least to the Greek astronomer-mathematician Hipparchus in the 2nd century BCE, apparent stellar brightness (m) is measured in magnitudes. Magnitudes are now defined such that a first-magnitude star is 100 times brighter than a star of sixth magnitude. The human eye cannot see stars fainter than about sixth magnitude, but modern instruments used with large telescopes can record stars as faint as about 30th magnitude. By convention, the absolute magnitude (M) is defined as the magnitude that a star would appear to have if it were located at a standard distance of 10 parsecs. These quantities are related through the expression $m - M = 5 \log_{10} r - 5$, in which r is the star's distance in parsecs.

The magnitude scale is anchored on a group of standard stars. An absolute measure of radiant power is luminosity, usually expressed in ergs per second (ergs/sec). (Sometimes the luminosity is stated in terms of the solar luminosity, 3.86×10^{33} ergs/sec.) Luminosity can be calculated when m and r are known. Correction might be necessary for the interstellar absorption of starlight.

For example, in the Sun the central density is 158 grams per cubic cm; the pressure is calculated to be more than one billion times the pressure of Earth's atmosphere at sea level and the temperature around 15 million K (27 million °F). At this temperature, all atoms are ionized, and so the solar interior consists of a plasma, an ionized gas with hydrogen nuclei (i.e., protons), helium nuclei, and electrons as major constituents. A small fraction of the hydrogen nuclei possess sufficiently high speeds that, on colliding, their electrostatic repulsion is overcome, resulting in the formation, by means of a set of fusion reactions, of helium nuclei and a release of energy. Some of this energy is carried away by neutrinos, but most of it is carried by photons to the surface of the Sun to maintain its luminosity.

Other stars, both more and less massive than the Sun, have broadly similar structures, but the size, central pressure and temperature, and fusion rate are functions of the star's mass and composition. The stars and their internal fusion (and resulting luminosity) are held stable against collapse through a delicate balance between the inward pressure produced by gravitational attraction and the outward pressure supplied by the photons produced in the fusion reactions.

Stars that are in this condition of hydrostatic equilibrium are termed main-sequence stars, and they occupy a well-defined band on the Hertzsprung-Russell (H-R) diagram, in which luminosity is plotted against colour index or temperature. Spectral classification, based initially on the colour index, includes the major spectral types O, B, A, F, G, K and M, each subdivided into 10 parts. Temperature is deduced from broadband spectral measurements in several standard wavelength intervals. Measurement of apparent magnitudes in two spectral regions, the *B* and *V* bands (centred on 4350 and 5550 angstroms, respectively), permits calculation of the colour index,

$$CI = m_B - m_V$$

from which the temperature can be calculated.

For a given temperature, there are stars that are much more luminous than main-sequence stars. Given the dependence of luminosity on the square of the radius and the fourth power of the temperature, greater luminosity implies larger radius, and such stars are termed giant stars or supergiant stars. Conversely, stars with luminosities much less than those of main-sequence stars of the same temperature must be smaller and are termed white dwarf stars. Surface temperatures of white dwarfs typically range from 10,000 to 12,000 K (18,000 to 21,000 °F), and they appear visually as white or blue-white.

The strength of spectral lines of the more abundant elements in a star's atmosphere allows additional subdivisions within a class. Thus, the Sun, a main-sequence star, is classified as G2 V, in which the V denotes main sequence. Betelgeuse, a red giant with a surface temperature about half that of the Sun but with a luminosity of about 10,000 solar units, is classified as M2 Iab. In this classification, the spectral type is M2, and

the Iab indicates a giant, well above the main sequence on the H-R diagram.

Star Formation and Evolution

The range of physically allowable masses for stars is very narrow. If the star's mass is too small, the central temperature will be too low to sustain fusion reactions. The theoretical minimum stellar mass is about 0.08 solar mass. An upper theoretical limit of approximately 100 solar masses has been suggested, but this value is not firmly defined. Stars as massive as this will have luminosities about one million times greater than that of the Sun.

A general model of star formation and evolution has been developed, and the major features seem to be established. A large cloud of gas and dust can contract under its own gravitational attraction if its temperature is sufficiently low. As gravitational energy is released, the contracting central material heats up until a point is reached at which the outward radiation pressure balances the inward gravitational pressure, and contraction ceases. Fusion reactions take over as the star's primary source of energy, and the star is then on the main sequence. The time to pass through these formative stages and onto the main sequence is less than 100 million years for a star with as much mass as the Sun. It takes longer for less massive stars and a much shorter time for those much more massive.

Once a star has reached its main-sequence stage, it evolves relatively slowly, fusing hydrogen nuclei in its core to form helium nuclei. Continued fusion not only releases the energy that is radiated but also results in nucleosynthesis, the production of heavier nuclei.

Stellar evolution has of necessity been followed through computer modeling because the timescales for most stages are generally too extended for measurable changes to be observed, even over a period of many years. One exception is the supernova, the violently explosive finale of certain stars. Different types of supernovas can be distinguished by their spectral lines and by changes in luminosity during and after the outburst. In Type Ia, a white dwarf star attracts matter from its nearby companion; when the white dwarf's mass exceeds about 1.4 solar masses, the star implodes and is completely destroyed. Type II supernovas are not as luminous as Type Ia and are the final evolutionary stage of stars more massive than about eight solar masses.

The nature of the final products of stellar evolution depend on stellar mass. Some stars pass through an unstable stage in which their dimensions, temperature, and luminosity change cyclically over periods of hours or days. These so-called Cepheid variables serve as standard candles for distance measurements. Some stars blow off their outer layers to produce planetary nebulas. The expanding material can be seen glowing in a thin shell as it disperses into the interstellar medium, while the remnant core, initially with a surface temperature as high as 100,000 K (180,000 °F), cools to become a white dwarf. The maximum stellar mass

that can exist as a white dwarf is about 1.4 solar masses and is known as the Chandrasekhar limit. More-massive stars may end up as either neutron stars or black holes.

The average density of a white dwarf is calculated to exceed one million grams per cubic cm. Further compression is limited by a quantum condition called degeneracy, in which only certain energies are allowed for the electrons in the star's interior. Under sufficiently great pressure, the electrons are forced to combine with protons to form neutrons. The resulting neutron star will have a density in the range of 10^{14}–10^{15} grams per cubic cm, comparable to the density within atomic nuclei. The behaviour of large masses having nuclear densities is not yet sufficiently understood to be able to set a limit on the maximum size of a neutron star, but it is thought to be in the region of three solar masses.

Still more-massive remnants of stellar evolution would have smaller dimensions and would be even denser than neutron stars. Such remnants are conceived to be black holes, objects so compact that no radiation can escape from within a characteristic distance called the Schwarzschild radius. This critical dimension is defined by

$$R_s = 2GM/c^2.$$

(R_s is the Schwarzschild radius, G is the gravitational constant, M is the object's mass, and c is the speed of light.) For an object of three solar masses, the Schwarzschild radius would be about

3 kilometres (1.8 miles). Radiation emitted from beyond the Schwarzschild radius can still escape and be detected.

Although no light can be detected coming from within a black hole, the presence of a black hole may be manifested through the effects of its gravitational field, as, for example, in a binary star system. If a black hole is paired with a normal visible star, it may pull matter from its companion toward itself. This matter is accelerated as it approaches the black hole and becomes so intensely heated that it radiates large amounts of X-rays from the periphery of the black hole before reaching the Schwarzschild radius. A few candidates for stellar black holes have been found—e.g., the X-ray source Cygnus X-1. Each of them has an estimated mass clearly exceeding that allowable for a neutron star, a factor crucial in the identification of possible black holes. (Supermassive black holes that do not originate as individual stars are thought to exist at the centres of active galaxies.)

Whereas the existence of stellar black holes has been strongly indicated, the existence of neutron stars was confirmed in 1968 when they were identified with the then newly discovered pulsars, objects characterized by the emission of radiation at short and extremely regular intervals, generally between 1 and 1,000 pulses per second and stable to better than a part per billion. Pulsars are considered to be rotating neutron stars, remnants of some supernovas.

STUDY OF THE MILKY WAY GALAXY

Stars are not distributed randomly throughout space. Many stars are in systems consisting of two or three members separated by less than 1,000 AU. On a larger scale, star clusters may contain many thousands of stars. Galaxies are much larger systems of stars and usually include clouds of gas and dust.

The solar system is located within the Milky Way Galaxy, close to its equatorial plane and about 7.9 kiloparsecs from the galactic centre. The galactic diameter is about 30 kiloparsecs, as indicated by luminous matter. There is evidence, however, for nonluminous matter—so-called dark matter—extending out nearly twice this distance. The entire system is rotating such that, at the position of the Sun, the orbital speed is about 220 km per second (almost 500,000 miles per hour) and a complete circuit takes roughly 240 million years. Application of Kepler's third law leads to an estimate for the galactic mass of about 100 billion solar masses. The rotational velocity can be measured from the Doppler shifts observed in the 21-cm (8-inch) emission line of neutral hydrogen and the lines of millimetre wavelengths from various molecules, especially carbon monoxide. At great distances from the galactic centre, the rotational velocity does not drop off as expected but rather increases slightly. This behaviour appears to require a much larger galactic mass than can be accounted for by the known (luminous)

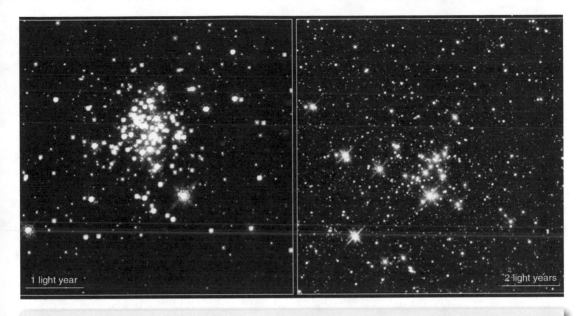

The Hubble Telescope afforded views of the Arches (left) *and Quintuplet star clusters, located near the center of the Milky Way Galaxy.* NASA Goddard Space Flight Center

matter. Additional evidence for the presence of dark matter comes from a variety of other observations. The nature and extent of the dark matter (or missing mass) constitutes one of today's major astronomical puzzles.

There are about 100 billion stars in the Milky Way Galaxy. Star concentrations within the galaxy fall into three types: open clusters, globular clusters, and associations. Open clusters lie primarily in the disk of the galaxy; most contain between 50 and 1,000 stars within a region no more than 10 parsecs in diameter. Stellar associations tend to have somewhat fewer stars; moreover, the constituent stars are not as closely grouped as those in the clusters and are

for the most part hotter. Globular clusters, which are widely scattered around the galaxy, may extend up to about 100 parsecs in diameter and may have as many as a million stars.

The importance to astronomers of globular clusters lies in their use as indicators of the age of the galaxy. Because massive stars evolve more rapidly than do smaller stars, the age of a cluster can be estimated from its H-R diagram. In a young cluster the main sequence will be well-populated, but in an old cluster the heavier stars will have evolved away from the main sequence. The extent of the depopulation of the main sequence provides an index of age. In this way, the oldest globular clusters have been found to be about 14 billion ± 1 billion years old, which should therefore be the minimum age for the galaxy.

Investigations of Interstellar Matter

The interstellar medium, composed primarily of gas and dust, occupies the regions between the stars. On average, it contains less than one atom in each cubic centimetre, with about 1 percent of its mass in the form of minute dust grains. The gas, mostly hydrogen, has been mapped by means of its 21-cm (8-inch) emission line. The gas also contains numerous molecules. Some of these have been detected by the visible-wavelength absorption lines that they impose on the spectra of more-distant stars, while others have been identified by their own emission lines at millimetre wavelengths. Many of the interstellar molecules are found in giant molecular clouds, wherein complex organic molecules have been discovered.

In the vicinity of a very hot O- or B-type star, the intensity of ultraviolet radiation is sufficiently high to ionize the surrounding hydrogen out to a distance as great as 100 parsecs to produce an H II region, known as a Strömgren sphere. Such regions are strong and characteristic emitters of radiation at radio wavelengths, and their dimensions are well calibrated in terms of the luminosity of the central star. Using radio interferometers, astronomers are able to measure the angular

diameters of H II regions even in some external galaxies and can thereby deduce the great distances to those remote systems. This method can be used for distances up to about 30 megaparsecs.

Interstellar dust grains scatter and absorb starlight, with the effect being roughly inversely proportional to wavelength from the infrared to the near ultraviolet. As a result, stellar spectra tend to be reddened. Absorption amounts typically to about one magnitude per kiloparsec but varies considerably in different directions. Some dusty regions contain silicate materials, identified by a broad absorption feature around a wavelength of 10 μm. Other prominent spectral features in the infrared range have been sometimes, but not conclusively, attributed to graphite grains and polycyclic aromatic hydrocarbons.

Starlight often shows a small degree of polarization (a few percent), with the effect increasing with stellar distance. This is attributed to the scattering of the starlight from dust grains that have been partially aligned in a weak interstellar magnetic field. The strength of this field is estimated to be a few microgauss, very close to the strength inferred from observations of nonthermal cosmic radio noise. This radio background has been identified as synchrotron radiation, emitted by cosmic-ray electrons traveling at nearly the speed of light and moving along curved paths in the interstellar magnetic field. The spectrum of the cosmic radio noise is close to what is calculated on the basis of measurements of the cosmic rays near Earth.

Cosmic rays constitute another component of the interstellar medium. Cosmic rays that are detected in the vicinity of Earth comprise high-speed nuclei and electrons. Individual particle energies, expressed in electron volts (eV; 1 eV = 1.6 × 10^{-12} erg), range with decreasing numbers from about 10^6 eV to more than 10^{20} eV. Among the nuclei, hydrogen nuclei are the most plentiful at 86 percent, helium nuclei next at 13 percent, and all other nuclei together at about 1 percent. Electrons are about 2 percent as abundant as the nuclear component. (The relative numbers of different nuclei vary somewhat with kinetic energy, while the electron proportion is strongly energy-dependent.)

A minority of cosmic rays detected in Earth's vicinity are produced in the Sun, especially at times of increased solar activity (as indicated by sunspots and solar flares). The origin of galactic cosmic rays has not yet been conclusively identified, but they are thought to be produced in stellar processes such as supernova explosions, perhaps with additional acceleration occurring in the interstellar regions.

OBSERVATIONS OF THE GALACTIC CENTRE

The central region of the Milky Way Galaxy is so heavily obscured by dust that direct observation has become possible only with the development of astronomy at nonvisual wavelengths—namely, radio, infrared, and, more recently, X-ray and gamma-ray wavelengths. Together, these observations have revealed a nuclear region of intense activity, with a large number of separate sources of emission and a great deal of dust. Detection of gamma-ray emission at a line energy of 511,000 eV, which corresponds to the annihilation of electrons and positrons (the antimatter counterpart of electrons), along with radio mapping of a region no more than 20 AU across, points to a very compact and energetic source, designated Sagittarius A*, at the centre of the galaxy. Sagittarius A* is a supermassive black hole with a mass equivalent to 4,310,000 Suns.

STUDY OF OTHER GALAXIES AND RELATED PHENOMENA

Galaxies are normally classified into three principal types according to their appearance: spiral, elliptical, and irregular. Galactic diameters are typically in the tens of kiloparsecs and the distances between galaxies typically in megaparsecs.

Spiral galaxies, of which the Milky Way system is a characteristic example, tend to be flattened, roughly circular systems with their constituent stars strongly concentrated along spiral arms. These arms are thought to be produced by traveling density waves, which compress and expand the galactic material. Between the spiral arms exists a diffuse interstellar medium of gas and dust, mostly at very low temperatures (below 100 K [−280 °F, −170 °C]). Spiral galaxies are typically a few kiloparsecs in thickness; they have a central bulge and taper gradually toward the outer edges.

Ellipticals show none of the spiral features but are more densely packed stellar systems. They range in shape from nearly spherical to very flattened and contain little interstellar matter. Irregular galaxies number only a few percent of all stellar systems and exhibit none of the regular features associated with spirals or ellipticals.

Properties vary considerably among the different types of galaxies. Spirals typically have masses in the range of a billion to a trillion solar masses, with ellipticals having values from 10 times smaller to 10 times larger and the irregulars generally 10–100 times smaller. Visual galactic luminosities show similar spreads among the three types, but the irregulars tend to be less luminous. In contrast, at radio wavelengths the maximum luminosity for spirals is usually 100,000 times less than for ellipticals or irregulars.

Quasars are objects whose spectra display very large redshifts, thus implying (in accordance with the Hubble law) that they lie at the greatest distances. They were discovered in 1963 but remained enigmatic for many years. They appear as starlike (i.e., very compact) sources of radio waves—hence their initial designation as quasi-stellar radio sources, a term later shortened to *quasars*. They are now considered to be the exceedingly luminous cores of distant galaxies. These energetic cores, which emit copious quantities of X-rays and gamma rays, are termed active galactic nuclei and include the object Cygnus A and the nuclei of a class of galaxies called Seyfert galaxies. They are powered by the infall of matter into supermassive black holes.

The Milky Way Galaxy is one of the Local Group of galaxies, which contains more than three dozen members and extends over a volume about one megaparsec in diameter. Two of the closest

It's easy to see how a quasar (left), could be confused with a star (right). Astronomers now know that quasars are actually the cores of distant galaxies. Charles Steidel (California Institute of Technology, Pasadena) and NASA

members are the Magellanic Clouds, irregular galaxies about 53 kiloparsecs away. At about 740 kiloparsecs the Andromeda Galaxy is one of the most distant in the Local Group. Some members of the group are moving toward the Milky Way system, while others are traveling away from it. At greater distances all galaxies are moving away from the Milky Way Galaxy. Their speeds (as determined from the redshifted wavelengths in their spectra) are generally proportional to their distances. The Hubble law relates these two quantities. In the absence of any other method, the Hubble law continues to be used for distance determinations to the farthest objects—that is, galaxies and quasars for which redshifts can be measured.

COSMOLOGY

Cosmology is the scientific study of the universe as a unified whole, from its earliest moments through its evolution to its ultimate fate. The currently accepted cosmological model is the big bang. In this theory, the expansion of the universe started in an intense explosion 13.7 billion years ago. In this primordial fireball, the temperature exceeded one trillion K, and most of the energy was in the form of radiation. As the expansion proceeded (accompanied by cooling), the role of the radiation diminished, and other physical processes dominated in turn. Thus, after about three minutes, the temperature had dropped to the one-billion-K range, making it possible for nuclear reactions of protons to take place and produce nuclei of deuterium and helium. (At the higher temperatures that prevailed earlier, these nuclei would have been promptly disrupted by high-energy photons.)

With further expansion, the time between nuclear collisions had increased and the proportion of deuterium and helium nuclei had stabilized. After a few hundred thousand years, the temperature must have dropped sufficiently for electrons to remain attached to nuclei to constitute atoms. Galaxies are thought to have begun forming after a few million years, but this stage is very poorly understood. Star formation probably started much later, after at least a billion years, and the process continues today.

Observational support for this general model comes from several independent directions. The expansion has been documented by the redshifts observed in the spectra of galaxies. Furthermore, the radiation left over from the original fireball would have cooled with the expansion. Confirmation of this relic energy came in 1965 with one of the most striking cosmic discoveries of the 20th century—the observation, at short radio wavelengths, of a widespread cosmic radiation corresponding to a temperature of almost 3 K (about -454 °F or -270 °C). The shape of the observed spectrum is an excellent fit to the theoretical Planck blackbody spectrum. (The present best value for this temperature is 2.735 K, but it is still called three-degree radiation or the cosmic microwave background.) The spectrum of this cosmic radio noise peaks at

GRAVITY WAVES

Variations in the gravitational field can be transmitted as waves. According to general relativity, the curvature of space-time is determined by the distribution of masses, while the motion of masses is determined by the curvature. In consequence, variations of the gravitational field should be transmitted from place to place as waves, just as variations of an electromagnetic field travel as waves. If the masses that are the source of a field change with time, they should radiate energy as waves of curvature of the field.

Superficially, there are many similarities between gravity and electromagnetism. For example, Newton's law for the gravitational force between two point masses and Coulomb's law for the electric force between two point charges indicate that both forces vary as the inverse square of the separation distance. Yet in Scottish physicist James Clerk Maxwell's theory for electromagnetism, accelerated charges emit signals (electromagnetic radiation) that travel at the speed of light, whereas in Newton's theory of gravitation accelerated masses transmit information (action at a distance) that travels at infinite speed. This dichotomy is repaired by Einstein's theory of gravitation, wherein accelerated masses also produce signals (gravitational waves) that travel only at the speed of light. Just as electromagnetic waves can make their presence known by the pushing to and fro of electrically charged bodies, so too should gravitational waves be detected, in principle, by the tugging to and fro of massive bodies. However, because the coupling of gravitational forces to masses is intrinsically much weaker than the coupling of electromagnetic forces to charges, the generation and detection of gravitational radiation are much more difficult than those of electromagnetic radiation. Indeed, there has yet to be a single instance of the detection of gravitational waves that is direct and undisputed.

Nevertheless, there are strong grounds for believing that such radiation exists. The most convincing concerns radio-timing observations of a pulsar, PSR 1913+16, located in a binary star system with an orbital period of 7.75 hours. This object has a pulse period of about 59 milliseconds that varies by about one part in 1,000 every 7.75 hours. Interpreted as Doppler shifts, these variations imply orbital velocities on the order of 1/1,000 the speed of light. It is now believed that the system is composed of two neutron stars, each having a mass of about 1.4 solar masses, with a semimajor axis separation of only 2.8 solar radii. According to general relativity, such a system ought to be losing orbital energy through the radiation of gravitational waves at a rate that would cause them to spiral together on a timescale of about 3×10^8 years. The observed decrease in the orbital period in the years since PSR 1913+16's discovery is exactly the predicted rate. Gravitational radiation is the only known means by which that could happen.

The implosion of the core of a massive star to form a neutron star prior to a supernova explosion, if it takes place in a nonspherically symmetric way, ought to provide a powerful burst of gravitational radiation. Simple estimates yield the release of a fraction of the mass-energy deficit, roughly 10^{53} ergs, with the radiation primarily coming out at wave periods between the vibrational period of the neutron star, approximately 0.3 millisecond, and the gravitational-radiation damping time, about 300 milliseconds.

Three types of detectors have been designed to look for gravitational radiation. The changes of curvature of space-time would correspond to a dilation in one direction and a contraction at right angles to that direction. One scheme, first tried out about 1960, employs a massive cylinder that might be set in mechanical oscillation by a gravitational signal. The builders of this apparatus argued that signals had been detected, but their claim has not been substantiated.

In a second scheme an optical interferometer is set up with freely suspended reflectors at the ends of long paths that are at right angles to each other. Shifts of interference fringes corresponding to an increase in length of one arm and a decrease in the other would indicate the passage of gravitational waves. One such interferometer is the Laser Interferometer Gravitational-Wave Observatory (LIGO), which consists of two interferometers with arm lengths of 4 km (2 miles), one in Hanford, Wash., and the other in Livingston, La. LIGO and other interferometers have not yet directly observed gravitational radiation. A planned third scheme, the Laser Interferometer Space Antenna (LISA), would use three separate, but not independent, interferometers installed in three spacecraft located at the corners of a triangle with sides of some 5 million km (3 million miles).

Instrumentation inside the tunnels of the Laser Interferometer Gravitational-Wave Observatory (LIGO) in Louisiana can detect wave forces as little as one-billionth the diameter of a hydrogen atom. Joe McNally/Getty Images

approximately one-millimetre wavelength, which is in the far infrared, a difficult region to observe from Earth. However, the spectrum has been well mapped by the Cosmic Background Explorer (COBE) and the Wilkinson Microwave Anisotropy Probe satellites. Additional support for the big bang theory comes from the observed cosmic abundances of deuterium and helium. Normal stellar nucleosynthesis cannot produce their measured quantities, which fit well with calculations of production during the early stages of the big bang.

Early surveys of the cosmic background radiation indicated that it is extremely uniform in all directions (isotropic). Calculations have shown that it is difficult to achieve this degree of isotropy unless there was a very early and rapid inflationary period before the expansion settled into its present mode. Nevertheless, the isotropy posed problems for models of galaxy formation. Galaxies originate from turbulent conditions that produce local fluctuations of density, toward which more matter would then be gravitationally attracted. Such density variations were difficult to reconcile with the isotropy required by observations of the 3 K radiation. This problem was solved when the COBE satellite was able to detect the minute fluctuations in the cosmic background from which the galaxies formed.

The very earliest stages of the big bang are less well understood. The conditions of temperature and pressure that prevailed prior to the first microsecond require the introduction of theoretical ideas of subatomic particle physics. Subatomic particles are usually studied in laboratories with giant accelerators, but the region of particle energies of potential significance to the question at hand lies beyond the range of accelerators currently available. Fortunately, some important conclusions can be drawn from the observed cosmic helium abundance, which is dependent on conditions in the early big bang. The observed helium abundance sets a limit on the number of families of certain types of subatomic particles that can exist.

The age of the universe can be calculated in several ways. Assuming the validity of the big bang model, one attempts to answer the question: How long has the universe been expanding in order to have reached its present size? The numbers relevant to calculating an answer are Hubble's constant (i.e., the current expansion rate), the density of matter in the universe, and the cosmological constant, which allows for change in the expansion rate. In 2003 a calculation based on a fresh determination of Hubble's constant yielded an age of 13.7 billion ± 200 million years, although the precise value depends on certain assumed details of the model used. Independent estimates of stellar ages have yielded values less than this, as would be expected, but other estimates, based on supernova distance measurements, have arrived at values of about 15 billion years, still consistent, within the errors. In the big bang model the age is proportional to the reciprocal of Hubble's constant, hence the importance of determining H as reliably as possible. For example, a value for H of 100 km/sec/Mpc would lead to an age less than that of many stars, a physically unacceptable result.

A small minority of astronomers have developed alternative cosmological theories that are seriously pursued. The overwhelming professional opinion, however, continues to support the big bang model.

Finally, there is the question of the future behaviour of the universe. Scientists question whether the universe is open, meaning it will expand indefinitely, or closed, such that the expansion will slow down and eventually reverse, resulting in contraction. (The final collapse of such a contracting universe is sometimes termed the "big crunch.") The density of the universe seems to be at the critical density; that is, the universe is neither open nor closed, but "flat." So-called dark energy, a kind of repulsive force that is now believed to be a major component of the universe, appears to be the decisive factor in predictions of the long-term fate of the cosmos.

If this energy is a cosmological constant (as proposed in 1917 by Albert Einstein to correct certain problems in his model of the universe), then the result would be a "big chill." In this scenario, the universe would continue to expand, but its density would decrease. While old stars would burn out, new stars would no longer form. The universe would become cold and dark. The dark (nonluminous) matter component of the universe, whose composition remains unknown, is not considered sufficient to close the universe and cause it to collapse; it now appears to contribute only a fourth of the density needed for closure.

An additional factor in deciding the fate of the universe might be the mass of neutrinos. For decades the neutrino had been postulated to have zero mass, although there was no compelling theoretical reason for this to be so. From the observation of neutrinos generated in the Sun and other celestial sources such as supernovas, in cosmic-ray interactions with Earth's atmosphere, and in particle accelerators, investigators have concluded that neutrinos have some mass, though only an extremely small fraction of the mass of an electron. Although there are vast numbers of neutrinos in the universe, the sum of such small neutrino masses appears insufficient to close the universe.

ASTROBIOLOGY

Astrobiology is a multidisciplinary field dealing with the nature, existence, and search for extraterrestrial life (life beyond Earth). It encompasses areas of biology, astronomy, and geology.

Although no compelling evidence of extraterrestrial life has yet been found, the possibility that biota might be a

Global map of Mars in epithermal (intermediate-energy) neutrons created from data collected by the 2001 Mars Odyssey spacecraft. The darker areas have the lowest levels of neutrons indicate the presence of high levels of hydrogen, which is suggestive of large reservoirs of water ice below the surface. NASA/JPL/University of Arizona/Los Alamos National Laboratories

common feature of the universe has been strengthened by the discovery of extra-solar planets (planets around other stars) and by the strong suspicion that several moons of Jupiter and Saturn might have vast reserves of liquid water. The first development indicates that habitats for life may be numerous, and the second suggests that even in the solar system there may be other worlds on which life evolved. The principal areas of astrobiology research can be classified as (1) understanding the conditions under which life can arise, (2) looking for habitable worlds, and (3) searching for evidence of life.

For life like that on Earth (based on complex carbon compounds) to exist, a world must have liquid water. Because planets either too close to or too far from their host stars will be at temperatures that cause water either to boil or to freeze, astrobiologists define a "habitable zone," a range of orbital distances within which planets can support liquid water on their surfaces. In the solar system, only Earth is inside the Sun's habitable zone. However, photographs and other data from spacecraft orbiting Mars indicate that water once flowed on the surface of the red planet and is still present in large quantities underground. Consequently, there is a sustained international effort to use robotic probes to examine Mars for evidence of past, and even present, life that could have retreated to subsurface, liquid aquifers.

Also, discoveries primarily due to the Galileo space probe (launched in 1989) suggest that some of the moons of Jupiter—principally Europa but also Ganymede and Callisto—as well as Saturn's moon Enceladus, might have long-lived liquid oceans under their icy outer skins. These oceans can be kept warm despite their great distance from the Sun because of gravitational interactions between the moons and their host planet, and they might support the kind of life found in deep sea vents on Earth.

Even Titan, a large moon of Saturn with a thick atmosphere, might conceivably have some unusual biology on its cold surface, where lakes of liquid methane and ethane may exist. The European space probe Huygens landed on Titan on Jan. 14, 2005, and saw signs of liquid flow on its surface. Such discoveries as these have strongly promoted the emergence of astrobiology as a field of study by broadening the range of possible extraterrestrial habitats far beyond the conventional notion of a "habitable zone."

An additional impetus has been the discovery since 1995 of hundreds of extra-solar planets around other normal stars. Most of these are giant worlds, similar to Jupiter and therefore unlikely to be suitable for life themselves, although they could have moons on which life might arise. However, this work has shown that at least 5 to 10 percent (and possibly as much as 50 percent or more) of all Sun-like stars have planets, implying many billions of solar systems in the Milky Way Galaxy. The discovery of these planets has encouraged astrobiology and in particular has motivated proposals for several space-based telescopes designed (1) to search for smaller, Earth-size worlds and (2) if such worlds are found, to analyze spectrally the light reflected by the planets' atmospheres in the hope of detecting oxygen, methane, or other substances that would indicate the presence of biota.

While no one can say with certainty what sort of life might be turned up by these experiments, the usual assumption is that it will be microbial, as single-celled life is adaptable to a wide range of environments and requires less energy. However, telescopic searches for extraterrestrial intelligence (SETI) are also part of astrobiology's extensive research palette.

CHAPTER 3

ASTRONOMICAL OBJECTS AND THEIR MOTIONS

Ordinary classical mechanics can describe the motion of a car on a highway, a baseball clearing the outfield fence, or an apple falling from a tree. The same equations that describe the motion of the car, the baseball, and the apple can be applied to the motion of celestial bodies acted on by any of several types of forces. By far the most important force experienced by these bodies, and much of the time the only important force, is that of their mutual gravitational attraction. But other forces can be important as well, such as atmospheric drag on artificial satellites, the pressure of radiation on dust particles, and even electromagnetic forces on dust particles if they are electrically charged and moving in a magnetic field.

CELESTIAL MECHANICS

The term *celestial mechanics* is sometimes assumed to refer only to the analysis developed for the motion of point mass particles moving under their mutual gravitational attractions, with emphasis on the general orbital motions of solar system bodies. This science has evolved from an ad hoc collection of rules of thumb to describe the planetary motions to a finely tuned description of astronomical motion based on Newton's laws and their fullest description in Einstein's theory of general relativity.

The term *astrodynamics* is often used to refer to the celestial mechanics of artificial satellite motion. *Dynamic astronomy* is a much broader term, which, in addition to celestial mechanics and astrodynamics, is usually interpreted to include all aspects of celestial body motion (e.g., rotation, tidal evolution, mass and mass distribution determinations for stars and galaxies, fluid motions in nebulas, and so forth).

EARLY THEORIES

Celestial mechanics has its beginnings in early astronomy, in which the motions of the Sun, the Moon, and the five planets visible to the unaided eye—Mercury, Venus, Mars, Jupiter, and Saturn—were observed and analyzed. The word *planet* is derived from the Greek word for wanderer. It was natural for some cultures to elevate these objects moving against the fixed background of the sky to the status of gods. This status survives in some sense today in astrology, where the positions of the planets and Sun are thought to somehow influence the lives of individuals on Earth. The divine status of the planets and their supposed influence on human activities may have been the primary motivation for careful, continued observations of planetary motions and for the development of elaborate schemes for predicting their positions in the future.

The Greek astronomer Ptolemy proposed a system of planetary motion in which Earth was fixed at the centre and all the planets, the Moon, and the Sun orbited around it. As seen by an observer on Earth, the planets move across the sky at a variable rate. They even reverse their direction of motion occasionally but resume the dominant direction of motion after a while. To describe this variable motion, Ptolemy assumed that the planets revolved around small circles called epicycles at a uniform rate while the centre of the epicyclic circle orbited Earth on a large circle called a deferent. Other variations in the motion were accounted for by offsetting the centres of the deferent for each planet from Earth by a short distance. By choosing the combination of speeds and distances appropriately, Ptolemy was able to predict the motions of the planets with considerable accuracy. His scheme was adopted as absolute dogma and survived more than 1,000 years until the time of Copernicus.

Nicolaus Copernicus assumed that Earth was just another planet that orbited the Sun along with the other planets. He showed that this heliocentric (centred on the Sun) model was consistent with all observations and that it was far simpler than Ptolemy's scheme. His belief that planetary motion had to be a combination of uniform circular motions forced him to include a series of epicycles to match the motions in the noncircular orbits. The epicycles were like terms in the Fourier series that are used to represent planetary motions today. (A Fourier series is an infinite sum of periodic terms that oscillate between positive and negative values in a smooth way, where the frequency of oscillation changes from term to term. They represent better and better approximations to other functions as more and more terms are kept.) Copernicus also determined the relative scale of his heliocentric solar system, with results that are remarkably close to the modern determination.

Tycho Brahe (1546–1601), who was born three years after Copernicus's death and three years after the publication of the latter's heliocentric model of the solar system, still embraced a geocentric model, but he had only the Sun and the Moon orbiting Earth and all the other planets orbiting the Sun. Although this model is mathematically equivalent to the heliocentric model of Copernicus, it represents an unnecessary complication and is physically incorrect. Tycho's greatest contribution was the more than 20 years of celestial observations he collected; his measurements of the positions of the planets and stars had an unprecedented accuracy of approximately 2 arc minutes. (An arc minute is $\frac{1}{60}$ of a degree.)

KEPLER'S LAWS OF PLANETARY MOTION

Tycho's observations were inherited by Johannes Kepler (1571–1630), who was employed by Tycho shortly before the latter's death. From these precise positions of the planets at correspondingly accurate times, Kepler empirically determined his famous three laws describing planetary motion: (1) the orbits of the planets

are ellipses with the Sun at one focus; (2) the radial line from the Sun to the planet sweeps out equal areas in equal times; and (3) the ratio of the squares of the periods of revolution around the Sun of any two planets equal the ratio of the cubes of the semimajor axes of their respective orbital ellipses.

An ellipse is a plane curve defined such that the sum of the distances from any point G on the ellipse to two fixed points (S and S') is constant. The two points S and S' are called foci, and the straight line on which these points lie between the extremes of the ellipse at A and P is referred to as the major axis of the ellipse. Hence, $GS + GS' = AP = 2a$, where a is the semimajor axis of the ellipse. A focus is separated from the centre C of the ellipse by the fractional part of the semimajor axis given by the product ae, where $e < 1$ is called the eccentricity. Thus, $e = 0$ corresponds to a circle. If the Sun is at the focus S of the ellipse, the point P at which the planet is closest to the Sun is called the perihelion, and the most distant point in the orbit A is the aphelion. The term *helion* refers specifically to the Sun as the primary body about which the planet is orbiting. As the points P and A are also called apses, periapse and apoapse are often used to designate the corresponding points in an orbit about any primary body, although more specific terms, such as perigee and apogee for Earth, are often used to indicate the primary body. If G is the instantaneous location of a planet in its orbit, the angle f, called the true anomaly, locates this point relative to the perihelion P with the Sun (or focus S) as the origin, or vertex, of the angle. The angle u, called the eccentric anomaly, also locates G relative to P but with the centre of the ellipse as the origin rather than the focus S. An angle called the mean anomaly l is also measured from P with S as the origin; it is defined to increase uniformly with time and to equal the true anomaly f at perihelion and aphelion.

Kepler's second law relates to the form of an ellipse. If the time required for the planet to move from two points on the ellipse P to F is the same as that to move from two other points D to E, the areas of the two shaded regions will be equal according to the second law. The validity of the second law means a planet must have a higher than average velocity near perihelion and a lower than average velocity near aphelion. The angular velocity (rate of change of the angle f) must vary around the orbit in a similar

German astronomer Johannes Kepler made many discoveries in optics, general physics, and geometry. Arguably his most renowned achievement is the discovery of the laws of planetary motion, named in his honor. Hulton Archive/Getty Images

way. The average angular velocity, called the mean motion, is the rate of change of the mean anomaly l defined above.

The third law can be used to determine the distance of a planet from the Sun if one knows its orbital period, or vice versa. In particular, if time is measured in years and distance in units of AU, the third law can be written $\tau^2 = a^3$, where τ is the orbital period.

NEWTON'S LAWS OF MOTION

The empirical laws of Kepler describe planetary motion, but Kepler made no attempt to define or constrain the underlying physical processes governing the motion. It was Isaac Newton who accomplished that feat in the late 17th century. Newton defined momentum as being proportional to velocity with the constant of proportionality being defined as mass. (As described earlier, momentum is a vector quantity in the sense that the direction of motion as well as the magnitude is included in the definition.) Newton then defined force (also a vector quantity) in terms of its effect on moving objects and in the process formulated his three laws of motion: (1) The momentum of an object is constant unless an outside force acts on the object; this means that any object either remains at rest or continues uniform motion in a straight line unless acted on by a force. (2) The time rate of change of the momentum of an object is equal to the force acting on the object. (3) For every action (force) there is an equal and opposite reaction (force). The first

law is seen to be a special case of the second law. Galileo, the great Italian contemporary of Kepler who adopted the Copernican point of view and promoted it vigorously, anticipated Newton's first two laws with his experiments in mechanics. But it was Newton who defined them precisely, established the basis of classical mechanics, and set the stage for its application as celestial mechanics to the motions of bodies in space.

According to the second law, a force must be acting on a planet to cause its path to curve toward the Sun. Newton and others noted that the acceleration of a body in uniform circular motion must be directed toward the centre of the circle; furthermore, if several objects were in circular motion around the same centre at various separations r and their periods of revolution varied as $r^{3/2}$, as Kepler's third law indicated for the planets, then the acceleration—and thus, by Newton's second law, the force as well—must vary as $1/r^2$. By assuming this attractive force between point masses, Newton showed that a spherically symmetric mass distribution attracted a second body outside the sphere as if all the spherically distributed mass were contained in a point at the centre of the sphere. Thus the attraction of the planets by the Sun was the same as the gravitational force attracting objects to Earth. Newton further concluded that the force of attraction between two massive bodies was proportional to the inverse square of their separation and to the product of their masses, known as the law of universal gravitation. Kepler's

EPHEMERIS

An ephemeris (plural ephemerides) is a table giving the positions of one or more celestial bodies, often published with supplementary information. Ephemerides were constructed as early as the 4th century BCE and are still essential today to the astronomer and navigator.

Modern ephemerides are calculated when a theory (mathematical description) of the motion of a heavenly body has been evolved, based on observations. Heavy computing and careful checking are involved. Until the 20th century, tables of logarithms were the chief aid to computation. The gradual introduction of mechanical calculators increased the speed and accuracy of the work. Of greater effect was the development of electronic calculators and computers. These have made feasible the solution of problems formerly considered impossible because of the tremendous labour involved. The simultaneous integration of the equations of motion of the five outer planets, for every 40th day, from the year 1653 to 2060 is typical.

A number of national ephemerides are published regularly. The oldest is the Connaissance des temps, *founded in Paris in 1679 as the direct successor to a series of ephemerides originally begun by the German astronomer Johannes Kepler in 1617. The British* Nautical Almanac and Astronomical Ephemeris *commenced through the initiative of Nevil Maskelyne in 1766. The American Ephemeris and Nautical Almanac was first published in Washington, D.C., in 1852 for the year 1855. From 1877, under the direction of the astronomer Simon Newcomb, it became the best of the national ephemerides. To avoid duplication of costs, it has since 1960 been unified with the British national publication, which at the same time was renamed* The Astronomical Ephemeris. *The two are of identical content, reproduced separately in each country; the work of computing is shared. Beginning in 1981, both national ephemerides were renamed* The Astronomical Almanac. Ephemerides of Minor Planets, *compiled and published annually by the Institute of Theoretical Astronomy, St. Petersburg, represents further international cooperation.*

laws are derivable from Newton's laws of motion with a central force of gravity varying as $1/r^2$ from a fixed point, and Newton's law of gravity is derivable from Kepler's laws if one assumes Newton's laws of motion.

In addition to formulating the laws of motion and of gravity, Newton also showed that a point mass moving about a fixed centre of force, which varies as the inverse square of the distance away from the centre, follows an elliptical path if the initial velocity is not too large, a hyperbolic path for high initial velocities, and a parabolic path for intermediate velocities. In other words, a sequence of orbits with the perihelion distance SP fixed but with the velocity at P increasing from orbit to orbit is characterized by a corresponding increase in the orbital eccentricity e from orbit to orbit such that $e < 1$ for bound elliptical orbits, $e = 1$ for a parabolic orbit, and $e > 1$ for a hyperbolic orbit. Many comets have nearly parabolic orbits for their first pass into the inner solar system, whereas spacecraft may have nearly hyperbolic orbits relative to a planet they are flying by while they are close to the planet.

Throughout history, the motion of the planets in the solar system has served as a laboratory to constrain and guide the development of celestial mechanics in particular and classical mechanics in general. In modern times, increasingly precise observations of celestial bodies have been matched by increasingly precise predictions for future positions—a combination that became a test for Newton's law of gravitation itself. Although the lunar motion (within observational errors) seemed consistent with a gravitational attraction between point masses that decreased exactly as $1/r^2$, this law of gravitation was ultimately shown to be an approximation of the more complete description of gravity given by the theory of general relativity. Similarly, a discrepancy of roughly 40 arc seconds per century between the observed rate of advance of Mercury's perihelion and that predicted by planetary perturbations with Newtonian gravity is almost precisely accounted for with Einstein's general theory of relativity. That this small discrepancy could be confidently asserted as real was a triumph of quantitative celestial mechanics.

PERTURBATIONS AND PROBLEMS OF TWO BODIES

The motions of two bodies in their mutual gravitational attraction are the simplest that can be described by celestial mechanics. However, there are no two astronomical bodies that exist in isolation. Any celestial object is affected, however slightly, by the other objects in the universe. Such small effects are called perturbations.

THE APPROXIMATE NATURE OF KEPLER'S LAWS

The constraints placed on the force for Kepler's laws to be derivable from Newton's laws were that the force must be directed toward a central fixed point and that the force must decrease as the inverse square of the distance. In actuality, however, the Sun, which serves as the source of the major force, is not fixed but experiences small accelerations because of the planets, in accordance with Newton's second and third laws. Furthermore, the planets attract one another, so that the total force on a planet is not just that due to the Sun; other planets perturb the elliptical motion that would have occurred for a particular planet if that planet had been the only one orbiting an isolated Sun. Kepler's laws therefore are only approximate. The motion of the Sun itself means that, even when the attractions by other planets are neglected, Kepler's third law must be replaced by $(M + m_i)\tau^2 \propto a^3$, where m_i is one of the planetary masses and M is the Sun's mass. That Kepler's laws are such good approximations to the actual planetary motions results from the fact that all the planetary masses are very small compared to that of the Sun.

The perturbations of the elliptic motion are therefore small, and the coefficient $M + m_i \approx M$ for all the planetary masses m_i means that Kepler's third law is very close to being true.

Newton's second law for a particular mass is a second-order differential equation that must be solved for whatever forces may act on the body if its position as a function of time is to be deduced. The exact solution of this equation, which resulted in a derived trajectory that was an ellipse, parabola, or hyperbola, depended on the assumption that there were only two point particles interacting by the inverse square force. Hence, this "gravitational two-body problem" has an exact solution that reproduces Kepler's laws. If one or more additional bodies also interact with the original pair through their mutual gravitational interactions, no exact solution for the differential equations of motion of any of the bodies involved can be obtained. As was noted above, however, the motion of a planet is almost elliptical, since all masses involved are small compared to the Sun. It is then convenient to treat the motion of a particular planet as slightly perturbed elliptical motion and to determine the changes in the parameters of the ellipse that result from the small forces as time progresses. It is the elaborate developments of various perturbation theories and their applications to approximate the exact motions of celestial bodies that has occupied celestial mechanicians since Newton's time.

PERTURBATIONS OF ELLIPTICAL MOTION

So far the following orbital parameters, or elements, have been used to describe elliptical motion: the orbital semimajor axis a, the orbital eccentricity e, and, to specify position in the orbit relative to the perihelion, either the true anomaly f, the eccentric anomaly u, or the mean anomaly l. Three more orbital elements are necessary to orient the ellipse in space, since that orientation will change because of the perturbations. These additional parameters are referred to relative to a reference plane, where the reference plane is chosen arbitrarily to be the plane of the ecliptic, which is the plane of Earth's orbit defined by the path of the Sun on the sky. (For motion of a near-Earth artificial satellite, the most convenient reference plane would be that of Earth's Equator.) Angle i is the inclination of the orbital plane to the reference plane. The line of nodes is the intersection of the orbit plane with the reference plane, and the ascending node is that point where the planet travels from below the reference plane (south) to above the reference plane (north). The ascending node is described by its angular position measured from a reference point on the ecliptic plane, such as the vernal equinox; the angle Ω is called the longitude of the ascending node. Angle ω (called the argument of perihelion) is the angular distance from the ascending node to the perihelion measured in the orbit plane.

For the two-body problem, all the orbital parameters a, e, i, Ω, and ω are constants. A sixth constant T, the time of perihelion passage (i.e., any date at which the object in orbit was known to be at perihelion), may be used to replace f, u, or l, and the position of the planet in its fixed elliptic orbit can be determined uniquely at subsequent times. These six constants are determined uniquely by the six initial conditions of three components of the position vector and three components of the velocity vector relative to a coordinate system that is fixed with respect to the reference plane. When small perturbations are taken into account, it is convenient to consider the orbit as an instantaneous ellipse whose parameters are defined by the instantaneous values of the position and velocity vectors, since for small perturbations the orbit is approximately an ellipse. In fact, however, perturbations cause the six formerly constant parameters to vary slowly, and the instantaneous perturbed orbit is called an osculating ellipse; that is, the osculating ellipse is that elliptical orbit that would be assumed by the body if all the perturbing forces were suddenly turned off.

First-order differential equations describing the variation of the six orbital parameters can be constructed for each planet or other celestial body from the second-order differential equations that result by equating the mass times the acceleration of a body to the sum of all the forces acting on the body (Newton's second law). These equations are sometimes called the Lagrange planetary equations after their derivation by the great Italian-French mathematician Joseph-Louis Lagrange (1736–1813). As long as the forces are conservative and do not depend on the velocities—i.e., there is no loss of mechanical energy through such processes as friction—they can be derived from partial derivatives of a function of the spatial coordinates only, called the potential energy, whose magnitude depends on the relative separations of the masses.

In the case where all the forces are derivable from such potential energy, the total energy of a system of any number of particles—i.e, the kinetic energy plus the potential energy—is constant. The kinetic energy of a single particle is one-half its mass times the square of its velocity, and the total kinetic energy is the sum of such expressions for all the particles being considered. The conservation of energy principle is thus expressed by an equation relating the velocities of all the masses to their positions at any time. The partial derivatives of the potential energy with respect to spatial coordinates are transformed into particle derivatives of a disturbing function with respect to the orbital elements in the Lagrange equations, where the disturbing function vanishes if all bodies perturbing the elliptic motion are removed. Like Newton's equations of motion, Lagrange's differential equations are exact, but they can be solved only numerically on a computer or analytically by successive approximations. In the latter process, the disturbing function is represented by a Fourier series, with convergence of the series (successive decrease in size and importance of the terms) depending on the size of the orbital eccentricities and inclinations. Clever changes of variables and other mathematical tricks are used to increase the time span over which the solutions (also represented by series) are good approximations to the real motion. These series solutions usually diverge, but they still represent the actual motions remarkably well for limited periods of time. One of the major triumphs of celestial mechanics using these perturbation techniques was the discovery of Neptune in 1846 from its perturbations of the motion of Uranus.

EXAMPLES OF PERTURBATIONS

Some of the variations in the orbital parameters caused by perturbations can be understood in simple terms. The lunar orbit is inclined to the ecliptic plane by about 5°, and the longitude of its ascending node on the ecliptic plane (Ω) is observed to regress (Ω decreasing) a complete revolution in 18.61 years. The Sun is the dominant cause of this regression of the lunar node. When the Moon is closer to the Sun than Earth, the Sun accelerates the Moon slightly more than it accelerates Earth. This difference in the accelerations is what perturbs the lunar motion around Earth. The Moon does not fly off in this situation since the acceleration of the Moon toward Earth is much larger than

the difference between the Sun's accelerations of Earth and the Moon.

The Sun, of course, is always in the ecliptic plane, since its apparent path among the stars defines the plane. This means that the perturbing acceleration just defined will always be pointed slightly toward the ecliptic plane whenever the Moon is below or above this plane in its orbital motion about Earth. This tendency to pull the Moon toward the ecliptic plane means that the Moon will cross the plane on each half orbit at a longitude that is slightly smaller than the longitude at which it would have crossed if the Sun had not been there. Thus, the line of nodes will have regressed. The instantaneous rate at which the node regresses varies as the geometry changes during the Moon's motion around Earth, and during the Earth-Moon system's motion around the Sun, but there is always a net regression. Such a change that is always in the same direction as time increases is called a secular perturbation. Superposed on the secular perturbation of the longitude of the node are periodic perturbations (periodically changing their direction), which are revealed by the fact that the rate of secular regression of the node is not constant in time. The Sun causes a secular increase in the longitude of the lunar perigee ($\Omega + \omega$) of one complete revolution in 8.85 years, as well as periodic perturbations in the inclination, eccentricity, and mean motion.

For near-Earth artificial satellites, the deviation of Earth's mass distribution from spherical symmetry is the dominant cause of the perturbations from pure elliptic motion. The most important deviation is the equatorial bulge of Earth due to its rotation. If, for example, Earth were a sphere with a ring of mass around its Equator, the ring would give to a satellite whose orbit is inclined to the Equator a component of acceleration toward the Equator plane whenever the satellite was above or below this plane. By an argument similar to that for the Moon acted on by the Sun, this acceleration would cause the line of nodes of a close satellite orbit to regress a little more than 5° per day.

As a final example, the distribution of continents and oceans and the varying mass densities in Earth's mantle (the layer underlying the crust) lead to a slight deviation of Earth's gravitational force field from axial symmetry. Usually this causes only short-period perturbations of low amplitude for near-Earth satellites. However, communications or weather satellites that are meant to maintain a fixed longitude over the Equator (i.e., geostationary satellites, which orbit synchronously with Earth's rotation) are destabilized by this deviation except at two longitudes. If the axial asymmetry is represented by a slightly elliptical Equator, the difference between the major and minor axis of the ellipse is about 64 metres (210 feet), with the major axis located about 35° W. A satellite at a position slightly ahead of the long axis of the elliptical Equator will experience a component of acceleration opposite its direction of orbital motion (as if a large mountain were pulling it back). This acceleration makes the satellite fall closer to Earth and increases its mean motion, causing it to drift further ahead of the axial bulge on the Equator. If the satellite is slightly behind the axial bulge, it experiences an acceleration in the direction of its motion. This makes the satellite move away from Earth with a decrease in its mean motion, so that it will drift further behind the axial bulge. The synchronous Earth satellites are thus repelled from the long axis of the equatorial ellipse and attracted to the short axis, and compensating accelerations, usually from onboard jets, are required to stabilize a satellite at any longitude other than the two corresponding to the ends of the short axis of the axial bulge. (The jets are actually required for any longitude, as they must also compensate for other perturbations such as radiation pressure.)

THE THREE-BODY PROBLEM

The inclusion of solar perturbations of the motion of the Moon results in a "three-body problem" (Earth-Moon-Sun), which is the simplest complication of the completely solvable two-body problem discussed above. When Earth, the Moon, and the Sun are considered to be point masses, this particular three-body problem is called "the main problem of the lunar theory," which has been studied extensively with a variety of methods beginning with Newton. Although the three-body problem has no complete analytic solution in closed form, various series solutions by successive approximations achieve such accuracy that complete theories of the lunar motion must include the effects of the nonspherical mass distributions of both Earth and the Moon as well as the effects of the planets if the precision of the predicted positions is to approach that of the observations. Most of the schemes for the main problem are partially numerical and therefore apply only to the lunar motion. An exception is the completely analytic work of the French astronomer Charles-Eugène Delaunay (1816–72), who exploited and developed the most elegant techniques of classical mechanics pioneered by his contemporary, the Irish astronomer and mathematician William R. Hamilton (1805–65). Delaunay could predict the position of the Moon to within its own diameter over a 20-year time span. Since his development was entirely analytic, the work was applicable to the motions of satellites about other planets where the series expansions converged much more rapidly than they did for the application to the lunar motion.

Delaunay's work on the lunar theory demonstrates some of the influence that celestial mechanics has had on the development of the techniques of classical mechanics. This close link between the development of classical mechanics and its application to celestial mechanics was probably no better demonstrated than in the work of the French mathematician

Henri Poincaré (1854–1912). Poincaré, along with other great mathematicians such as George D. Birkhoff (1884–1944), Aurel Wintner (1903–58), and Andrey N. Kolmogorov (1903–87), placed celestial mechanics on a more sound mathematical basis and was less concerned with quantitatively accurate prediction of celestial body motion. Poincaré demonstrated that the series solutions in use in celestial mechanics for so long generally did not converge but that they could give accurate descriptions of the motion for significant periods of time in truncated form. The elaborate theoretical developments in celestial and classical mechanics have received more attention recently with the realization that a large class of motions are of an irregular or chaotic nature and require fundamentally different approaches for their description.

THE RESTRICTED THREE-BODY PROBLEM

The simplest form of the three-body problem is called the restricted three-body problem, in which a particle of infinitesimal mass moves in the gravitational field of two massive bodies orbiting according to the exact solution of the two-body problem. (The particle with infinitesimal mass, sometimes called a massless particle, does not perturb the motions of the two massive bodies.) There is an enormous literature devoted to this problem, including both analytic and numerical developments. The analytic work was devoted mostly to the circular, planar restricted three-body problem, where all particles are confined to a plane and the two finite masses are in circular orbits around their centre of mass (a point on the line between the two masses that is closer to the more massive). Numerical developments allowed consideration of the more general problem.

In the circular problem, the two finite masses are fixed in a coordinate system rotating at the orbital angular velocity, with the origin (axis of rotation) at the centre of mass of the two bodies. Lagrange showed that in this rotating frame there were five stationary points at which the massless particle would remain fixed if placed there. There are three such points lying on the line connecting the two finite masses: one between the masses and one outside each of the masses. The other two stationary points, called the triangular points, are located equidistant from the two finite masses at a distance equal to the finite mass separation. The two masses and the triangular stationary points are thus located at the vertices of equilateral triangles in the plane of the circular orbit.

There is a constant of the motion in the rotating frame that leads to an equation relating the velocity of the massless particle in this frame to its position. For given values of this constant it is possible to construct curves in the plane on which the velocity vanishes. If such a zero-velocity curve is closed, the particle cannot escape from the interior of the closed zero-velocity curve if placed there

with the constant of the motion equal to the value used to construct the curve. These zero-velocity curves can be used to show that the three collinear stationary points are all unstable in the sense that, if the particle is placed at one of these points, the slightest perturbation will cause it to move far away. The triangular points are stable if the ratio of the finite masses is less than 0.04, and the particle would execute small oscillations around one of the triangular points if it were pushed slightly away. Since the mass ratio of Jupiter to the Sun is about 0.001, the stability criterion is satisfied, and Lagrange predicted the presence of the Trojan asteroids at the triangular points of the Sun-Jupiter system 134 years before they were observed. Of course, the stability of the triangular points must also depend on the perturbations by any other bodies. Such perturbations are sufficiently small not to destabilize the Trojan asteroids. Single Trojan-like bodies have also been found orbiting at leading and trailing triangular points in the orbit of Saturn's satellite Tethys, at the leading triangular point in the orbit of another Saturnian satellite, Dione, and at the trailing point in the orbit of Mars.

ORBITAL RESONANCES

There are stable configurations in the restricted three-body problem that are not stationary in the rotating frame. If, for example, Jupiter and the Sun are the two massive bodies, these stable configurations occur when the mean motions of

Jupiter and the small particle—here an asteroid—are near a ratio of small integers. The orbital mean motions are then said to be nearly commensurate, and an asteroid that is trapped near such a mean motion commensurability is said to be in an orbital resonance with Jupiter. For example, the Trojan asteroids librate (oscillate) around the 1:1 orbital resonance (i.e., the orbital period of Jupiter is in a 1:1 ratio with the orbital period of the Trojan asteroids); the asteroid Thule librates around the 4:3 orbital resonance; and several asteroids in the Hilda group librate around the 3:2 orbital resonance. There are several such stable orbital resonances among the satellites of the major planets and one involving Pluto and the planet Neptune. The analysis based on the restricted three-body problem cannot be used for the satellite resonances, however, except for the 4:3 resonance between Saturn's satellites Titan and Hyperion, since the participants in the satellite resonances usually have comparable masses.

Although the asteroid Griqua librates around the 2:1 resonance with Jupiter, and Alinda librates around the 3:1 resonance, the orbital commensurabilities 2:1, 7:3, 5:2, and 3:1 are characterized by an absence of asteroids in an otherwise rather highly populated, uniform distribution spanning all of the commensurabilities. These are the Kirkwood gaps in the distribution of asteroids, and the recent understanding of their creation and maintenance has introduced into celestial mechanics an entirely new concept of irregular, or chaotic, orbits in a system whose equations of motion are entirely deterministic.

CHAOTIC ORBITS

The French astronomer Michel Hénon and the American astronomer Carl Heiles discovered that when a system exhibiting periodic motion, such as a pendulum, is perturbed by an external force that is also periodic, some initial conditions lead to motions where the state of the system becomes essentially unpredictable (within some range of system states) at some time in the future, whereas initial conditions within some other set produce quasiperiodic or predictable behaviour. The unpredictable behaviour is called chaotic, and initial conditions that produce it are said to lie in a chaotic zone. If the chaotic zone is bounded, in the sense that only limited ranges of initial values of the variables describing the motion lead to chaotic behaviour, the uncertainty in the state of the system in the future is limited by the extent of the chaotic zone; that is, values of the variables in the distant future are completely uncertain only within those ranges of values within the chaotic zone. This complete uncertainty within the zone means the system will eventually come arbitrarily close to any set of values of the variables within the zone if given sufficient time. Chaotic orbits were first realized in the asteroid belt.

A periodic term in the expansion of the disturbing function for a typical asteroid orbit becomes more important in influencing the motion of the asteroid if the frequency with which it changes sign is very small and its coefficient is relatively large. For asteroids orbiting near a mean motion commensurability with Jupiter, there are generally several terms in the disturbing function with large coefficients and small frequencies that are close but not identical. These "resonant" terms often dominate the perturbations of the asteroid motion so much that all the higher-frequency terms can be neglected in determining a first approximation to the perturbed motion. This neglect is equivalent to averaging the higher-frequency terms to zero; the low-frequency terms change only slightly during the averaging. If one of the frequencies vanishes on the average, the periodic term becomes nearly constant, or secular, and the asteroid is locked into an exact orbital resonance near the particular mean motion commensurability. The mean motions are not exactly commensurate in such a resonance, however, since the motion of the asteroid orbital node or perihelion is always involved (except for the 1:1 Trojan resonances).

For example, for the 3:1 commensurability, the angle

$$\theta = \lambda_A - 3\lambda_J + \varpi_A$$

is the argument of one of the important periodic terms whose variation can vanish (zero frequency). Here

$$\lambda = \Omega + \omega + l$$

is the mean longitude, the subscripts A and J refer to the asteroid and Jupiter, respectively, and $\varpi = \Omega + \omega$ is the longitude of perihelion. Within resonance, the angle θ librates, or oscillates, around a constant value as would a pendulum around its equilibrium position at the bottom of its swing. The larger the amplitude of the equivalent pendulum, the larger its velocity at the bottom of its swing. If the velocity of the pendulum at the bottom of its swing, or, equivalently, the maximum rate of change of the angle θ, is sufficiently high, the pendulum will swing over the top of its support and be in a state of rotation instead of libration. The maximum value of the rate of change of θ for which θ remains an angle of libration (periodically reversing its variation) instead of one of rotation (increasing or decreasing monotonically) is defined as the half-width of the resonance.

Another term with nearly zero frequency when the asteroid is near the 3:1 commensurability has the argument $\theta' = \lambda_A - \lambda_J + 2\varpi_J$. The substitution of the longitude of Jupiter's perihelion for that of the asteroid means that the rates of change of θ and θ' will be slightly different. As the resonances are not separated much in frequency, there may exist values of the mean motion of the asteroid where both θ and θ' would be angles of libration if either resonance existed in the absence of the other. The resonances are said to overlap in this case, and the attempt by the system to librate simultaneously about both resonances for some initial conditions leads to chaotic orbital behaviour. The important characteristic of the chaotic zone for asteroid motion near a mean motion commensurability with Jupiter is that it includes a region where the asteroid's orbital eccentricity is large. During the variation of the elements over the entire chaotic zone as time increases, large eccentricities must occasionally be reached. For asteroids near the 3:1 commensurability with Jupiter, the orbit then crosses that of Mars, whose gravitational interaction in a close encounter can remove the asteroid from the 3:1 zone.

By numerically integrating many orbits whose initial conditions spanned the 3:1 Kirkwood gap region in the asteroid belt, Jack Wisdom, an American dynamicist who developed a powerful means of analyzing chaotic motions, found that the chaotic zone around this gap precisely matched the physical extent of the gap. There are no observable asteroids with orbits within the chaotic zone, but there are many just outside extremes of the zone. Preliminary work has indicated that the other Kirkwood gaps can be similarly accounted for. The realization that orbits governed by Newton's laws of motion and gravitation could have chaotic properties and that such properties could solve a long-standing problem in the celestial mechanics of the solar system is a major breakthrough in the subject.

THE *N*-BODY PROBLEM

The general problem of n bodies, where n is greater than three, has been attacked vigorously with numerical techniques on powerful computers. Celestial mechanics in the solar system is ultimately an n-body problem, but the special configurations and relative smallness of the perturbations have allowed quite accurate descriptions of motions (valid for limited time periods) with various approximations and procedures without any attempt to solve the complete problem of n bodies. Examples are the restricted three-body problem to determine the effect of Jupiter's perturbations of the asteroids and the use of successive approximations of series solutions to sequentially add the effects of smaller and smaller perturbations for the motion of the Moon.

In the general n-body problem, all bodies have arbitrary masses, initial velocities, and positions; the bodies interact through Newton's law of gravitation, and one attempts to determine the subsequent motion of all the bodies. Many numerical solutions for the motion of quite large numbers of gravitating particles have been successfully completed where the precise motion of individual particles is usually less important than the statistical behaviour of the group.

NUMERICAL SOLUTIONS

Numerical solutions of the exact equations of motion for n bodies can be formulated. Each body is subject to the gravitational attraction of all the others, and it may be subject to other forces as well. It is relatively easy to write the expression for the instantaneous acceleration (equation of motion) of each body if the position of all the other bodies is known, and expressions for all the other forces can be written (as they can for gravitational forces) in terms of the relative positions of the particles and other defining characteristics of the particle and its environment. Each particle is allowed to move under its instantaneous acceleration for a short time step. Its velocity and position are thereby changed, and the new values of the variables are used to calculate the acceleration for the next time step, and so forth.

Of course, the real position and velocity of the particle after each time step will differ from the calculated values by errors of two types. One type results from the fact that the acceleration is not really constant over the time step, and the other from the rounding off or truncation of the numbers at every step of the calculation. The first type of error is decreased by taking shorter time steps. But this means more numerical operations must be carried out over a given span of time, and this increases the round-off error for a given precision of the numbers being carried in the calculation. The design of numerical algorithms, as well as the choice of precisions and step sizes that maximize the speed of the calculation while keeping the errors within reasonable bounds, is almost an art form developed by extensive experience and ingenuity. For example, a scheme exists for extrapolating the step size to zero in order to find the change in the variables over a relatively short time span, thereby minimizing the accumulation of error from this source. If the total energy of the system is theoretically conserved, its evaluation for values of the variables at the beginning and end of a calculation is a measure of the errors that have accumulated.

The motion of the planets of the solar system over time scales approaching its 4.6-billion-year age is a classic n-body problem, where $n = 9$ with the Sun included. The question of whether or not the solar system is ultimately stable—whether the current configuration of the planets will be maintained indefinitely under their mutual perturbations, or whether one or another planet will eventually be lost from the system or otherwise have its orbit drastically altered—is a long-standing one that might someday be answered through numerical calculation. The interplay of orbital resonances and chaotic orbits discussed above can be investigated numerically, and this interplay may be crucial in determining the stability of the solar system. Already it appears that the parameters defining the orbits of several planets vary over narrow chaotic zones, but whether or not this chaos can lead to instability if given enough time is still uncertain.

If accelerations are determined by summing all the pairwise interactions for the n particles, the computer time per time step increases as n^2. Practical computations for the direct calculation of the interactions between all the particles are thereby limited to $n < 10,000$. Therefore, for larger values of n, schemes are used where a particle is assumed to move in the force field of the remaining particles approximated by that due to a continuum mass distribution, or a "tree structure" is used where the effects of nearby particles are considered individually while larger and larger groups of particles are considered collectively as their distances increase. These later schemes have the capability of calculating the evolution of a very large system of particles using a reasonable amount of computer time with reasonable approximation. Values of n near 100,000 have been used in calculations determining the evolution of galaxies of stars. Also, the consequences for distribution of stars when two galaxies closely approach one another or even collide has been determined. Even calculations of the n-body problem where n changes with time have been completed in the study of the accumulation of larger bodies from smaller bodies via collisions in the process of the formation of the planets.

In all n-body calculations, very close approaches of two particles can result in accelerations so large and so rapidly changing that large errors are introduced or the calculation completely diverges. Accuracy can sometimes be maintained in such a close approach, but only at the expense of requiring very short time steps, which drastically slows the calculation. When n is small, as in some solar system calculations where two-body orbits still dominate, close approaches are sometimes handled by a change to a set of variables, usually involving the eccentric anomaly u, that vary much less rapidly during the encounter. In this process, called regularization, the encounter is traversed in less computer time while preserving reasonable accuracy. This process is impractical when n is large, so accelerations are usually artificially bounded on close approaches to prevent instabilities in the numerical calculation and to prevent slowing the calculation. For example, if several sets of particles were trapped in stable, close binary orbits, the very short time steps required to follow this rapid motion would bring the calculation to a virtual standstill, and such binary motion is not important in the overall evolution of, say, a galaxy of stars.

ALGEBRAIC MAPS

In numerical calculations for conservative systems with modest values of n over long time spans, such as those seeking a determination of the stability of the solar system, the direct solution of the differential equations governing the motions requires excessive time on any computer and accumulates excessive round-off error in the process. Excessive time is also required to explore thoroughly a complete range of orbital parameters in numerical experiments in order to determine the extent of chaotic zones in various configurations (e.g., those in the asteroid belt near orbital mean motion commensurabilities with Jupiter).

A solution to this problem is the use of an algebraic map, which maps the space of system variables onto itself in such a way that the values of all the variables at one instant of time are expressed by algebraic relations in terms of the values of the variables at a fixed time in the past. The values at the next time step are determined by applying the same map to the values just obtained, and so on. The map is constructed by assuming that the motions of all the bodies are unperturbed for a given short time but are periodically "kicked" by the perturbing forces for only an instant. The continuous perturbations are thus replaced by periodic impulses. The values of the variables are "mapped" from one time step to the next by the fact that the unperturbed part of the motion is available from the exact solution of the two-body problem, and it is easy to solve the equations with all the perturbations over the short time of the impulse. Although this approximation does not produce exactly the same values of all the variables at some time in the future as those produced by a numerical solution of the differential equations starting with the same initial conditions, the qualitative behaviour is indistinguishable over long time periods. As computers can perform the algebraic calculations as much as 1,000 times faster than they can solve the corresponding differential equations, the computational time savings are enormous and problems otherwise impossible to explore become tractable.

TIDAL EVOLUTION

This discussion has so far treated the celestial mechanics of bodies accelerated by conservative forces (total energy being conserved), including perturbations of elliptic motion by nonspherical mass distributions of finite-size bodies. However, the gravitational field of one body in close orbit about another will tidally distort the shape of the other body. Dissipation of part of the energy stored in these tidal distortions leads to a coupling that causes secular changes (always in the same direction) in the orbit and in the spins of both bodies. Since tidal dissipation accounts for the current spin states of several planets, the spin states of most of the planetary satellites and some of their orbital configurations, and the spins and orbits of close binary stars, it is appropriate that tides and their consequences be included in this discussion.

The twice-daily high and low tides in the ocean are known by all who have lived near a coast. Few are aware, however, that the solid body of the Earth also experiences twice-daily tides with a maximum amplitude of about 30 centimetres (11 inches). George Howard Darwin (1845–1912), the second son of Charles Darwin, the naturalist, was an astronomer-geophysicist who understood quantitatively the generation of the tides in the gravitational fields of tide-raising bodies, which are primarily the Moon and Sun for Earth; he pointed out that the dissipation of tidal energy resulted in a slowing of Earth's rotation while the Moon's orbit was gradually expanded. That any mass raises a tide on every other mass within its gravitational field follows from the fact that the gravitational force between two masses decreases as the inverse square of the distance between them.

The accelerations due to mass m_s of three mass elements in the spherical mass m_p are proportional to the inverse square of the distance from m_s. The element nearest m_s is accelerated more than the element at the centre of m_p and tends to leave the centre element behind; the element at the centre of m_p is accelerated more than the element farthest from m_s, and the latter tends to be left further behind. The point of view of a fictitious observer at the centre of m_p can be realized by subtracting the acceleration of the central mass element from that of each of the other two mass elements. If the mass elements were free, this observer would see the two extreme mass elements being accelerated in opposite directions away from his position at the centre.

But the mass elements are not free; they are gravitationally attracted to one another and to the remaining mass in m_p. The gravitational acceleration of the mass elements on the surface of m_p toward the centre of m_p far exceeds the differential acceleration due to the gravitational attraction of m_s, thus the elements do not fly off. If m_p were incompressible and perfectly rigid, the mass elements on the surface would weigh a little less than they would if m_s were not there but would not move relative to the centre of m_p. If m_p were fluid or otherwise not rigid, it would distort into an oval shape in the presence of m_s. The reason for this distortion is that the mass elements making up m_p that do not lie on the line joining the centres of m_p and m_s also experience a differential acceleration. Such differential accelerations are not perpendicular to the surface, however, and are therefore not compensated by the self-gravity that accelerates mass elements toward the centre of m_p.

The differential accelerations can be resolved into two components, one perpendicular and one tangential to the surface. The perpendicular component is compensated by the self-gravity; the tangential component is not. If m_p were entirely fluid, the uncompensated tangential components of the differential accelerations due to m_s would cause mass to flow toward the points on m_p that were either closest to m_s or farthest from m_s until m_p would resemble an oval. In this shape the self-gravity is no longer perpendicular to the surface but has a component opposite the tangential component of the differential acceleration. Only in this distorted shape will all the differential accelerations be compensated and the entire body accelerated like the centre. If m_p is not fluid but is rigid like rock or iron, part of the compensating acceleration will be provided by internal stress forces, and the body will distort less. As no material is perfectly rigid, there is always some tidal bulge, and compressibility of the material will farther enhance this bulge. Note that the tidal distortion is independent of the orbital motion and would also occur if m_p and m_s were simply falling toward each other.

If m_p rotates relative to m_s, an observer on the surface of m_p would successively rotate through the maxima and minima of the tidal distortion, which would tend to remain aligned with the direction to m_s. The observer would thereby experience two high and two low tides a day, as observed on Earth. Some of the energy of motion of any fluid parts of m_p and some of the energy stored as distortion of the solid parts as the tides wax and wane is converted into heat, and this dissipation of mechanical energy causes a delay in the response of the body to the tide-raising force. This means that high tide would occur at a given point on m_p as it rotates relative to m_s after m_s passes overhead. (On Earth, the continents alter the motion of the fluid ocean so much that ocean tides at continental coasts do not always lag the passage of the Moon overhead.) If m_p rotates in the same direction as m_s revolves in its orbit, the tidal bulge is carried ahead of m_s. Again, because the gravitational force between two masses varies as the inverse square of their separation, the tidal bulge closest to m_s experiences a greater attraction toward m_s (F_1) than does the bulge farthest away (F_2). As these two forces are not aligned with the centre of m_p, there is a twisting effect, or torque, on m_p that retards its rate of rotation. This retardation will continue until the rotation is synchronous with the mean orbital motion of m_s. This has happened for the Moon, which keeps the same face toward Earth.

From Newton's third law, there are equal and opposite forces acting on m_s corresponding to F_1 and F_2. These forces can be resolved into two components, one directed toward the centre of m_p and the other perpendicular to this direction. The inequality of these forces causes a net acceleration of m_s in its orbit, which thereby expands, as is observed for the Moon. Both the observed increase in the length of one day of 0.0016 second per century and the observed recession of the Moon of 3 to 4 centimetres (1.18 to 1.57 inches) per year are understood as consequences of the tides raised on Earth.

It has been assumed that the spin axis of m_p is perpendicular to the plane of the orbit of m_s. If the spin axis is inclined to this plane, the tidal bulge is carried out of the plane as well as ahead of m_s. This means that there is a twist, or torque, that changes the direction of the spin axis, so both the magnitude of spin and the direction of the spin axis experience a tidal evolution. The end point of tidal evolution for the spin state of one body of an isolated pair is rotation synchronous with the mean orbital motion with the spin axis perpendicular to the orbit plane. This simple picture is complicated somewhat if other perturbations cause the orbital plane to precess. This precession for the lunar orbit causes its spin axis to be inclined 6°41' to the orbit plane as the end point of tidal evolution.

In addition to those of the Earth-Moon pair, numerous other consequences of tidal dissipation and the resulting evolution can be observed in the solar system and elsewhere in the Milky Way Galaxy. For example, all the major and close planetary satellites but one are observed to be rotating synchronously with their orbital motion. The exception is Saturn's satellite Hyperion. Tidal friction has indeed retarded Hyperion's initial spin rate to a value near that of synchronous rotation, but the combination of Hyperion's unusually asymmetric shape and its high orbital eccentricity leads to gravitational torques that make synchronous rotation unstable. As a result, the tides have brought Hyperion to a state where it tumbles chaotically with large changes in the direction and magnitude of its spin on time scales comparable to its orbital period of about 21 days.

The assembly and maintenance of several orbital resonances among the satellites because of differential tidal expansion of the orbits have also been observed. The orbital resonances among Jupiter's satellites Io, Europa, and Ganymede, where the orbital periods are nearly in the ratio 1:2:4, maintain Io's orbital eccentricity at the value of 0.0041. This rather modest eccentricity causes sufficient variation in the magnitude and direction of Io's enormous tidal bulge to have melted a significant fraction of the satellite through dissipation of tidal energy in spite of Io's synchronous rotation. As a result, Io is the most volcanically active body in the solar system. The orbital eccentricity would normally be damped to zero by this large dissipation, but the orbital resonances with Europa and Ganymede prevent this from happening.

The distant dwarf planet Pluto and its satellite Charon have almost certainly reached the ultimate end point where further tidal evolution has ceased altogether (the tiny tides raised by the Sun and other planets being neglected). In this state the orbit is circular, with both bodies rotating synchronously with the orbital motion and both spin axes perpendicular to the orbital plane.

The spin of the planet Mercury has been slowed by tides raised by the Sun to a final state where the spin angular velocity is exactly 1.5 times the orbital mean motion. This state is stable against further change because Mercury's high orbital eccentricity (0.206) allows restoring torques on the permanent (nontidal) axial asymmetry of the planet, which keeps the longest equatorial axis aligned with the direction to the Sun at perihelion. The tidal reduction of Mercury's average eccentricity (near 0.2) will cause insufficient change during the remaining lifetime of the Sun to disrupt this spin-orbit resonance. Finally, many close binary stars are observed to have circular orbits and synchronized spins—an example of tidal evolution elsewhere in the Milky Way Galaxy.

CHAPTER 4

OBSERVATORIES AND TELESCOPES

Astronomers are in the business of observing planets, stars, and galaxies. It makes perfect sense, then, that the facilities from which they conduct their research would be called observatories. An observatory is any structure containing instruments with which to study celestial objects. Of all the tools available to astronomers, the most useful and pervasive would have to be the telescope. There are several types of telescopes, ranging from the simple reflecting telescope of the most humble amateur astronomer to satellites that study various forms of radiation.

ASTRONOMICAL OBSERVATORIES

Observatories can be classified on the basis of the part of the electromagnetic spectrum in which they are designed to observe. The largest number of observatories are optical; i.e., they are equipped to observe in and near the region of the spectrum visible to the human eye. Some are instrumented to detect cosmic emitters of radio waves, while still others, known as orbiting astronomical observatories, consist of Earth satellites that carry special telescopes and detectors to study celestial sources of such forms of high-energy radiation as gamma rays and X-rays from high above the atmosphere.

Optical observatories have a long history. The predecessors of astronomical observatories were monolithic structures that tracked the positions of the Sun, Moon, and other celestial bodies for timekeeping or calendrical purposes. The most famous of these ancient structures is Stonehenge, constructed in England over the period from 2500 BCE to 1700 BCE. At about the same time, astrologer-priests in Babylonia observed the motions of the Sun, Moon, and planets from atop their terraced towers known as ziggurats. No astronomical instruments appear to have been used. The Indians of the Yucatan Peninsula in Mexico carried out the same practice at El Caracol, a dome-shaped structure somewhat resembling a modern optical observatory. There is again no evidence of any scientific instrumentation, even of a rudimentary nature.

Perhaps the first observatory that utilized instruments for accurately measuring the positions of celestial objects was built about 150 BCE on the island of Rhodes by the greatest of the pre-Christian astronomers, Hipparchus. There he discovered precession and developed the magnitude system used to indicate the brightness of celestial objects. The true predecessors of the modern observatory were those established in the Islamic world. Observatories were built at

The design of its monolithic structures suggests to some that Stonehenge may once have been used to predict lunar and solar eclipses. Shutterstock.com

Damascus and Baghdad as early as the 9th–10th century CE. A splendid one was built at Marāgheh (now in Iran) about 1260 CE, and substantial modifications in Ptolemaic astronomy were introduced there. The most productive Islamic observatory was that erected by the Timurid prince Ulūgh Beg at Samarkand in about 1420. He and his assistants made a catalog of stars from observations with a large quadrant. The first notable premodern European observatory was that at Uraniborg on the island of Hven, built by King Frederick of Denmark for Tycho Brahe in 1576 CE.

The first major centres for astronomical study utilized a telescope movable only in one plane, with motion solely along the local meridian (the "transit," or "meridian circle"). Such centres were founded in the 18th and 19th centuries at Greenwich (London), Paris, Cape Town, and Washington, D.C. By timing the passage of stars as the local meridian was swept past them by Earth's rotation, astronomers were able to improve the accuracy of position measurements of celestial objects from a few minutes of arc (before the advent of the telescope) to less than a tenth of a second of arc.

One notable observatory built and operated by an individual was that of William Herschel, assisted by his sister Caroline, in Slough, Eng. Known as Observatory House, its largest instrument had a mirror made of speculum metal, with a diameter of 122 cm (48 inches) and a focal length of 17 m (40 feet).

Completed in 1789, it became one of the technical wonders of the 18th century.

Today, Kitt Peak National Observatory—located near Tucson, Ariz., in the southwestern United States—is the site of the world's largest grouping of optical telescopes. Most notable among this array of instruments are the 4-metre (157-inch) Mayall telescope and the McMath solar telescope, the largest of its type in the world.

With the advent of the space age, the capability of astronomical instruments to orbit above Earth's absorbing and distorting atmosphere has enabled astronomers to build telescopes sensitive to regions of the electromagnetic spectrum besides those of visible light and radio waves. Since the 1960s, orbiting observatories have been launched to observe gamma rays (Orbiting Solar Observatory and the Small Astronomy Satellite-2), X rays (Uhuru and the High Energy Astronomical Observatory), ultraviolet radiation (International Ultraviolet Explorer), and infrared radiation (Infrared Astronomical Satellite). Several of these functions were combined in the Hubble Space Telescope, launched in 1990.

THE EVOLUTION OF THE OPTICAL TELESCOPE

Galileo is credited with having developed telescopes for astronomical observation in 1609. While the largest of his instruments was only about 120 cm (47 inches) long and had an objective diameter of 5 cm (2 inches), it was equipped with an eyepiece that provided an upright (i.e., erect) image. Galileo used his modest instrument to explore such celestial phenomena as the valleys and mountains of the Moon, the phases of Venus, and the four largest Jovian satellites, which had never been systematically observed before.

The reflecting telescope was developed in 1668 by Newton, though John Gregory had independently conceived of an alternative reflector design in 1663. Laurent Cassegrain introduced another variation of the reflector in 1672. Near the end of the century, others attempted to construct refractors as long as 61 metres (200 feet), but these instruments were too awkward to be effective.

The most significant contribution to the development of the telescope in the 18th century was that of Sir William Herschel. Herschel, whose interest in telescopes was kindled by a modest 5-cm (2-inch) Gregorian, persuaded the king of England to finance the construction of a reflector with a 12-metre (39-foot) focal length and a 120-cm (47-inch) mirror. Herschel is credited with having used this instrument to lay the observational groundwork for the concept of extragalactic "nebulas"—i.e., galaxies outside the Milky Way system.

Reflectors continued to evolve during the 19th century with the work of William Parsons, the 3rd Earl of Rosse, and William Lassell. In 1845 Lord Rosse constructed in Ireland a reflector with a 185-cm (73-inch) mirror and a focal length of about 16 metres (52 feet). For 75 years this telescope ranked as the largest in the world and was used to explore thousands of nebulas and star clusters. Lassell built several reflectors, the largest of which was on Malta. This instrument had a 124-cm (49-inch) primary mirror and a focal length of more than 10 metres (33 feet). His telescope had greater reflecting power than that of Rosse, and it enabled him to catalog 600 new nebulas as well as to discover several satellites of the outer planets—Triton (Neptune's largest moon), Hyperion (Saturn's 8th moon), and Ariel and Umbriel (two of Uranus' moons).

Refractor telescopes, too, underwent development during the 18th and 19th centuries. The last significant one to be built was the 1-metre (40-inch) refractor at Yerkes Observatory. Installed in 1897, it remains the largest refracting system in the world. Its objective was designed and constructed by the optician Alvan Clark, while the mount was built by the firm of Warner & Swasey.

The reflecting telescope has predominated in the 20th century. The rapid proliferation of larger and larger instruments of this type began with the installation of the 2.5-metre (8.2-foot) reflector at the Mount Wilson Observatory near Pasadena, Calif. The technology for mirrors underwent a major advance when the Corning Glass Works (in Steuben County, N.Y.) developed Pyrex. This borosilicate glass, which undergoes substantially less expansion than ordinary glass, was used in the 5-metre (16-foot) Hale reflector built in 1950 at the Palomar Observatory. Pyrex also was utilized in the main mirror of the world's largest telescope, the 6-metre (20-foot) reflector of the Special Astrophysical Observatory in Zelenchukskaya, Rus.

In recent years, much better materials for mirrors have become available. Cer-Vit, for example, was used for the 4.2-metre (13.8-foot) William Herschel Telescope of the Roque de los Muchachos Observatory in the Canary Islands, and Zerodur for the 3.5-metre (11.5-foot) reflector at the German-Spanish Astronomical Center in Calar Alto, Spain.

REFRACTING TELESCOPES

Optical telescopes commonly known as refractors are used to examine the visible-light region of the electromagnetic spectrum. Typical uses include viewing the Moon, other objects of the solar system such as Jupiter and Mars, and double stars. The name refractor is derived from the term *refraction*, which is the bending of light when it passes from one medium to another of different density—e.g., from air to glass. The glass is referred to as a lens and may have one or more components. The physical shape of the components may be convex, concave, or plane-parallel. The focus is the point, or plane, at which light rays from infinity converge after passing through a lens and traveling a distance of one focal length. In a refractor, the first lens through which light from a celestial object passes is called the objective lens. It should be

noted that the light will be inverted at the focal plane. A second lens, referred to as the eyepiece lens, is placed behind the focal plane and enables the observer to view the enlarged, or magnified, image. Thus, the simplest form of refractor consists of an objective and an eyepiece.

The diameter of the objective is referred to as the aperture; it typically ranges from a few centimetres for small spotting telescopes up to one metre for the largest refractor in existence. The objective, as well as the eyepiece, may have several components. Small spotting telescopes may contain an extra lens behind the eyepiece to erect the image so that it does not appear upside-down. When an object is viewed with a refractor, the image may not appear sharply defined, or it may even have a predominant colour in it. Such distortions, or aberrations, are sometimes introduced when the lens is polished into its design shape. The major kind of distortion in a refractor is chromatic aberration, which is the failure of the differently coloured light rays to come to a common focus. Chromatic aberration can be minimized by adding components to the objective. In lens-design technology, the coefficients of expansion of different kinds of glass are carefully matched to minimize the aberrations that result from temperature changes of the telescope at night.

Eyepieces have a wide variety of applications and provide observers with the ability to select the magnification of their instruments. The magnification, sometimes referred to as magnifying power, is determined by dividing the focal length of the objective by the focal length of the eyepiece. For example, if the objective has a focal length of 254 cm (100 inches) and the eyepiece has a focal length of 2.54 cm (1 inch), then the magnification will be 100. Large magnifications are very useful for observing the Moon and the planets; however, since stars appear as point sources owing to their great distances, magnification provides no additional advantage when viewing them. Another important factor that one must take into consideration when attempting to view at high magnification is the stability of the telescope mounting. Any vibration in the mounting will also be magnified and may severely reduce the quality of the observed image. Thus, great care is usually taken to provide a stable platform for the telescope. This problem should not be associated with that of atmospheric seeing, which may introduce a disturbance to the image due to fluctuating air currents in the path of the light from a celestial or terrestrial object. Generally, most of the seeing disturbance arises in the first 30 metres (100 feet) of air above the telescope. Large telescopes are frequently installed on mountain peaks in order to get above the seeing disturbances.

LIGHT GATHERING AND RESOLUTION

The most important of all the powers of an optical telescope is its light-gathering power. This capacity is strictly a function of the diameter of the clear objective— that is, the aperture—of the telescope. Comparisons of different-sized apertures for their light-gathering power are calculated by the ratio of their diameters squared; for example, a 25-cm (10-inch) objective will collect four times the light of a 12.5-cm (5-inch) objective [(25 × 25) ÷ (12.5 × 12.5)] = 4. The advantage of collecting more light with a larger-aperture telescope is that one can observe fainter stars, nebulas, and very distant galaxies.

Resolving power is another important feature of a telescope. This is the ability of the instrument to distinguish clearly between two points whose angular separation is less than the smallest angle that the observer's eye can resolve. The resolving power of a telescope can be calculated by the formula

resolving power = 11.25 seconds of arc/d

where d is the diameter of the objective expressed in centimetres. Thus, a 25-cm-diameter objective has a theoretical resolution of 0.45 second of arc and a 250-cm (98-inch) telescope has one of 0.045 second of arc. An important application of resolving power is in the observation of visual binary stars. Here, one star is routinely observed as it revolves around a second star. Many observatories conduct extensive visual binary observing programs and publish catalogs of their observational results. One of the major contributors in this field

Telescopes with superior resolving power are best suited for recording the orbits of visual binary stars, like these depicted based on information from NASA's Chandra X-ray Observatory. NASA/Tod Strohmayer (GSFC)/Dana Berry (Chandra X-Ray Observatory)

is the United States Naval Observatory in Washington, D.C.

Most refractors currently in use at observatories have equatorial mountings. (The mounting describes the orientation of the physical bearings and structure that permits a telescope to be pointed at a celestial object for viewing.) In the equatorial mounting, the polar axis of the telescope is constructed parallel to Earth's axis. The polar axis supports the declination axis of the instrument. Declination is measured on the celestial sky north or south from the celestial equator. The

declination axis makes it possible for the telescope to be pointed at various declination angles as the instrument is rotated about the polar axis with respect to right ascension. Right ascension is measured along the celestial equator from the vernal equinox (i.e., the position on the celestial sphere where the Sun crosses the celestial equator from south to north on the first day of spring).

Declination and right ascension are the two coordinates that define a celestial object on the celestial sphere. Declination is analogous to latitude, and right

SEEING

The sharpness of a telescopic image is defined by a parameter called seeing, which is dependent upon the degree of turbulence in Earth's atmosphere for a given telescope. Scintillation, the "twinkling" of stars as seen by the unaided eye, is a commonly known result of turbulence in the higher reaches of the atmosphere. Poor seeing in telescopes is more a result of turbulence in the lower atmosphere. This turbulence sets a limit on the features that a telescope can resolve.

Turbulence, whether in the upper or lower atmosphere, generates unstable regions of varying densities, diminishing the atmosphere's ability to allow a beam of light to pass straight through with unchanging intensity. When the light from a celestial object is moved about in a rapid and random fashion by atmospheric turbulence, the image formed by a small telescope flutters and dances about. In a larger telescope, the distortions are magnified and the image becomes more diffuse. Seeing is expressed in units of seconds of arc, or 1/3,600 of a degree. The best observatory sites have seeing between 0.5 and 1 second of arc.

ascension is analogous to longitude. Graduated dials are mounted on the axis to permit the observer to point the telescope precisely. To track an object, the telescope's polar axis is driven smoothly by an electric motor at a sidereal rate—namely, at a rate equal to the rate of rotation of Earth with respect to the stars. Thus, one can track or observe with a telescope for long periods of time if the sidereal rate of the motor is very accurate. High-accuracy, motor-driven systems have become readily available with the rapid advancement of quartz-clock technology. Most major observatories now rely on either quartz or atomic clocks to provide accurate sidereal time for observations as well as to drive telescopes at an extremely uniform rate.

A notable example of a refracting telescope is the 66-cm (26-inch) refractor of the U.S. Naval Observatory. This instrument was used by the astronomer Asaph Hall to discover the two moons of Mars, Phobos and Deimos, in 1877. Today, the telescope is used primarily for observing double stars. The 91-cm (36-inch) refractor at Lick Observatory on Mount Hamilton, Calif., and the one-metre instrument at Yerkes Observatory in Williams Bay, Wis., are the largest refracting systems currently in operation. (See Appendix D: Select Ground-Based Optical Telescopes on page 201.)

Another type of refracting telescope is the astrograph, which usually has an objective diameter of approximately 20 cm (8 inches). The astrograph has a photographic plateholder mounted in the focal plane of the objective so that photographs of the celestial sphere can be taken. The photographs are usually taken on glass plates. The principal application of the astrograph is to determine the positions of a large number of faint stars. These positions are then published in catalogs such as the *AGK*3 and serve as reference points for deep-space photography.

REFLECTING TELESCOPES

Reflectors are used not only to examine the visible region of the electromagnetic spectrum but also to explore both the shorter- and longer-wavelength regions adjacent to it (i.e., the ultraviolet and the infrared). The name of this type of instrument is derived from the fact that the primary mirror reflects the light back to a focus instead of refracting it. The primary mirror usually has a concave spherical or parabolic shape, and, as it reflects the light, it inverts the image at the focal plane. The formulas for resolving power, magnifying power, and light-gathering power, as discussed for refractors, apply to reflectors as well.

The primary mirror is located at the lower end of the telescope tube in a reflector and has its front surface coated with an extremely thin film of metal, such as aluminum. The back of the mirror is usually made of glass, although other materials have been used from time to time. Pyrex was the principal glass of choice for many of the older large

The 72-inch reflecting telescope at Birr Castle, County Offaly, Leinster, Ire., was the largest in the world at the time of its construction in the 1840s. Geray Sweeney/Tourism Ireland

telescopes, but new technology has led to the development and widespread use of a number of glasses with very low coefficients of expansion. A low coefficient of expansion means that the shape of the mirror will not change significantly as the temperature of the telescope changes during the night. Since the back of the mirror serves only to provide the desired form and physical support, it does not have to meet the high optical quality standards required for a lens.

Reflecting telescopes have a number of other advantages over refractors. They are not subject to chromatic aberration because reflected light does not disperse according to wavelength. Also, the telescope tube of a reflector is shorter than that of a refractor of the same diameter, which reduces the cost of the tube. Consequently, the dome for housing a reflector is smaller and more economical to construct. So far only the primary mirror for the reflector has been discussed.

One might wonder about the location of the eyepiece. The primary mirror reflects the light of the celestial object to the prime focus near the upper end of the tube. Obviously, if an observer put his eye there to observe with a modest-sized reflector, he would block out the light from the primary mirror with his head. Isaac Newton placed a small plane mirror at an angle of 45° inside the prime focus and thereby brought the focus to the side of the telescope tube. The amount of light lost by this procedure is very small when compared to the total light-gathering power of the primary mirror.

The Newtonian reflector is popular among amateur telescope makers.

A contemporary of Newton, Laurent Cassegrain of France, invented another type of reflector. Called the Cassegrainian telescope, this instrument employs a small convex mirror to reflect the light back through a small hole in the primary mirror to a focus located behind the primary. Some large telescopes of this kind do not have a hole in the primary mirror but use a small plane mirror in front of the primary to reflect the light outside the main tube and provide another place for observation. The Cassegrain design usually permits short tubes relative to their mirror diameter.

One more variety of reflector was invented by another of Newton's contemporaries, the Scottish astronomer James Gregory. Gregory placed a concave secondary mirror outside the prime focus to reflect the light back through a hole in the primary mirror. Notable is the fact that the Gregorian design was adopted for the Earth-orbiting space observatory, the Solar Maximum Mission (SMM), launched in 1980.

Most large reflecting telescopes that are currently in use have a cage at their prime focus that permits the observer to sit inside the telescope tube while operating the instrument. The 5-metre (16-foot) reflector at Palomar Observatory, near San Diego, Calif., is so equipped. While most reflectors have equatorial mounts similar to refractors, the world's largest reflector, the 6-metre (19-foot) instrument at the Special Astrophysical Observatory in

Zelenchukskaya, Rus., has an altitude-azimuth mounting. The significance of the latter design is that the telescope must be moved in both altitude and azimuth as it tracks a celestial object. Equatorial mountings, by contrast, require motion in only one coordinate while tracking, since the declination coordinate is constant. Reflectors, like refractors, usually have small guide telescopes mounted parallel to their main optical axis to facilitate locating the desired object. These guide telescopes have low magnification and a wide field of view, the latter being a desirable attribute for finding stars or other remote cosmic objects.

The parabolic shape of a primary mirror has a basic failing in that it produces a narrow field of view. This can be a problem when one wishes to observe extended celestial objects. To overcome this difficulty, most large reflectors now have a modified Cassegrain design. The central area of the primary mirror has its shape deepened from that of a paraboloid, and the secondary mirror is configured to compensate for the altered primary. The result is the Ritchey-Chrétien design, which has a curved rather than a flat focus. Obviously, the photographic medium must be curved to collect high-quality images across the curved focal plane. The one-metre telescope of the U.S. Naval Observatory in Flagstaff, Ariz., was one of the early examples of this design. The largest modern-day reflecting telescospes are the 10.4-metre (409-inch) Gran Telescopio Canarias reflector on La Palma, in the Canary Islands, Spain, and the two 10-metre (394-inch) Keck telescopes of the Mauna Kea Observatory, in Hawaii.

THE SCHMIDT TELESCOPE

For some astronomical applications, photographing large areas of the sky is mandatory. In 1930 Bernhard Schmidt, an optician at the Hamburg Observatory in Bergedorf, Ger., designed a catadioptric telescope that satisfied the requirement of photographing larger celestial areas. A catadioptric telescope design incorporates the best features of both the refractor and reflector—i.e., it has both reflective and refractive optics. The Schmidt telescope has a spherically shaped primary mirror. Since parallel light rays that are reflected by the centre of a spherical mirror are focused farther away than those reflected from the outer regions, Schmidt introduced a thin lens (called the correcting plate) at the radius of curvature of the primary mirror. Since this correcting plate is very thin, it introduces little chromatic aberration. The resulting focal plane has a field of view several degrees in diameter.

The *National Geographic Society-Palomar Observatory Sky Survey* made use of a 1.2-metre Schmidt telescope to photograph the northern sky in the red and blue regions of the visible spectrum. The survey produced 900 pairs of photographic plates (about 7° by 7° each) taken from 1949 to 1956. Schmidt telescopes of the European Southern Observatory in Chile and of the observatory at Siding Spring Mountain in Australia have photographed the remaining part of the sky that cannot be observed from Palomar Mountain. (The survey undertaken at the latter included photographs in the infrared as well as in the red and blue spectral regions.)

Multimirror Telescopes

The main reason astronomers build larger telescopes is to increase light-gathering power so that they can see deeper into the universe. Unfortunately, the cost of constructing larger single-mirror telescopes increases rapidly—approximately with the cube of the diameter of the aperture. Thus, in order to achieve the goal of increasing light-gathering power while keeping costs down, it has become necessary to explore new, more economical and nontraditional telescope designs.

The two 10-metre (33-foot) Keck multimirror telescopes represent such an effort. The first was installed on Mauna Kea on the island of Hawaii in 1992, and a second telescope was completed in 1996. Each of the Keck telescopes comprise 36 contiguous, adjustable mirror segments, all under computer control. Even larger multimirror instruments are currently being planned by American and European astronomers.

Special Types of Optical Telescopes

Some optical telescopes are optimized for special purposes. Some are designed to look only at the Sun. Others are designed to orbit Earth. Still others are built to make precise determinations of stellar positions.

Solar Telescopes

Either a refractor or reflector may be used for visual observations of solar features, such as sunspots or solar prominences. The main precaution that needs to be taken is to reduce the intensity of the image so that the observer's eye will not be damaged. Generally, this is done with a tinted eyepiece. Special solar telescopes have been constructed, however, for investigations of the Sun that require the use of such ancillary instruments as spectroheliographs and coronagraphs. These telescopes are mounted in towers and have very long focus objectives. Typical examples of tower solar telescopes are found at the Mount Wilson Observatory in California and the McMath-Hulbert Observatory in Michigan.

The long focus objective produces a very good scale factor, which in turn makes it possible to look at individual wavelengths of the solar electromagnetic spectrum in great detail. A tower telescope has an equatorially mounted plane mirror at its summit to direct the sunlight into the telescope objective. This plane mirror is called a coelostat. Bernard Lyot constructed another type of solar telescope in 1930 at Pic du Midi Observatory in France. This instrument was specifically designed for photographing the Sun's corona (the outer layer), which up to that time had been successfully photographed only during solar eclipses. The coronagraph, as this special telescope is called, must be located at a high altitude to be effective. The high altitude is required to reduce the scattered sunlight, which would reduce the quality of the photograph. The High Altitude Observatory in Colorado and the Sacramento Peak Observatory in New Mexico have coronagraphs.

Cutaway of the Hubble Space Telescope, revealing the Optical Telescope Assembly (OTA), the heart of this orbiting observational system. Courtesy of the Hughes Aircraft Company

EARTH-ORBITING SPACE TELESCOPES

While astronomers continue to seek new technological breakthroughs with which to build larger ground-based telescopes, it is readily apparent that the only solution to some scientific problems is to make observations from above Earth's atmosphere. Through the years a series of Orbiting Astronomical Observatories (OAOs) has been launched by the National Aeronautics and Space Administration (NASA). The OAO launched in 1972 (later named Copernicus) had an 81-cm (32-inch) telescope on board. The most sophisticated observational system placed in Earth orbit so far is the Hubble Space Telescope (HST). Launched in 1990, the HST is essentially an optical-ultraviolet telescope with a 2.4-metre (7.8-foot) primary mirror. It has been designed to enable astronomers to see into a volume of space 300 to 400 times larger than that permitted by other systems. At the same time, the HST is not impeded by any of the problems caused by the atmosphere. It was equipped with five principal scientific instruments: (1) a wide-field and planetary camera, (2) a faint-object spectrograph, (3) a high-resolution spectrograph, (4) a high-speed photometer, and (5) a faint-object camera. The HST was launched into orbit from the U.S. space shuttle at an altitude of more than 570 km (350 miles) above Earth. Shortly after its deployment in Earth orbit, HST project scientists found that a manufacturing error affecting the shape of the telescope's primary mirror severely impaired the instrument's focusing capability. The flawed mirror causes spherical aberration, which limits the ability of the HST to distinguish between cosmic objects that lie close together and to image distant galaxies and quasars. Project scientists devised measures that enabled them to compensate in part for the defective mirror and correct the imaging problem.

ASTRONOMICAL TRANSIT INSTRUMENTS

These small but extremely important telescopes play a vital role in mapping the celestial sphere. Without the transit instrument's very accurate determination of stellar and planetary positions, the larger deep-space telescopes would not be able to find their desired celestial object.

Astronomical transit instruments are usually refractors with apertures of 15 to 20 cm (6 to 8 inches). (Ole Rømer, a Danish astronomer, is credited with having invented this type of telescope system.) The main optical axis of the instrument is aligned on a north-south line such that its motion is restricted to the plane of the meridian of the observer. The observer's meridian is a great circle on the celestial sphere that passes through the north and south points of the horizon as well as through the zenith of the observer. Restricting the telescope to motion only in the meridian provides an added degree

of stability, but it requires the observer to wait for the celestial object to rotate across his meridian. The latter process is referred to as transiting the meridian, from which the name of the telescope is derived.

There are various types of transit instruments, as, for example, the transit circle telescope, the vertical circle telescope, and the horizontal meridian circle telescope. The transit circle determines the right ascension of celestial objects, while the vertical circle measures only their declinations. Transit circles and horizontal

The 15-centimetre transit circle instrument of the U.S. Naval Observatory. Official U.S. Navy photograph

meridian circles measure both right ascension and declination at the same time. The final output data of all transit instruments are included in star or planetary catalogs.

One of the most accurate astronomical transit instruments in the world is the U.S. Naval Observatory's 15-cm (6-inch) transit circle telescope. Other notable examples of this class of telescopes include the transit circle of the National Astronomical Observatory in Tokyo, the meridian circle of the Bordeaux Observatory in France, and the automatic meridian circle of the Roque de los Muchachos Observatory in the Canary Islands.

ASTROLABES

Another special type of telescopic instrument is the modern version of the astrolabe. Known as a prismatic astrolabe, it too is used for making precise determinations of the positions of stars and planets. It may sometimes be used inversely to determine the latitude and longitude of the observer, assuming the star positions are accurately known. The aperture of a prismatic astrolabe is small, usually only 8 to 10 cm (3 to 4 inches). A small pool of mercury and a refracting prism make up the other principal parts of the instrument. An image reflected off the mercury is observed along with a direct image to give the necessary position data.

The most notable example of this type of instrument is the French-constructed Danjon astrolabe. During the 1970s, however, the Chinese introduced various innovations that resulted in a more accurate and automatic kind of astrolabe, which is now in use at the Peking Observatory.

RADIO TELESCOPES

Radio telescopes are used to study naturally occurring radio emissions from

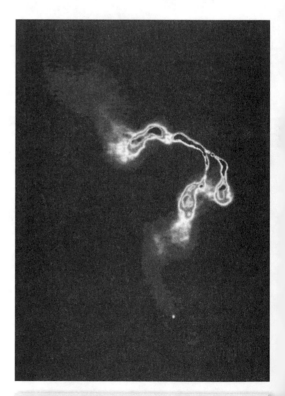

VLA (Very Large Array) image of an interacting twin-jet radio galaxy. The jets appear to interact and wrap around one another. Courtesy of the National Radio Astronomy Observatory/Associated Universities, Inc.

stars, galaxies, quasars, and other astronomical objects. Today's radio telescopes are capable of observing at most wavelength regions from a few millimetres to about 10 metres (33 feet). They vary in construction, though they are typically huge movable dishes.

DEVELOPMENT OF THE RADIO TELESCOPE

Extraterrestrial radio emission was first reported in 1933 by Karl Jansky, an engineer at the Bell Telephone Laboratories, while he was searching for the cause of shortwave interference. Jansky had mounted a directional radio antenna on a turntable so that he could point it at different parts of the sky to determine the direction of the interfering signals. He not only detected interference from distant thunderstorms but also located a source of radio "noise" from the centre of the Milky Way Galaxy. This first detection of cosmic radio waves received much attention from the public but only passing notice from the astronomical community.

Grote Reber, a radio engineer and amateur radio operator, built a 9.5-metre

RADAR ASTRONOMY

Radar astronomy is the study of celestial bodies by examination of the radio-frequency energy they reflect. Radio waves penetrate much of the gas and dust in space, as well as the clouds of planetary atmospheres, and pass through Earth's atmosphere with little distortion. Radio astronomers can therefore obtain a much clearer picture of stars and galaxies than is possible by means of optical observation. The construction of ever larger antenna systems and radio interferometers and improved radio receivers and data-processing methods have allowed radio astronomers to study fainter radio sources with increased resolution and image quality.

Using powerful radar systems, it is possible to detect radio signals reflected from nearby astronomical bodies such as the Moon, the nearby planets, some asteroids and comets, and the larger moons of Jupiter. Precise measurements of the time delay between the transmitted and reflected signal and the spectrum of the returned signal are used to precisely measure the distance to solar system objects and to image their surface features with a resolution of a few metres. The first successful detection of radar signals from the Moon occurred in 1946. This was quickly followed by experiments in the United States and the Soviet Union using powerful radar systems built for military and commercial applications. Both radio and radar studies of the Moon revealed the sandlike nature of its surface even before the Apollo landings were made. Radar echoes from Venus have penetrated its dense cloud cover surrounding the surface and have uncovered valleys and enormous mountains on the planet's surface. The first evidence for the correct rotation periods of Venus and of Mercury also came from radar studies.

(31-inch) parabolic reflector in his backyard in Wheaton, Ill., to continue Jansky's investigation of cosmic radio noise. In 1944 he published the first radio map of the sky. After World War II ended, the technology that had been developed for military radar was applied to astronomical research. Radio telescopes of increasing size and sophistication were built first in Australia and Great Britain and later in the United States and other countries.

PRINCIPLES OF OPERATION

Radio telescopes vary widely, but they all have two basic components: (1) a large radio antenna and (2) a sensitive radiometer, or radio receiver. The sensitivity of a radio telescope—i.e., the ability to measure weak sources of radio emission—depends both on the area and efficiency of the antenna and on the sensitivity of the radio receiver used to amplify and to detect the signals. For broadband continuum emission over a range of wavelengths, the sensitivity also depends on the bandwidth of the receiver. Because cosmic radio sources are extremely weak, radio telescopes are usually very large, up to hundreds of metres across, and use the most sensitive radio receivers available. Moreover, weak cosmic signals can be easily masked by terrestrial radio interference, and great effort is taken to protect radio telescopes from man-made emissions.

The most familiar type of radio telescope is the radio reflector consisting of a parabolic antenna, which operates in the same manner as a television satellite dish to focus the incoming radiation onto a small antenna called the feed, a term that originated with antennas used for radar transmissions. This type of telescope is also known as the dish, or filled-aperture, telescope. In a radio telescope the feed is typically a waveguide horn and transfers the incoming signal to the sensitive radio receiver. Solid-state amplifiers that are cooled to very low temperatures to reduce significantly their internal noise are used to obtain the best possible sensitivity.

In some radio telescopes the parabolic surface is equatorially mounted, with one axis parallel to the rotation axis of Earth. Equatorial mounts are attractive because they allow the telescope to follow a position in the sky as Earth rotates by moving the antenna about a single axis parallel to Earth's axis of rotation. But equatorially mounted radio telescopes are difficult and expensive to build. In most modern radio telescopes, a digital computer is used to drive the telescope about the azimuth and elevation axes to follow the motion of a radio source across the sky.

In the simplest form of radio telescope, the receiver is placed directly at the focal point of the parabolic reflector, and the detected signal is carried by cable along the feed support structure to a point near the ground where it can be recorded and analyzed. However, it is difficult in this type of system to access the instrumentation for maintenance and repair, and weight restrictions limit the size and number of individual receivers

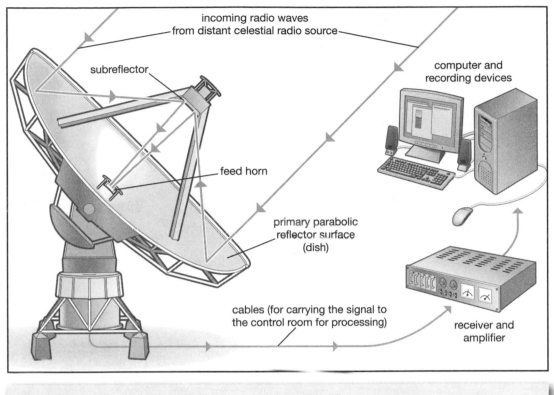

incoming radio waves
from distant celestial radio source

subreflector

computer and
recording devices

feed horn

primary parabolic
reflector surface
(dish)

cables (for carrying the signal to
the control room for processing)

receiver and
amplifier

Radio telescope system. Encyclopædia Britannica, Inc.

that can be installed on the telescope. More often, a secondary reflector is placed in front of (Cassegrain focus) or behind (Gregorian focus) the focal point of the paraboloid to focus the radiation to a point near the vertex, or centre, of the main reflector. Multiple feeds and receivers may be located at the vertex where there is more room, where weight restrictions are less stringent, and where access for maintenance and repair is more straightforward. Secondary focus systems also have the advantage that both the primary and secondary reflecting surfaces may be carefully shaped so as to improve the gain over that of a simple parabolic antenna.

Earlier radio telescopes used a symmetric tripod or quadrapod structure to hold the feed or secondary reflector, but such an arrangement blocks some of the incoming radiation, and the reflection of signals from the support legs back into the receiver distorts the response. In newer designs, the feed or secondary reflector is placed off the central axis and does not block the incoming signal. Off-axis radio telescopes are thus more sensitive and less affected by interference reflected from the support structure into the feed.

The Electromagnetic Spectrum

The entire distribution of electromagnetic radiation according to frequency or wavelength is called the electromagnetic spectrum. All electromagnetic waves travel with the same velocity in a vacuum—at the speed of light, which is 299,792,458 metres, or about 186,282 miles, per second. However, the entire distribution covers a wide range of frequencies and wavelengths, and it consists of many subranges, commonly referred to as portions of the electromagnetic spectrum. The various portions bear different names based on differences in behaviour in the emission, transmission, and absorption of the corresponding waves and also based on their different practical applications. There are no precise accepted boundaries between any of these contiguous portions, so the ranges tend to overlap.

The entire electromagnetic spectrum, from the lowest to the highest frequency (longest to shortest wavelength), includes all radio waves (e.g., commercial radio and television, microwaves, radar), infrared radiation, visible light, ultraviolet radiation, X-rays, and gamma rays.

The performance of a radio telescope is limited by various factors. The accuracy of a reflecting surface may depart from the ideal shape because of manufacturing irregularities. Wind load can exert force on the telescope. Thermal deformations cause differential expansion and contraction. As the antenna is pointed to different parts of the sky, deflections occur due to changes in gravitational forces. Departures from a perfect parabolic surface become important when they are a few percent or more of the wavelength of operation.

Since small structures can be built with greater precision than larger ones, radio telescopes designed for operation at millimetre wavelengths are typically only a few tens of metres across, whereas those designed for operation at centimetre wavelengths range up to 300 metres (1,000 feet) in diameter. For operation at relatively long metre wavelengths where the reflecting surface need not have an accuracy better than a few centimetres, it becomes practical to build very large fixed structures in which the reflecting surface can be made of simple "chicken wire" fencing or even parallel rows of wires.

Traditionally, the effect of gravity has been minimized by designing the movable structure to be as stiff as possible in order to reduce the deflections resulting from gravity. A more effective technique, based on the principle of homology, allows the structure to deform under the force of gravity, and the cross section and weight of each member of the movable structure are chosen to cause the gravitational forces to deform the reflecting structure into a new paraboloid with a slightly different focal point. It is then necessary only to move the feed or secondary reflector to maintain optimum performance. Homologous designs have become possible only since the development of computer-aided structural simulations known as the finite element method.

Some radio telescopes, particularly those designed for operation at very short wavelengths, are placed in protective enclosures called radomes that can nearly eliminate the effect of both wind loading and temperature differences throughout the structure. Special materials that exhibit very low absorption and reflection of radio waves have been developed for such structures, but the cost of enclosing a large antenna in a suitable temperature-controlled radome may be almost as much as the cost of the movable antenna itself.

The cost of constructing an antenna with a very large aperture can be greatly reduced by fixing the structure to the ground and moving either the feed or the secondary reflector to steer the beam in the sky. However, for parabolic reflecting surfaces, the beam can be steered in this way over only a limited range of angle without introducing aberration and a loss of signal strength.

Radio telescopes are used to measure broad-bandwidth continuum radiation as well as narrow-bandwidth spectroscopic features due to atomic and molecular lines found in the radio spectrum of astronomical objects. In early radio telescopes, spectroscopic observations were made by tuning a receiver across a sufficiently large frequency range to cover the various frequencies of interest. Because the spectrometer had a narrow frequency range, this procedure was extremely time-consuming and greatly restricted observations. Modern radio telescopes observe simultaneously at a large number of frequencies by dividing the signals up into as many as several thousand separate frequency channels that can range over a much larger total bandwidth of tens to hundreds of megahertz.

The most straightforward type of radio spectrometer employs a large number of filters, each tuned to a separate frequency and followed by a separate detector that combines the signal from the various filters to produce a multichannel, or multifrequency, receiver. Alternatively, a single broad-bandwidth signal may be converted into digital form and analyzed by the mathematical process of autocorrelation and Fourier transforms. In order to detect faint signals, the receiver output is often averaged over periods of up to several hours to reduce the effect of noise generated by thermal radiation in the receiver.

RADIO INTERFEROMETRY AND APERTURE SYNTHESIS

The angular resolution, or ability of a radio telescope to distinguish fine detail in the sky, depends on the wavelength of observations divided by the size of the instrument. Yet even the largest antennas, when used at their shortest operating wavelength, have an angular resolution of only a few arc seconds, which is about

10 times poorer than the resolution of ground-based optical telescopes. Because radio telescopes operate at much longer wavelengths than do optical telescopes, radio telescopes need to be much larger than optical telescopes to achieve the same angular resolution.

At radio wavelengths, the distortions introduced by the atmosphere are less important than at optical wavelengths, and so the theoretical angular resolution of a radio telescope can in practice be achieved even for the largest dimensions. Also, because radio signals are easy to distribute over large distances without distortion, it is possible to build radio telescopes of essentially unlimited dimensions. In fact, the history of radio astronomy has been one of solving engineering problems to construct radio telescopes of continually increasing angular resolution.

The high angular resolution of radio telescopes is achieved by using the principles of interferometry to synthesize a very large effective aperture from a number of antennas. In a simple two-antenna radio interferometer, the signals from an unresolved, or "point," source alternately arrive in phase (constructive interference) and out of phase (destructive interference) as Earth rotates and causes a change in the difference in path from the radio source to the two elements of the interferometer. This produces interference fringes in a manner similar to that in an optical interferometer. If the radio source has finite angular size, then the difference in path length to the elements of the interferometer varies across the source. The measured interference fringes from each interferometer pair thus depend on the detailed nature of the radio "brightness" distribution in the sky.

Each interferometer pair measures one "Fourier component" of the brightness distribution of the radio source. Work by Sir Martin Ryle and his colleagues in the 1950s and 1960s showed that movable antenna elements combined with the rotation of Earth can sample a sufficient number of Fourier components with which to synthesize the effect of a large aperture and thereby reconstruct high-resolution images of the radio sky. The laborious computational task of doing Fourier transforms to obtain images from the interferometer data is accomplished with high-speed computers and the fast Fourier transform (FFT), a mathematical technique that is specially suited for computing discrete Fourier transforms. In recognition of his contributions to the development of the Fourier synthesis technique, more commonly known as aperture synthesis, or earth-rotation synthesis, Ryle was awarded the 1974 Nobel Prize for Physics.

During the 1960s the Swedish physicist Jan Hogbom developed a technique called CLEAN, which is used to remove the spurious responses from a celestial radio image caused by the use of discrete, rather than continuous, spacings in deriving the radio image. Further developments, based on a technique introduced in the early 1950s by the British scientists Roger Jennison and Francis Graham Smith, led to the concept of self-calibration, which uses the observed source as its own calibrator in order to remove errors in a radio image due to uncertainties in the response of individual antennas as well as small errors introduced by the propagation of radio signals through the terrestrial atmosphere. In this way radio telescopes are able to achieve extraordinary angular resolution and image quality that are not possible in any other wavelength band.

Very Long Baseline Interferometry

In conventional interferometers and arrays, coaxial cable, waveguide, or even fibre-optic links are used to distribute a common local-oscillator reference signal to each antenna and also to return the received signal from an individual antenna to a central laboratory where it is correlated with the signals from other antennas. In cases in which antennas are spaced more than a few tens of kilometres apart, however, it becomes prohibitively expensive to employ real physical links to distribute the signals. Very high frequency (VHF) or ultrahigh frequency (UHF) radio links have been used, but the need for a large number of repeater stations makes this impractical for spacings greater than a few hundred kilometres.

Interferometer systems of essentially unlimited element separation can be formed by using the technique of very

long baseline interferometry (VLBI). In early VLBI systems the signals received at each element were recorded by broad-bandwidth videotape recorders located at each antenna. More recently, with the advent of inexpensive, reliable computer disk drives, the data are recorded on disks. The disks are then transported to a common location where they are replayed and the signals combined to form interference fringes. The successful operation of a VLBI system requires that the tape recordings be synchronized within a few millionths of a second and that the local oscillator reference signal be stable to better than one part in a trillion. Recorded data from just a few hours of observation typically contain about one trillion bits of information, which is roughly equivalent to storing the entire contents of a modest-sized library. Hydrogen maser frequency standards are used to give a timing accuracy of only a few billionths of a second and a frequency stability of one part in a million billion.

Radar Techniques

Techniques analogous to those used in military and civilian radar applications are sometimes employed with radio telescopes to study the surface of planets and asteroids in the solar system. By measuring the spectrum and the time of flight of signals reflected from planetary surfaces, it is possible to examine topographical features with a linear resolution as good as 1 km (3,280 feet), deduce rates of rotation, and determine with great accuracy the distance to the planets. Radio signals reflected from the planets are weak, and high-power radar transmitters are needed in order to obtain measurable signal detections. The time it takes for a radar signal to travel to Venus and back, even at the closest approach of the planet to Earth, is about five minutes. For Saturn, it is more than two hours.

MAJOR APPLICATIONS OF RADIO TELESCOPES

Radio telescopes permit astronomers to study many kinds of extraterrestrial radio sources. These astronomical objects emit radio waves by one of several processes, including (1) thermal radiation from solid bodies such as the planets, (2) thermal, or bremsstrahlung, radiation from hot gas in the interstellar medium, (3) synchrotron radiation from electrons moving at velocities near the speed of light in weak magnetic fields, (4) spectral line radiation from atomic or molecular transitions that occur in the interstellar medium or in the gaseous envelopes around stars, and (5) pulsed radiation resulting from the rapid rotation of neutron stars surrounded by an intense magnetic field and energetic electrons.

Radio telescopes are used to measure the surface temperatures of all the planets, as well as some of the moons of Jupiter and Saturn. Radar measurements have revealed the rotation of Mercury, which was previously thought to keep the same side toward the Sun. Astronomers have also used radar observations to image features on the surface of Venus, which is completely obscured from visual scrutiny by the heavy cloud cover that permanently enshrouds the planet. Accurate measurements of the travel time of radar signals reflected from Venus when it is on the other side of the Sun from Earth have indicated that radio waves passing close to the Sun slow down owing to gravity and thereby provide a new independent test of Albert Einstein's theory of general relativity.

Broadband continuum emission throughout the radio-frequency spectrum is observed from a variety of stars (especially binary, X-ray, and other active stars), from supernova remnants, and from magnetic fields and relativistic electrons in the interstellar medium. The discovery of pulsars (short for *pulsating radio stars*) in 1967 revealed the existence of rapidly rotating neutron stars throughout the Milky Way Galaxy and led to the first observation of the effect of gravitational radiation.

Using radio telescopes equipped with sensitive spectrometers, radio astronomers have discovered about 150 separate molecules, including familiar chemical compounds like water, formaldehyde, ammonia, methanol, ethyl alcohol, and carbon dioxide. The important spectral line of atomic hydrogen at 1,421.405 MHz (21 cm wavelength) is used to determine the motions of hydrogen clouds in the Milky Way Galaxy and other galaxies. This is done by measuring the change in the wavelength of the observed lines arising from the Doppler effect. It has been established from such measurements that the rotational velocities of the hydrogen clouds vary with distance from the galactic centre. The mass of a spiral galaxy can in turn be estimated using this velocity data. In this way radio telescopes show evidence for the presence of so-called dark matter by showing that the amount of starlight is insufficient to account for the large mass inferred from the rapid rotation curves.

Radio telescopes have discovered powerful radio galaxies and quasars far beyond the Milky Way Galaxy system. These cosmic objects have intense clouds of radio emission that extend hundreds of thousands of light-years away from a central energy source located in an active galactic nucleus (AGN), or quasar. Observations with high-resolution radio arrays show highly relativistic jets extending from an AGN to the radio lobes.

Measurements made in 1965 by Arno Penzias and Robert Wilson using an experimental communications antenna at 3 cm wavelength located at Bell Laboratories in Holmdel, N.J., detected the existence of a microwave cosmic background radiation with a temperature of 3 kelvins (K). This radiation, which comes from all parts of the sky, is thought to be the remaining radiation from the hot big bang, the primeval explosion from which the universe presumably originated 13.7 billion years ago. Satellite

and ground-based radio telescopes have been used to measure the very small deviations from isotropy of the cosmic microwave background. This work has led to refined determination of the size, geometry, and age of the universe.

Notable Radio Telescopes

The largest single radio telescope in the world is the 305-metre (1,000-foot) fixed spherical reflector operated by Cornell University at the Arecibo Observatory near Arecibo, P.R. The antenna has an enormous collecting area, but the beam can be moved through only a limited angle of about 20° from the zenith. It is used for planetary radar astronomy, as well as for studying pulsars and other galactic and extragalactic phenomena.

The Russian RATAN-600 telescope (RATAN stands for Radio Astronomical Telescope of the Academy of Sciences), located near Zelenchukskaya in the Caucasus Mountains, has 895 reflecting panels, each 7.4 metres (24.3 feet) high, arranged in a ring 576 metres (1,890 feet) in diameter. Using long parabolic cylinders, standing reflectors, or dipole elements, researchers in Australia, France, India, Italy, Russia, and Ukraine have also built antennas with very large collecting areas.

The largest fully steerable radio telescope in the world is the Robert C. Byrd Green Bank Telescope (GBT) located in Green Bank, W.Va. This 110-by-100-metre (360-by-330-foot) off-axis radio telescope was completed in 2000 and operates at wavelengths as short as a few millimetres. The moving structure, which weighs 7.3 million kg (16 million pounds), points to any direction in the sky with an accuracy of only a few arc seconds. The secondary reflector is held by an off-axis support structure to minimize radiation from the ground and unwanted reflections from support legs. Each of the 2,004 surface panels that make up the parabolic surface is held in place by computer-controlled actuators that keep the surface accurate to a few tenths of a millimetre. The GBT is located in the National Radio Quiet Zone, which offers unique protection for radio telescopes from local sources of man-made interference.

Other large, fully steerable, filled-aperture radio telescopes include the Max Planck Institut für Radioastronomie 100-metre-diameter (330-foot) antenna near Effelsberg, Ger.; the Australian Commonwealth Scientific and Industrial Research Organization (CSIRO) 64-metre (210-foot) dish near Parkes; and the 76-metre (250-foot) Lovell Telescope at Jodrell Bank in England. These filled-aperture radio telescopes are used for atomic and molecular spectroscopy over a wide range of frequency and for other galactic and extragalactic studies.

Several smaller, more precise radio telescopes for observing at millimetre wavelength have been installed high atop mountains or other high elevations, where clear skies and high altitudes minimize absorption and distortion of the incoming signals by the terrestrial atmosphere. A 45-metre (148-foot) radio dish near Nobeyama, Japan, is used for observations at wavelengths as short as 3 mm (0.12 inch). The French-Spanish Institut de Radio Astronomie Millimetrique (IRAM) in Grenoble, France, operates a 30-metre (100-foot) antenna at an altitude of 2,850 metres (9,350 feet) on Pico Veleta in the Spanish Sierra Nevada for observations at wavelengths as short as 1 mm (0.04 inch). Several radio telescopes that operate at submillimetre wavelengths are located near the summit

The 100-metre (330-foot) radio telescope at Effelsberg, near Bonn, Ger. Courtesy of the Max-Planck-Institut fur Radioastronomie; photographer, G. Hutschenreiter

of Mauna Kea, Hawaii, at elevations above 4,000 metres (13,000 feet) and on Mount Graham near Tucson, Ariz. The largest of these, the James Clerk Maxwell Telescope at the Mauna Kea Observatory, has a diameter of 15 metres (49 feet). (See Appendix E: Select Radio Telescopes on page 203.)

RADIO TELESCOPE ARRAYS

The world's most powerful radio telescope, in its combination of sensitivity, resolution, and versatility, is the U.S. Very Large Array (VLA) located on the Plains of San Agustin near Socorro, in central New Mexico. The VLA consists of 27 parabolic antennas, each measuring 25 metres (82 feet) in diameter. The total collecting area is equivalent to a single 130-metre (430-foot) antenna. However, the angular resolution is equivalent to a single antenna 36 km (22 miles) in diameter. Each element of the VLA can be moved by a transporter along a Y-shaped railroad track; it is possible to change the length of the arms between 600 metres (2,000 feet) and 21 km (13 miles) to vary the resolution. Each antenna is equipped with receivers that operate in eight different wavelength bands from approximately 7 mm (0.3 inch) to 4 metres (13 feet).

When used at the shorter wavelength in the largest antenna configuration, the angular resolution of the VLA is better than one tenth of an arc second, or about the same as the Hubble Space Telescope at optical wavelengths. The VLA is operated by the U.S. National Radio Astronomy Observatory as a facility of the National Science Foundation and is used by nearly 1,500 astronomers each year for a wide variety of research programs devoted to the study of the solar system, the Milky Way Galaxy, radio stars, pulsars, atomic and molecular gas in the Milky Way Galaxy and in other galaxies, radio galaxies, quasars, and the radio afterglow of gamma-ray bursters.

In Europe the Netherlands Foundation for Research in Astronomy operates the Westerbork Synthesis Radio Telescope, which is an east-west array of 14 antennas, each 25 metres (82 feet) in diameter and extending over 2.7 km (1.7 miles). In Australia the Commonwealth Scientific and Industrial Research Organization maintains the six-element Australian Telescope Compact Array at Narrabri, N.S.W., for studies of the southern skies, including in particular the nearby Magellanic Clouds.

Indian radio astronomers have built the Giant Metrewave Radio Telescope (GMRT) near Pune, India. The GMRT contains 30 antennas extending some 25 km (16 miles) in diameter. Each antenna element is 45 metres (148 feet) in diameter and is constructed using a novel, inexpensive system of wire trusses to replace the conventional steel beam backup structure of the parabolic surface. The GMRT operates at relatively long wavelengths between 20 cm (8 inches) and 6 metres (20 feet).

The Multi-Element Radio Linked Interferometer Network (MERLIN),

Very Large Array radio telescope system near Socorro, N.M. © Pixtal

operated by the Nuffield Radio Astronomy Laboratories at Jodrell Bank, is being upgraded to use fibre-optic, instead of microwave radio, links to connect seven antennas separated by up to 217 km (135 miles) in the southern part of England. It is used primarily to study compact radio sources associated with quasars, AGN, and cosmic masers with a resolution of a few hundredths of an arc second.

The Very Long Baseline Array (VLBA) consists of ten 25-metre (82-foot) dishes spread across the United States from the Virgin Islands to Hawaii. The VLBA operates at wavelengths from 3 mm (0.1 inch) to 1 metre (3 feet) and is used to study quasars, galactic nuclei, cosmic masers, pulsars, and radio stars with a resolution as good as 0.0001 arc second, or more than 100 times better than that of the Hubble Space Telescope. The 10 individual antenna elements of the VLBA do not have any direct connection; instead, signals are recorded on high-density computer disk drives that are then shipped to a special processing centre in New Mexico where they are replayed and the signals analyzed to form images. Precise timing between the elements is maintained by a hydrogen maser atomic clock located at each antenna site. The control and analysis centre for the VLBA is located in central New Mexico along with the VLA Operations centre, and the two instruments are sometimes used together to obtain increased sensitivity and angular resolution.

In 1997, Japanese radio astronomers working at the Institute for Space Science near Tokyo launched an 8-metre (26-foot) dish, known as the VLBI Space Observatory Program (VSOP), in Earth orbit. Working with the VLBA and other ground-based radio telescopes, VSOP gave interferometer baselines up to 33,000 km (21,000 miles). (VSOP was also known as Highly Advanced Laboratory for Communication and Astronomy [HALCA].) In 2003 the VSOP lost its ability to point accurately, and the program ended.

Interferometers and arrays are also used at millimetre and submillimetre wavelengths where they are used to study the formation of stars and galaxies with resolution better than can be obtained with simple filled-aperture antennas. The operation of arrays at millimetre and submillimetre wavelengths is very difficult and requires that the instrument be at very high and dry locations to minimize the phase distortions of signals as they propagate through the atmosphere. Some prominent millimetre interferometers and arrays are the Combined Array for Research in Millimeter-wave Astronomy (CARMA) near Big Pine, Calif., the IRAM Plateau de Bure facility in France, and the Japanese Nobeyama Radio Observatory. In 2003 the Harvard-Smithsonian Center for Astrophysics in collaboration with the Academia Sinica of Taiwan completed the Submillimeter Array (SMA) located near the summit of Mauna Kea, Hawaii, at an elevation of 4,080 metres (13,385 feet). This is an eight-element array of 6-metre (20-foot) dishes designed to work at wavelengths as short as 0.3 mm (0.01 inch). A major new international facility is under construction by the United States, Canada, Europe, and Japan in the Atacama Desert in northern Chile at an elevation of more than 5,000 metres (16,000 feet) and is expected to be completed around 2012. The Atacama Large Millimeter Array (ALMA) will consist of fifty 12-metre (39-foot) dishes operating at wavelengths as short as 0.3 mm (0.01 inch), as well as a more compact array of four 12-metre and sixteen 7-metre (23-foot) dishes.

EARTH-ORBITING RADIO TELESCOPES

Most radio waves pass relatively undistorted through Earth's atmosphere, and so there is little need to place radio telescopes in space. The exceptions are for observations at very long wavelengths that are distorted by Earth's ionosphere, for observations at very short wavelengths that are affected by water vapour and oxygen in the atmosphere, and for precision observations at all wavelengths that might be affected by thermal radiation from the ground. The first radio astronomy satellite was the U.S.-British Ariel 2, launched in 1964, which studied long-wavelength radio noise from Earth's ionosphere and the Milky Way Galaxy. Ariel 2 was followed by two more satellites in the Ariel series and by the U.S. satellites Radio Astronomy Explorers 1 and 2, launched in 1968 and 1973, respectively.

Subsequent radio astronomy satellites performed observations that were difficult to make from the ground or were enhanced by being made from space (such as VSOP mentioned above). The U.S. Submillimeter Wave Astronomy Satellite (SWAS) and the Swedish-Canadian-French-Finnish ODIN, launched in 1998 and 2001, respectively, observed at very short, submillimetre wavelengths. By observing the cosmic microwave background radiation left over from the big bang, the U.S. satellites Cosmic Background Explorer (launched in 1989) and the Wilkinson Microwave Anistropy Probe (launched in 2001) detected very small fluctuations in the background radiation corresponding to the early structures from which galaxies would be formed and accurately determined the age and composition of the universe.

OTHER TYPES OF TELESCOPES

Telescopes are not only used to observe both visible light and radio waves. There are telescopes for every region of the electromagnetic spectrum from infrared rays to gamma rays.

INFRARED TELESCOPES

Telescopic systems of this type do not really differ significantly from reflecting telescopes designed to observe in the visible region of the electromagnetic spectrum. The main difference is in the physical location of the infrared telescope, since infrared photons have lower energies than those of visible light. The infrared rays are readily absorbed by the water vapour in Earth's atmosphere, and most of this water vapour is located at the lower atmospheric regions—i.e., near sea level. Earth-bound infrared telescopes have been successfully located on high mountaintops, as, for example, Mauna Kea in Hawaii. The other obvious placement of infrared instruments is in a satellite such as the Infrared Astronomical Satellite (IRAS), which mapped the celestial sky in the infrared in 1983, or Herschel, which was launched in 2009. The Kuiper Airborne Observatory, operated by NASA, consists of a 0.9-metre (3.0-foot) telescope that is flown in a special airplane above the water vapour to collect infrared data. Much of the infrared data is collected with an electronic camera, since ordinary film is unable to register the low-energy photons.

Another example of an infrared telescope is the United Kingdom Infrared Telescope (UKIRT), which has a 3.8-metre (12.5-foot) mirror made of Cer-Vit, a glass ceramic that has a very low coefficient of expansion. This instrument is configured in a Cassegrain design and employs a thin monolithic primary mirror with a

Comet Hale-Bopp streaks across the pre-dawn sky over Mauna Kea, an observatory in Hawaii that is home to a multitude of extremely powerful telescopes. D. Nunuk/Photo Researchers, Inc.

lightweight support structure. This telescope is located at Mauna Kea Observatory. The 3-metre (10-foot) Infrared Telescope Facility (IRTF), also located at Mauna Kea, is sponsored by NASA and operated by the University of Hawaii.

ULTRAVIOLET TELESCOPES

These telescopes are used to examine the shorter wavelengths of the electromagnetic spectrum immediately adjacent to the visible portion. Like the infrared telescopes, the ultraviolet systems also employ reflectors as their primary collectors.

Ultraviolet radiation is composed of higher-energy photons than infrared radiation, which means that photographic techniques as well as electronic detectors can be used to collect astronomical data. The Earth's stratospheric ozone layer, however, blocks all wavelengths shorter than 3000 angstroms from reaching ground-based telescopes. As this ozone layer lies at an altitude of 20 to 40 km (12 to 25 miles), astronomers have to resort to rockets and satellites to make observations from above it. From 1978 to 1996 an orbiting observatory known as the International Ultraviolet Explorer (IUE) studied celestial sources of ultraviolet radiation. The IUE telescope was equipped with a 45-cm (18-inch) mirror and recorded data electronically down to 1000 angstroms. The IUE was in a synchronous orbit (i.e., its period of revolution around Earth was identical to the period of the planet's rotation) in view of NASA's Goddard Space Flight Center in Greenbelt, Md., and so data could be transmitted to the ground station at the end of each observing tour and examined immediately on a television monitor.

Another Earth-orbiting spacecraft, the Extreme Ultraviolet Explorer (EUVE) satellite, which was in operation from 1992 to 2001, was designed to survey the sky in the extreme ultraviolet region between 400 and 900 angstroms. It had four telescopes with gold-plated mirrors, the design of which was critically dependent on the transmission properties of the filters used to define the EUV band passes. The combination of the mirrors and filters was selected to maximize the telescope's sensitivity to detect faint EUV sources. Three of the telescopes had scanners that were pointed in the satellite's spin plane. The fourth telescope, the Deep Survey/Spectrometer Telescope, was directed in an anti-Sun direction. It conducted a photometric deep-sky survey in the ecliptic plane for part of the mission and then collected spectroscopic observations in the final phase of the mission.

The Far Ultraviolet Spectroscopic Explorer (FUSE) observed the universe in far-ultraviolet light (wavelengths between 905 and 1,195 angstroms) from 1999 to 2007. FUSE was just one telescope with a spectrometer designed to study the far-ultraviolet region. It studied the composition of the interstellar and intergalactic mediums.

X-RAY TELESCOPES

The X-ray telescope is used to examine the shorter-wavelength region of the electromagnetic spectrum adjacent to the ultraviolet region. The design of this type of telescope must be radically different from that of a conventional reflector. Since X-ray photons have so much energy, they would pass right through the mirror of a standard reflector. X rays must be bounced off a mirror at a very low angle if they are to be captured. (This technique is referred to as grazing incidence.) For this reason, the mirrors in X-ray telescopes are mounted with their surfaces only slightly off a parallel line with the incoming X rays. Application of the grazing-incidence principle makes it possible to focus X rays from a cosmic object into an image that can be recorded electronically.

NASA launched a series of three High-Energy Astronomy Observatories (HEAOs) during the late 1970s to explore cosmic X-ray sources. HEAO-1 mapped the X-ray sources with high sensitivity and high resolution. Some of the more interesting of these objects were studied in detail by HEAO-2 (named the Einstein

Observatory). HEAO-3 was used primarily to investigate cosmic rays and gamma rays.

The European X-ray Observatory Satellite (EXOSAT), developed by the European Space Agency (ESA), was capable of greater spectral resolution than the Einstein Observatory and was more sensitive to X-ray emissions at shorter wavelengths. EXOSAT remained in orbit from 1983 to 1986. A much larger X-ray astronomy satellite was launched in June 1990 as part of a cooperative program involving the United States, Germany, and the United Kingdom. This satellite, called the Röntgensatellit (ROSAT), had two parallel grazing-incidence telescopes. One of them, the X-ray telescope (XRT), bore many similarities to the equipment of the Einstein Observatory but had a larger geometric area and better mirror resolution. The other telescope, the extended ultraviolet wide-field camera, had an imaging detector much like the X-ray HRI. A positive sensitive proportional counter made it possible to survey the sky at X-ray wavelengths for the purpose of producing a catalog of 100,000 sources with a positional accuracy of better than 30 arc seconds. A wide-field camera with a 5°-diameter field of view was also part of the ROSAT instrument package. It produced an extended ultraviolet survey with arc minute source positions in this wavelength region, making it the first instrument with such capability. The ROSAT mirrors were gold-coated and permitted detailed examination of the sky from 6 to 100 angstroms.

X-ray astronomy has its equivalent of the Hubble Space Telescope in the Chandra X-ray Observatory. Chandra's mirrors are made of iridium and have an aperture of 10 metres (33 feet). It can obtain high-resolution spectra and images of astronomical objects.

GAMMA-RAY TELESCOPES

These instruments require the use of grazing-incidence techniques similar to those employed with X-ray telescopes. Gamma rays are the shortest (about 0.1 angstrom or less) known waves in the electromagnetic spectrum. As mentioned above, HEAO-3 was developed to collect data from cosmic gamma-ray sources. NASA and collaborative international agencies have numerous ongoing and planned projects in the area of gamma-ray astronomy. The scientific objectives of the programs include determining the nature and physical parameters of high-energy (up to 10 gigaelectron volts) astrophysical systems. Examples of such systems include stellar coronas, white dwarfs, neutron stars, black holes, supernova remnants, clusters of galaxies, and diffuse gamma-ray background. In addition to satellite investigations of these cosmic high-energy sources, NASA has an extensive program that involves the design and development of gamma-ray telescope systems for deployment in high-altitude balloons. All mirrors in gamma-ray telescopes have gold coatings similar to those in X-ray telescope mirrors.

ADVANCES IN AUXILIARY INSTRUMENTATION

Almost as important as the telescope itself are the auxiliary instruments that the astronomer uses to exploit the light received at the focal plane. Examples of such instruments are the camera, the spectrograph, the photomultiplier tube, and the charge-coupled device.

CAMERAS

John Draper of the United States photographed the Moon as early as 1840 by applying the daguerreotype process. The French physicists A.-H.-L. Fizeau and J.-B.-L. Foucault succeeded in making a photographic image of the Sun in 1845. Five years later, astronomers at Harvard Observatory took the first photographs of the stars.

The use of photographic equipment in conjunction with telescopes has benefited astronomers greatly, giving them two distinct advantages. First, photographic images provide a permanent record of celestial phenomena and, second, photographic plates integrate the light from celestial sources over long periods of time and thereby permit astronomers to see much fainter objects than they would be able to observe visually. Typically, the camera's photographic plate (or film) is mounted in the focal plane of the telescope. The plate (or film) consists of glass or of a plastic material that is covered with a thin layer of a silver compound. The light striking the photographic medium causes the silver compound to undergo a chemical change. When processed, a negative image results—i.e., the brightest spots (the Moon and the stars, for example) appear as the darkest areas on the plate or the film. Since the 1980s the charge-coupled device has supplanted photography in the production of astronomical images.

SPECTROGRAPHS

Newton noted the interesting way in which a piece of glass can break up light into different bands of colour, but it was not until 1814 that the German physicist Joseph von Fraunhofer discovered the lines of the solar spectrum and laid the basis for spectroscopy. The spectrograph consists of a slit, a collimator, a prism for dispersing the light, and a focusing lens. The collimator is an optical device that produces parallel rays from a focal plane source—i.e., gives the appearance that the source is located at an infinite distance. The spectrograph enables astronomers to analyze the chemical composition of planetary atmospheres, stars, nebulas, and other celestial objects. A bright line in the spectrum indicates the presence of a glowing gas radiating at a wavelength characteristic of the chemical element in the gas. A dark line in the spectrum usually means that a cooler gas has intervened and absorbed the lines of the element characteristic of the intervening material.

The Doppler effect—the apparent difference between the frequency at which sound or light waves leave a source and that at which they reach an observer—was named for its discoverer, astronomer Christian Doppler. Imagno/Hulton Archive/Getty Images

The lines may also be displaced to either the red end or the blue end of the spectrum. This effect was first noted in 1842 by the Austrian physicist Christian Johann Doppler. When a light source is approaching, the lines are shifted toward the blue end of the spectrum, and when the source is receding, the lines are shifted toward its red end. This effect, known as the Doppler effect, permits astronomers to study the relative motions of celestial objects with respect to Earth's motion.

The slit of the spectrograph is placed at the focal plane of the telescope. The resulting spectrum may be recorded photographically or with some kind of electronic detector, such as a photomultiplier tube, CCD, or CID. If no recording device is used, then the optical device is technically referred to as a spectroscope.

PHOTOMULTIPLIER TUBES

The photomultiplier tube is an enhanced version of the photocell, which was first used by astronomers to record data electronically. The photocell contains a photosensitive surface that generates an electric current when struck by light from a celestial source. The photosensitive surface is positioned just behind the focus. A diaphragm of very small aperture is usually placed in the focal plane to eliminate as much of the background light of the sky as possible. A small lens is used to focus the focal plane image on the photosensitive surface, which, in the case of a photomultiplier tube, is referred to as the photocathode. In the photomultiplier tube a series of special sensitive plates are arranged geometrically to amplify or multiply the electron stream. Frequently, magnifications of a million are achieved by this process.

The photomultiplier tube has a distinct advantage over the photographic plate. With the photographic plate the relationship between the brightness of the celestial source and its registration on the plate is not linear. In the case of the photomultiplier tube, however, the release of electrons in the tube is directly proportional to the intensity of light from the celestial source. This linear relationship is very useful for working over a wide range of brightness. A disadvantage of the photomultiplier tube is that only one object can be recorded at a time. The output from such a device is sent to a recorder or digital storage device to produce a permanent record.

CHARGE-COUPLED DEVICES

The charge-coupled device (CCD) uses a light-sensitive material on a silicon chip to electronically detect photons in a way similar to the photomultiplier tube. The principal difference is that the chip also contains integrated microcircuitry required to transfer the detected signal along a row of discrete picture elements (or pixels) and thereby scan a celestial object or objects very rapidly. When individual pixels are arranged simply in a single row, the detector is referred to as a linear array. When the pixels are arranged in rows and columns, the assemblage is called a two-dimensional array.

Pixels can be assembled in various sizes and shapes. The Hubble Space Telescope has a CCD detector with a 1,600 × 1,600 pixel array. Actually, there

PHOTOMETRY

In astronomy, photometry is the measurement of the brightness of stars and other celestial objects (nebulae, galaxies, planets, etc.). Such measurements can yield large amounts of information on the objects' structure, temperature, distance, age, etc.

The earliest observations of the apparent brightness of the stars were made by Greek astronomers. The system used by Hipparchus about 130 BCE divided the stars into classes called magnitudes; the brightest were described as being of first magnitude, the next class were second magnitude, and so on in equal steps down to the faintest stars visible to the unaided eye, which were said to be of sixth magnitude. The application of the telescope to astronomy in the 17th century led to the discovery of many fainter stars, and the scale was extended downward to seventh, eighth, etc., magnitudes.

In the early 19th century it was established by experimenters that the apparently equal steps in brightness were in fact steps of constant ratio in the light energy received and that a difference in brightness of five magnitudes was roughly equivalent to a ratio of 100. In 1856 Norman Robert Pogson suggested that this ratio should be used to define the scale of magnitude, so that a brightness difference of one magnitude was a ratio of 2.512 in intensity and a five-magnitude difference was a ratio of $(2.51188)^5$, or precisely 100. Steps in brightness of less than a magnitude were denoted by using decimal fractions. The zero point on the scale was chosen to cause the minimum change for the large number of stars traditionally established as of sixth magnitude, with the result that several of the brightest stars proved to have magnitudes less than 0 (i.e., negative values).

The introduction of photography provided the first nonsubjective means of measuring the brightness of stars. The fact that photographic plates are sensitive to violet and ultraviolet radiation, rather than to the green and yellow wavelengths to which the eye is most sensitive, led to the establishment of two separate magnitude scales, the visual and the photographic. The difference between the magnitudes given by the two scales for a given star was later termed the colour index and was recognized to be a measure of the temperature of the star's surface.

Photographic photometry relied on visual comparisons of images of starlight recorded on photographic plates. It was somewhat inaccurate because the complex relationships between the size and density of photographic images of stars and the brightness of those optical images were not subject to full control or accurate calibration.

Beginning in the 1940s astronomical photometry was vastly extended in sensitivity and wavelength range, especially by the use of the more accurate photoelectric rather than photographic detectors. The faintest stars observed with photoelectric tubes had magnitudes around 24. In photoelectric photometry, the image of a single star is passed through a small diaphragm in the focal plane of the telescope. After further passing through an appropriate filter and a field lens, the light of the stellar image passes into a photomultiplier, a device that produces a relatively strong electric current from a weak light input. The output current may then be measured in a variety of ways. This type of photometry owes its extreme accuracy to the highly linear relation between the amount of incoming radiation and the electric current it produces, and to the precise techniques that can be used to measure the current.

Photomultiplier tubes have since been supplanted by CCDs. Magnitudes are now measured not only in the visible part of the spectrum but also in the ultraviolet and infrared.

The dominant photometric classification system, the UBV system introduced in the early 1950s by Harold L. Johnson and William Wilson Morgan, uses three wave bands, one in the ultraviolet, one in the blue, and the other in the dominant visual range. More elaborate systems can use many more measurements, usually by dividing the visible and ultraviolet regions into narrower slices or by extension of the range into the infrared. Routine accuracy of measurement is now of the order of 0.001 magnitude, and the principal experimental difficulty in much modern work is that the sky itself is luminous, due principally to photochemical reactions in the upper atmosphere.

Photometric work is always a compromise between the time taken for an observation and its complexity. A small number of broad-band measurements can be done quickly, but as more colours are used for a set of magnitude determinations for a star, more can be deduced about the nature of that star. The simplest measurement is that of effective temperature, while data over a wider range allow the observer to separate giant from dwarf stars, to assess whether a star is metal-rich or deficient, to determine the surface gravity, and to estimate the effect of interstellar dust on a star's radiation.

are four 800 × 800 pixel arrays mosaicked together. The sensitivity of a CCD is 100 times greater than a photographic plate and so has the ability to quickly scan objects such as planets, nebulas, and star clusters and record the desired data. Another feature of the CCD is that the detector material may be altered to provide more sensitivity at different wavelengths. Thus, some detectors are more sensitive in the blue region of the spectrum than in the red region. Today, most large observatories use CCDs to record data electronically.

CHAPTER 5

ASTRONOMERS THROUGH THE AGES

Many scientists throughout human history have sought to understand the heavens using astronomical techniques. The history of astronomy described here stretches from ancient Babylon to the present day.

ANCIENT

NABU-RIMANNI
(fl. *c.* 491 BCE, Babylonia)

Nabu-rimanni was the earliest Babylonian astronomer known by name. He devised the so-called System A, a group of ephemerides, or tables, giving the positions of the Moon, Sun, and planets at any given moment. Based on centuries of observation, these tables were nonetheless somewhat crude and were superseded about a century later by Kidinnu's System B, a refined mathematical method for finding celestial positions more accurately. Both systems were in use simultaneously between 250 and 50 BCE. Nabu-rimanni also calculated the length of the synodic month (from New Moon to New Moon) to be 29.530614 days, as compared with the modern value of 29.530596 days.

SOSIGENES OF ALEXANDRIA
(fl. 1st century BCE)

The Greek astronomer and mathematician Sosigenes of Alexandria was employed by Julius Caesar to devise the Julian calendar. He is sometimes confused with Sosigenes the Peripatetic (fl. 2nd century CE), the tutor of the Greek philosopher Alexander of Aphrodisias.

At the conclusion of the Roman civil war (49–45 BCE), Caesar set out to replace the multitude of inaccurate and diverse calendars of the Roman commonwealth with a single official calendar. At the suggestion of Sosigenes, he adopted a modification of the 365-day Egyptian solar calendar but with an extra day every fourth year, the leap year. The Julian calendar went into effect in 45 BCE. Through a misunderstanding of Sosigenes' prescription (probably due to the Roman practice of inclusive counting), leap days were at first inserted every three years rather than every four—an error that was corrected during the reign of Augustus. Sosigenes may also have devised the astronomical calendar that Caesar published to accompany the reform. With minor modifications the Julian calendar is the same as the modern Gregorian calendar.

Sosigenes is said to have written three calendrical treatises, but these have been lost. The Roman scholar Pliny the Elder wrote that he agreed with the Babylonian astronomer Kidinnu that Mercury is never more than 22° from the Sun. Some historians have therefore surmised, on inadequate grounds, that Sosigenes taught that Mercury revolves around the Sun.

17TH CENTURY

John Bainbridge
(b. 1582, Ashby-de-la-Zouch, Leicestershire, Eng.—d. Nov. 3, 1643, Oxford, Oxfordshire)

John Bainbridge was noted for his observations of comets.

Bainbridge practiced medicine at Ashby-de-la-Zouch from 1614 to 1618. Soon after he moved to London, he was appointed (1619) Savilian professor of astronomy at the University of Oxford, largely on the basis of his *Astronomical Description of the Comet of 1618* (published in 1619). Although this work accepted to a point the superstitious belief that comets appear as signs of impending disaster, in *Antiprognosticon* (1642) he recanted and vigorously denounced astrological superstition that based predictions on conjunctions of the planets and appearances of comets.

His other publication includes the translation of ancient Greek astronomical works: *Procli Sphaera et Ptolomaei de Hypothesibus Planetarum* (1620; "The Sphere of Proclus and Ptolemy's 'On the Hypotheses of Planets'"). Ptolemy's book was an influential cosmological work of the 2nd century CE. The *Sphere*, an elementary teaching text falsely attributed to Proclus, consists of several chapters of Geminus's *Introduction to the Phenomena* (1st century BCE).

Giuseppe Campani
(b. 1635, Castel San Felice [Italy]— d. July 28, 1715, Rome)

The Italian optical-instrument maker Giuseppe Campani invented a lens-grinding lathe.

Of peasant origin, Campani studied in Rome. There he learned to grind lenses and, with his two brothers, invented a silent night clock that, when presented to Pope Alexander VII, brought him fame. Thereafter, he became a full-time lens grinder for about 50 years, constructing telescopes and lenses for important persons and for the Royal Observatory in Paris.

In 1664 he developed his lens-grinding lathe, with which he made superior lenses for telescopes. He also improved telescope tubes, constructing them of wood rather than of cardboard covered with leather; though somewhat unwieldy, these designs proved durable, and wooden telescopes continued in use until the 19th century. With his own instruments he observed the moons of Jupiter and the rings of Saturn in 1664–65. Subsequently, he devised a screw-barrel microscope that could be adjusted by rotating it within a threaded ring. That device supplanted sliding barrel types held only by friction, permitting far more precise adjustment.

EUSTACHIO DIVINI
(b. Oct. 4, 1610, San Severino delle Marche, near Ancona [Italy]— d. 1685, Rome)

The Italian scientist Eustachio Divini was one of the first to develop the technology necessary for producing scientific optical instruments.

After some scientific training under Benedetto Castelli, a disciple of Galileo, Divini established himself in Rome in 1646 as a maker of clocks and lenses. He constructed a number of compound microscopes and long-focus telescopes, the latter consisting of wooden tubes with four lenses, with a focal length of more than 15 m (50 feet).

In 1649 Divini published a copper engraving of a map of the Moon, based on his own observations made with his invention. He also made a number of astronomical observations, including some of the rings of Saturn and the spots and satellites of Jupiter. Many of his microscopes and telescopes have survived in museums in Florence, Rome, Padua, and elsewhere.

JOHANNES FABRICIUS
(b. Jan. 8, 1587, Resterhafe, Neth.— d. c. 1615)

Johannes Fabricius was a Dutch astronomer who may have been the first observer of sunspots (1610–11) and was the first to publish information on such observations. He did so in his *Narratio de maculis in sole observatis et appurente earum cum sole conversione* (1611; "Account of Spots Observed on the Sun and of Their Apparent Rotation with the Sun"). The son of the astronomer David Fabricius, Johannes used a camera obscura as well as a telescope in his study of the Sun.

HANS LIPPERSHEY
(b. c. 1570, Wesel, Ger.—d. c. 1619, Middelburg, Neth.)

The spectacle maker Hans Lippershey from the United Netherlands is traditionally credited with inventing the telescope (1608).

Lippershey applied to the States General of the Netherlands for a 30-year patent for his instrument, which he called a *kijker* ("looker"), or else an annual pension, in exchange for which he offered not to sell telescopes to foreign kings. Two other claimants to the invention came forward, Jacob Metius and Sacharias Jansen. The States General ruled that no patent should be granted because so many people knew about it and the device was so easy to copy. However, the States General granted Lippershey 900 florins for the instrument but required its modification into a binocular device. His telescopes were made available to Henry IV of France and others before the end of 1608. The potential importance of the instrument in astronomy was recognized by, among others, Jacques Bovedere of Paris; he reported the invention to Galileo, who promptly built his own telescope.

CHRISTIAN LONGOMONTANUS
(b. Oct. 4, 1562, Longberg, Den.—d. Oct. 8, 1647, Copenhagen)

The Danish astronomer and astrologer Christian Longomontanus is best known for his association with and published support of Tycho Brahe. In 1600, when Johannes Kepler went to Prague to work with Tycho, he found Tycho and Longomontanus engaged in extensive observations and studies of Mars. This turned out to be fortuitous, for, as Kepler later wrote, "Had Christian been treating a different planet, I would have started on it as well." It was these observations of Mars that eventually enabled Kepler to discover the true laws of planetary motion. Longomontanus later used Tycho's data to compile the *Astronomia danica* (1622), an exposition of the Tychonic system, which holds that the Sun revolves around Earth and the other planets revolve around the Sun. He began the construction of the Copenhagen Observatory in 1632 but died before its completion.

NICCOLÒ ZUCCHI
(b. Dec. 6, 1586, Parma, duchy of Parma and Piacenza [Italy]—d. May 21, 1670, Rome)

In approximately 1616 the Italian astronomer Niccolò Zucchi designed one of the earliest reflecting telescopes, antedating those of James Gregory and Sir Isaac Newton. A professor at the Jesuit College in Rome, Zucchi developed an interest in astronomy from a meeting with Johannes Kepler. With this telescope Zucchi discovered the belts of the planet Jupiter (1630) and examined the spots on Mars (1640). He also demonstrated (in 1652) that phosphors generate rather than store light. His book *Optica philosophia experimentalis et ratione a fundamentis constituta* (1652–56) inspired Gregory and Newton to build improved telescopes.

18TH CENTURY

JAMES BRADLEY

(b. March 1693, Sherborne,
Gloucestershire, Eng.—d. July 13, 1762,
Chalford, Gloucestershire)

In 1728 the English astronomer James Bradley announced his discovery of the aberration of starlight, an apparent slight change in the positions of stars caused by the yearly motion of Earth. That finding provided the first direct evidence for the revolution of Earth around the Sun.

Bradley was educated at Balliol College, Oxford, where he received a B.A. in 1714 and an M.A. in 1717. He was instructed in observational astronomy at Wanstead, Essex, by his uncle, the Rev. James Pound, clergyman and skilled amateur astronomer, who introduced him to the famous astronomer Edmond Halley.

Bradley's scientific acumen was stimulated by his membership in the Royal Society, to which he was elected a fellow in 1718 on the recommendation of Halley. Bradley took church orders and became vicar of Bridstow in 1719. The income from that position was augmented by a sinecure as an absentee rector in a parish in Pembrokeshire, Wales, which was procured for him by his friend and astronomical collaborator, Samuel Molyneux. Bradley resigned his church offices when he was appointed in 1721 to the Savilian chair of astronomy at Oxford and thenceforth devoted his full time to astronomy.

After the publication of *De revolutionibus orbium coelestium libri VI* ("Six Books Concerning the Revolutions of the Heavenly Orbs") by Copernicus in 1543, it became increasingly imperative for astronomers to be able to observe and measure the parallactic displacement of a star—the change in a star's position over a six-month period—to confirm the orbital motion of Earth around the Sun. Such information would provide the empirical

Eighteenth-century astronomer James Bradley's study of starlight lent credence to heliocentric models of the universe, where Earth revolved around the Sun. Hulton Archive/Getty Images

evidence needed to augment the mathematical and conceptual arguments thitherto advanced for the idea that the Sun does not revolve around Earth. In the absence of such evidence for parallax, Tycho Brahe, the 16th-century astronomer, had not been favourably disposed to Copernican theory. Ole Rømer, a Danish astronomer, measured an apparent displacement of the stars Sirius and Vega in the 17th century, but his observations were found to be erroneous. Robert Hooke, one of the founding members of the Royal Society, measured the star Gamma Draconis in a series of observations in 1669 for a similar attempt but was forced to report failure.

In 1725, using Molyneux's house as an observatory, Bradley attempted to repeat Hooke's measurements on Gamma Draconis with a telescope aimed so as to avoid any error resulting from the refraction of light. Although he failed to detect parallax because the star was too far away, Bradley made one of the two discoveries for which he is famous. He observed that Gamma Draconis shifted south in position by an astonishing 1" of arc in three days—the wrong direction and by too large an amount to be accounted for by parallax. It is said that the explanation for this phenomenon came to Bradley as he sailed on the Thames, observing how the wind vane on the mast shifted position with the varying motion of the boat, even though the wind had not changed direction. He concluded that the apparent stellar shift was brought about by the aberration of light, which was a result of the finite speed of light and the forward motion of Earth in its orbit. Bradley communicated this discovery to the Royal Society in 1728, shortly after the death of Molyneux. On the basis of his quantitative observations of aberration, Bradley confirmed the velocity of light to be 295,000 kilometres (183,000 miles) per second and gave a proof for the Copernican theory.

Bradley's star measurements in 1727–32 also revealed what he called the "annual change of declination in some of the fixed stars," which could not be accounted for by aberration. He concluded that this was caused by the slight and uneven nodding motion of the Earth's axis (nutation) that resulted from the changing direction of the gravitational pull of the Moon. But he withheld this announcement until he had made careful confirmatory observations during one complete set of revolutions of the Moon in its orbit. For this achievement the Royal Society of London awarded him the Copley Medal in 1748.

Members of the Royal Society in their function as "visitors and directors" of the Royal Greenwich Observatory recommended Bradley in 1742 to succeed Halley in the post of astronomer royal. Bradley received £250 a year and the then sizable grant of £1,000 for instruments, notably an 8-foot (2.4-metre) quadrant for more precise measurements. In 1744 he married Susannah Peach, by whom he had one daughter. He held his important scientific, administrative, and consultative position at Greenwich until his death.

The bulk of Bradley's observations was published after his death in an atmosphere of acrimony. Dispute between his heirs and the British Admiralty over the ownership of his work delayed publication until 1798–1805. The German mathematician Friedrich Bessel analyzed and organized his data, correcting for the small errors in Bradley's instruments, and then computing star positions.

GEORGE DOLLOND
(b. Jan. 25, 1774, London, Eng.—d. May 13, 1852, London)

The British optician George Dollond invented a number of precision instruments used in astronomy, geodesy, and navigation.

Throughout most of his life, he worked for the family firm of mathematical instrument makers, assuming full control after the retirement in 1819 of his uncle Peter Dollond. His micrometer made of rock crystal, announced in 1821, was used by the English astronomer William Rutter Dawes in measuring close double stars. Other inventions followed, including improvements to astronomical and navigation devices. Dollond received the council medal of the Great Exhibition of 1851 for his atmospheric recorder that simultaneously measured and recorded on paper tape temperature, atmospheric pressure, wind speed and direction, evaporation, and electrical phenomena.

JOHN DOLLOND
(b. June 10, 1706, London, Eng.— d. Nov. 30, 1761, London)

John Dollond was a British maker of optical and astronomical instruments who developed an achromatic (non-colour-distorting) refracting telescope and a practical heliometer, a telescope used to measure the Sun's diameter and the angles between celestial bodies.

The son of Huguenot refugees, Dollond learned the family trade of silk weaving. He became proficient in optics and astronomy and, in 1752, joined his eldest son, Peter, in an optical business. Two years later he introduced his heliometer.

In 1747 a controversy arose over Newton's statement that chromatic aberration in lenses could not be corrected. After later experiments proved otherwise, Dollond devised an achromatic lens made of flint and crown glasses for use in telescopes. The invention earned him the Copley Medal of the Royal Society, but the prior discovery by Chester Moor Hall of England was later recognized.

PETER DOLLOND
(b. 1730, London, Eng.—d. July 2, 1820, Kennington, London)

The British optician Peter Dollond, though lacking a theoretical background, invented the triple achromatic lens still in wide use, made substantial improvements in the astronomical refracting telescope, and improved navigation instruments of his day. In 1765 he combined two convex lenses of crown glass with one double-concave lens of flint glass to make a triple achromatic lens that rendered images free from extraneous colour and greatly reduced the spherical error of existing equipment.

John Hadley
(b. April 16, 1682, Hertfordshire, Eng.—d. Feb. 14, 1744, East Barnet, Hertfordshire)

John Hadley was a British mathematician and inventor who improved the reflecting telescope, producing the first such instrument of sufficient accuracy and power to be useful in astronomy.

Hadley's first Newtonian reflector, built in 1721, had a mirror about 6 inches (15 cm) in diameter. The favourable response it evoked inspired him to build another equally large one, with numerous improvements. His telescopes played a major part in bringing reflectors into general use by astronomers.

In 1730, independently of Thomas Godfrey of Philadelphia, Hadley invented a quadrant (actually a double-reflecting octant) for measuring the altitude of the Sun or a star above the horizon to find geographic position at sea. His double-reflecting principle made accurate determinations of location much easier. Hadley also fixed a spirit level to the instrument so that a meridian altitude at sea could be taken when the horizon was not visible. His device later evolved into the sextant.

Chester Moor Hall
(b. Dec. 9, 1703, Leigh, Essex, Eng.— d. March 17, 1771, Sutton, Surrey)

The English jurist and mathematician Chester Moor Hall invented the achromatic lens, which he utilized in building the first refracting telescope free from chromatic aberration (colour distortion).

Convinced from study of the human eye that achromatic lenses were feasible, Hall experimented with different kinds of glass until he found a combination of crown glass and flint glass that met his requirements in 1729. In 1733 he built several telescopes with apertures of 2.5 inches (6.5 cm) and focal lengths of 20 inches (50 cm).

John Dollond of London received the Copley Medal of the Royal Society in 1758 for the invention, but his right was contested by yet another inventor in 1766. It was Hall, however, who was established as the originator of the achromatic lens, although he was largely indifferent to priority claims.

Pierre Mechain
(b. Aug. 16, 1744, Laon, France—d. Sept. 20, 1804, Castellón de la Plana, Spain)

The French astronomer and hydrographer Pierre-François-André Mechain, with Jean Delambre, measured the meridian arc from Dunkirk, France, to Barcelona. The measurement was made between 1792 and 1798 to establish a basis for the unit of length in the metric system called for by the French national legislature. Mechain also discovered 11 comets and calculated the orbits of these and other known comets.

Born the son of a master ceiling plasterer, Mechain early in life showed mathematical prowess and worked as a hydrographer for the Naval Map Archives at Versailles during the 1770s. He turned to astronomy, and in 1782 his work with comets won him admission to the Académie Royale des Sciences. In addition, Mechain discovered numerous nebulae that were later incorporated by Charles Messier into his famous catalog of clusters and nebulae.

SAMUEL MOLYNEUX
(b. July 18, 1689, Chester, Cheshire, Eng.—d. April 13, 1728, Kew, Surrey)

Samuel Molyneux received his B.A. (1708) and M.A. (1710) from Trinity College, Dublin. He was elected to the Royal Society in 1712. Besides pursuing a career as an astronomer, he was also active in politics, as a member of both the English parliament (1715, 1726, 1727) and the Irish parliament (1727) and as a lord of the Admiralty (1727–28).

Molyneux collaborated (1723–25) with James Bradley to improve the construction of reflecting telescopes. Molyneux worked further with Bradley in 1725, setting up a zenith-pointing telescope to try to observe stellar parallax (apparent displacement by which the distances of stars can be calculated). Although they were unsuccessful in this effort, Bradley later used the same method to discover the aberration of starlight.

GEORG VON REICHENBACH
(b. Aug. 24, 1772, Durlach, Baden [Ger.]—d. May 21, 1826, Munich)

The German maker of astronomical instruments Georg von Reichenbach introduced the meridian, or transit, circle, a specially designed telescope for measuring both the time when a celestial body is directly over the meridian (the longitude of the instrument) and the angle of the body at meridian passage. By 1796 he was engaged in the construction of a dividing engine, a machine used to mark off equal intervals accurately, usually on precision instruments. In 1804 he was one of the founders of an instrument-making business in Munich, and in 1809 he helped establish at Benediktbeuern an optical works that was later moved to Munich.

In 1819 he built for the German astronomer Friedrich Bessel a transit circle, combining the transit, an instrument used for determining longitude and time, with the mural circle, an instrument mounted on a wall for zenith measurement. This combination had been introduced earlier but had not been adopted. Reichenbach's form of the instrument came into general use.

James Short
(b. June 10, 1710, Edinburgh, Scot.—d. June 14, 1768, London, Eng.)

James Short was a British optician and astronomer who produced the first truly parabolic—hence nearly distortionless—mirrors for reflecting telescopes.

Short entered the University of Edinburgh as a candidate for the ministry, but he was inspired to study optics instead by the lectures of the Scottish mathematician Colin Maclaurin. Maclaurin, realizing Short's mathematical talents, encouraged his interest in mathematics and optics, even providing him with an optical workshop. Short settled in London in 1738 and soon gained renown and wealth for his fine work. He manufactured metallic mirrors for more than 1,000 reflecting telescopes that were among the best then available. (The British mathematician John Hadley had experimented with parabolization of mirrors, but Short invented a better technique, the details of which are not precisely known.) Secretive about his craft, he ordered his tools destroyed shortly before he died.

19th Century

Giovanni Battista Amici
(b. March 25, 1786, Modena, duchy of Modena [Italy]—d. April 10, 1863, Florence)

The Italian astronomer and optician Giovanni Battista Amici made important improvements in the mirrors of reflecting telescopes and also developed prisms for use in refracting spectroscopes (instruments used to separate light into its spectral components).

Amici served as professor of mathematics at the University of Modena from 1815 to 1825 and then became astronomer to the Grand Duke of Tuscany and director of the observatory at the Royal Museum in Florence, where he also lectured at the museum of natural history. He made major advancements in compound-microscope design and introduced (1840) the oil-immersion technique, in which the objective lens is immersed in a drop of oil placed atop the specimen under observation in order to minimize light aberrations.

His name is most often associated with improvements in the microscope and reflecting telescope, but he also put his instruments to good use. His observations of Jupiter's satellites and certain double stars were highly esteemed. Using an improved micrometer of his own design, he made accurate measurements of the polar and equatorial diameters of the Sun. With his improved compound microscope he made discoveries about the circulation of sap in plants and the processes of plant reproduction.

Francis Baily
(b. April 28, 1774, Newbury, Berkshire, Eng.—d. Aug. 30, 1844, London)

Francis Baily detected the phenomenon called "Baily's beads" during an annular eclipse of the Sun on May 15, 1836. His vivid description aroused new interest in the study of eclipses.

Baily retired from a successful business career in 1825 and turned his energies to science. He had already, in 1820, taken a leading part in the foundation of the Royal Astronomical Society, which awarded him its Gold Medal in 1827 for his preparation of the society's catalog of 2,881 stars. His protests regarding the *British Nautical Almanac*, then notorious for its errors, were instrumental in bringing about its reform. Baily revised several star catalogs, repeated Henry Cavendish's experiments to determine the density of Earth, and measured its elliptical shape.

PETER BARLOW
(b. Oct. 13, 1776, Norwich, Norfolk, Eng.—d. March 1, 1862, Kent)

Peter Barlow was an optician and mathematician who invented two varieties of achromatic (non-colour-distorting) telescope lenses known as Barlow lenses.

Self-educated, he became assistant mathematics master at the Royal Military Academy, Woolwich, in 1801. He published numerous mathematical works, including *New Mathematical Tables* (1814). Later known as *Barlow's Tables*, this compilation of factors and functions of all numbers from 1 to 10,000 was considered so accurate and so useful that it has been regularly reprinted ever since.

In 1819 Barlow began work on the problem of deviation in ship compasses caused by the presence of iron in the hull. For his method of correcting the deviation by juxtaposing the compass with a suitably shaped piece of iron, he was awarded the Copley Medal of the Royal Society. He also conducted early investigations into the development and efficiency of the electric telegraph.

Barlow constructed (1827–32) his first achromatic telescope lens by enclosing liquid carbon disulfide between two pieces of glass. His second lens (1833) was a combination of flint and crown glass. The Barlow lens has come into general use for increasing the eyepiece power of any optical instrument.

WILHELM BEER
(b. Jan. 4, 1797, Berlin [Ger.]—d. March 27, 1850, Berlin)

The German banker and amateur astronomer Wilhelm Beer (with Johann Heinrich von Mädler) constructed the most complete map of the Moon of his time, *Mappa Selenographica* (1836). The first lunar map to be divided into quadrants, it contained a detailed representation of the Moon's face and was accompanied, in 1837, by a volume providing micrometric measurements of the diameters of 148 craters and the elevations of 830 mountains.

The *Mappa Selenographica* remained unsurpassed until 1878, when J.F. Julius Schmidt's more detailed map appeared. Beer and Mädler also published (1830) a description and map of Mars that was the first to depict the light and dark areas.

Alexis Bouvard
(b. June 27, 1767, Contamines,
France—d. June 7, 1843, Paris)

Alexis Bouvard was director of the Paris Observatory and is noted for discovering eight comets and writing *Tables astronomiques* of Jupiter and Saturn (1808) and of Uranus (1821). Bouvard's tables accurately predicted orbital locations of Jupiter and Saturn, but his tables for Uranus failed, leading him to hypothesize that irregularities in Uranus' motion were caused by the influence of an unknown celestial body. In 1846, three years after Bouvard's death, his hypothesis was confirmed by the discovery of Neptune by John Couch Adams and Urbain-Jean-Joseph Le Verrier. Bouvard was elected to the Academy of Sciences in 1803 and the Royal Society in 1826.

Richard Carrington
(b. May 26, 1826, London, Eng.—d. Nov. 27, 1875, Churt, near Farnham, Surrey)

It was the English astronomer Richard Christopher Carrington who, by observing the motions of sunspots, discovered the equatorial acceleration of the Sun— i.e., that it rotates faster at the equator than near the poles. He also discovered the movement of sunspot zones toward the Sun's equator as the solar cycle progresses.

The son of a brewer, Carrington was educated at Cambridge and in 1853 established his own observatory at Redhill,

Reigate, Surrey. He published *A Catalogue of 3,735 Circumpolar Stars* (1857), but in 1865 his health failed and he did little work thereafter.

Seth Carlo Chandler
(b. Sept. 17, 1846, Boston, Mass., U.S.—d. Dec. 31, 1913, Wellesley Hills, Mass.)

Seth Carlo Chandler was best known for his discovery (1884–85) of the Chandler Wobble, a movement in Earth's axis of rotation that causes latitude to vary with a period of about 433 days. A wandering of the rotation axis had been predicted by Swiss mathematician Leonhard Euler in 1765. Chandler's detection of this effect was facilitated by his invention of the almucantar, a device for measuring the positions of stars relative to a circle centred at the zenith rather than to the meridian. The North Pole of Earth's rotation axis wanders in an irregular, quasi-circular path with a radius of about 8–10 metres (26–33 feet).

Chandler initially worked for the U.S. Coast Survey (1864–70). He then worked as an actuary until he joined the Harvard University Observatory in 1881. From 1896 to 1909 he edited *The Astronomical Journal*.

Clark Family
Alvan Clark (b. March 8, 1804, Ashfield, Mass., U.S.—d. Aug. 19, 1887, Cambridge, Mass.), George Bassett Clark (b. Feb. 14, 1827, Lowell, Mass.— d. Dec. 20, 1891, Cambridge, Mass.), and Alvan Graham Clark (b. July 10,

1832, Fall River, Mass.—d. June 9, 1897, Cambridge, Mass.)

The Clark family of telescope makers and astronomers supplied unexcelled lenses to many observatories in the United States and Europe during the heyday of the refracting telescope.

Alvin Clark built a career as a portrait painter and engraver, but at the age of 40 he became interested in optics. With his son George Bassett Clark, he opened the optics firm Alvan Clark & Sons in Cambridge, Mass., in 1846. Alvan Graham Clark joined his father and brother in the business in the early 1850s.

Recognition of the family's superb lenses was slow to come. The discovery of two double stars by the elder Alvan Clark in the late 1850s, however, attracted attention abroad, and the firm began to flourish. They made the 36-inch (91-cm) lens for the Lick Observatory, Mt. Hamilton, Calif. (1888); the 30-inch (76-cm) lens for the Pulkovo Observatory, near St. Petersburg in Russia (1878); the 28-inch (71-cm) lens for the University of Virginia, Charlottesville (1883); and 24-inch (61-cm) lenses for the U.S. Naval Observatory, Washington, D.C. (1873), and the Lowell Observatory, Flagstaff, Ariz. (1896). All these telescopes remain in operation except that at Pulkovo, which was destroyed during World War II.

The younger Alvan Clark directed the fabrication of the 40-inch (101-cm) lens of the Yerkes Observatory, Williams Bay, Wis., the largest refractor lens in the world. Using telescopes of his own construction, he discovered the companion of the star Sirius as well as 16 double stars.

JOHN DALLMEYER
(b. Sept. 6, 1830, Loxten, Westphalia [Germany]—d. Dec. 30, 1883, at sea off New Zealand)

John Henry Dallmeyer was a British inventor and manufacturer of lenses.

Showing an aptitude for science, Dallmeyer was apprenticed to an Osnabrück optician, and in 1851 he went to London, where he obtained work with an optician and later with Andrew Ross, a lens and telescope manufacturer. After a year spent in a commercial post, he was reengaged by Ross as scientific adviser. He married Ross's second daughter, Hannah, and in 1859 inherited part of his employer's large fortune and the telescope-manufacturing portion of the business. Turning to the making of photographic lenses, he introduced improvements in both portrait and landscape lenses, in object glasses for the microscope, and in condensers for the optical lantern. He constructed several photoheliographs (telescopes adapted for photographing the Sun).

His son Thomas Rudolphus Dallmeyer (1859–1906) introduced telephoto lenses into ordinary practice (patented 1891) and wrote a standard book on the subject (*Telephotography*, 1899).

William Dawes
(b. March 19, 1799, London, Eng.—
d. Feb. 15, 1868, Haddenham,
Buckinghamshire)

The English astronomer William Rutter Dawes was known for his extensive measurements of double stars and for his meticulous planetary observations.

Trained as a physician, Dawes practiced at Haddenham and (from 1826) Liverpool; subsequently he became a Nonconformist clergyman. In 1829 he set up a private observatory at Ormskirk, Lancashire, where he measured more than 200 double stars before taking charge of George Bishop's Observatory at South Villa, Regent's Park, London, in 1839. He later set up private observatories at Cranbrook, Kent (1844); Wateringbury, Kent (1850); and Haddenham (1857). He was one of several independent discoverers of the "crepe ring" of Saturn (1850); he observed Jupiter's Great Red Spot (1857) several years before its existence was generally recognized; and he prepared exceptionally accurate drawings of Mars in 1864. Dawes received the Gold Medal of the Royal Astronomical Society in 1855 and was elected a fellow of the Royal Society in 1865. A crater on the Moon is named after him.

Henri-Alexandre Deslandres
(b. July 24, 1853, Paris, France—d. Jan. 15,
1948, Paris)

In 1894 the French physicist and astrophysicist Henri-Alexandre Deslandres invented a spectroheliograph, an instrument that photographs the Sun in monochromatic light.

After graduating from the École Polytechnique ("Polytechnic School") in 1874 and spending seven years in the army, Deslandres worked in the laboratories of the École Polytechnique and the Sorbonne. From 1886 to 1891 he studied the spectra of radiation emitted by molecules. Joining the Paris Observatory in 1889, he turned his energies to astrophysics, first studying molecular spectra and then the spectra of planets, the Sun, and other stars. He continued his work at the Meudon Observatory and in 1908 was appointed its director. The Paris and Meudon observatories merged in 1926, and he remained in charge of them until his retirement in 1929. During his career, Deslandres was elected to several scientific societies, including the Académie des Sciences, the Royal Astronomical Society and the Royal Society in Britain, and the National Academy of Sciences of the United States.

Giovanni Donati
(b. Dec. 16, 1826, Pisa [Italy]—d. Sept. 20,
1873, Florence)

Giovanni Battista Donati was an Italian astronomer who, on Aug. 5, 1864, was the first to observe the spectrum of a comet (Comet 1864 II). This observation indicated correctly that comet tails contain luminous gas and do not shine merely by reflected sunlight.

Between 1854 and 1864 Donati discovered six comets, one of which, first seen on June 2, 1858, bears his name. These discoveries led to his appointment as professor of astronomy and director of the observatory at Florence in 1864. He also contributed to early classification systems for stellar spectra. Donati was supervising the building of a new observatory at Arcetri, near Florence, when he died.

HENRY DRAPER
(b. March 7, 1837, Prince Edward County, Va., U.S.—d. Nov. 20, 1882, New York City)

In 1872 American physician and amateur astronomer Henry Draper made the first photograph of the spectrum of a star (Vega). He was also the first to photograph a nebula, the Orion Nebula, in 1880. His father, John William Draper, in 1840 had made the first photograph of the Moon.

Henry Draper was appointed to the medical staff of Bellevue Hospital, New York City, in 1859 and in 1866 became dean of the medical faculty of the University of the City of New York. For his photography of the transit of Venus in 1874, Congress ordered a gold medal struck in his honour. His widow established the Henry Draper Memorial Fund at Harvard Observatory, financing the making of the great *Henry Draper Catalogue* of stellar spectra.

NILS CHRISTOFER DUNÉR
(b. May 21, 1839, Billeberga, Swed.— d. Nov. 10, 1914, Stockholm)

Swedish astronomer Nils Christofer Dunér studied the rotational period of the Sun.

Dunér was senior astronomer (1864–88) at the Royal University Observatory in Lund, Sweden. In 1867 he began his investigations of binary stars. He also performed pioneering stellar spectroscopy studies (studies of the individual characteristic wavelengths of light).

Shortly after he became professor of astronomy at the University of Uppsala and director of the Uppsala Observatory in 1888, Dunér undertook a now-classic study of the Sun's rotation. Using the Doppler shift, he established that the Sun's rotational period is about 25 ½ days near the Equator but up to 38 ½ days near the Sun's poles.

STEPHEN GROOMBRIDGE
(b. Jan. 7, 1755, Goudhurst, Kent, Eng.—d. March 30, 1832, London)

The English astronomer Stephen Groombridge compiled a star catalog known by his name.

Groombridge began observations at Blackheath, London, in 1806 and retired from the West Indian trade in 1815 to devote full time to the project. *A Catalogue of Circumpolar Stars*, listing 4,243 stars situated within 50° of the North Pole and having apparent magnitudes greater than 9, was published in 1838 after having been edited by the Royal Astronomer Sir George Airy. Groombridge was elected a fellow of the Royal Society of London in 1812, and eight years later he was a founding member of the Astronomical Society of London (later the Royal Astronomical Society).

Asaph Hall
(b. Oct. 15, 1829, Goshen, Conn., U.S.— d. Nov. 22, 1907, Annapolis, Md.)

American astronomer Asaph Hall discovered the two moons of Mars, Deimos and Phobos, in 1877 and calculated their orbits.

Hall came from an impoverished family and was largely self-taught, though he did study briefly at Central College, McGrawville, N.Y., and at the University of Michigan. By 1858 he had acquired a minor position at the Harvard University observatory, where he did research and wrote papers. In 1863 he was appointed professor of mathematics at the U.S. Naval Observatory, in Washington, D.C., a position he held until his retirement in 1891. There he was chiefly concerned with planetary astronomy, the orbits of double stars, and determinations of stellar parallax. From 1896 to 1901 he was professor of astronomy at Harvard.

Peter Hansen
(b. Dec. 8, 1795, Tondern, Den.— d. March 28, 1874, Gotha, Ger.)

Peter Andreas Hansen was a Danish-born German astronomer whose most important work was the improvement of the theories and tables of the orbits of the principal bodies in the solar system.

Hansen became director of the Seeberg Observatory, near Gotha, in 1825, and in 1857 a new observatory was built for him. He worked on theoretical geodesy, optics, and probability theory. His most important books on the theory of the motion of the Moon are the *Fundamenta nova investigationis orbitae verae quam Luna perlustrat* (1838; "New Foundations of the Investigation of the True Orbit That the Moon Traverses") and the *Darlegung der theoretischen Berechnung der in den Mondtafeln angewandten Störungen* (1862–64; "Explanation of the Theoretical Calculation of Perturbations Used in Lunar Tables").

Asaph Hall. U.S. Naval Observatory Library

The systematic character of Hansen's methods carried celestial mechanics to a new level of power and precision. The tables based on his theory were printed in Great Britain in 1857 and were used until 1923. From his theory of the Moon, Hansen deduced a value close to that now accepted for the distance between Earth and the Sun. Assisted by the astronomer Christian Olufsen, Hansen in 1853 compiled new tables of the Sun's positions at various times.

KARL LUDWIG HARDING
(b. Sept. 29, 1765, Lauenburg [Germany]—d. Aug. 31, 1834, Göttingen)

In 1804 the German astronomer Karl Ludwig Harding discovered and named Juno, third minor planet to be detected. He studied at the University of Göttingen under Georg Lichtenberg and later served as assistant to J.H. Schröter at Schröter's Lilienthal Observatory. In 1805 Harding returned as a professor to Göttingen, where he remained until his death. He is credited with the discovery of three comets, in 1813, 1824, and 1832. His most important published work was the *Atlas novus coelestis* (1808–23), which catalogued more than 120,000 stars.

KARL LUDWIG HENCKE
(b. April 8, 1793, Driesen, Brandenburg [now Drezdenko, Pol.]—d. Sept. 21, 1866, Marienwerder, Prussia [now Kwidzyn, Pol.])

Karl Ludwig Hencke was an amateur astronomer who found the fifth and sixth minor planets to be discovered. Professional astronomers had largely given up the search for asteroids in 1816, when four were known. Hencke, a post office employee in Driesen who eventually became postmaster, began his systematic search in 1830 and found Astraea (minor planet 5) on Dec. 8, 1845, and Hebe (minor planet 6) on July 1, 1847.

THOMAS HENDERSON
(b. Dec. 28, 1798, Dundee, Angus, Scot.—d. Nov. 23, 1844, Edinburgh)

As royal astronomer at the Cape of Good Hope (1831–33), the Scottish astronomer Thomas Henderson made measurements that later allowed him to determine the parallax of a star (Alpha Centauri). He announced his findings in 1839, a few months after both German astronomer Friedrich Bessel and Russian astronomer Friedrich Struve had received credit for first measuring stellar parallaxes.

Henderson was elected a fellow of the Royal Astronomical Society (1832), the Royal Society of Edinburgh (1834), and the Royal Society of London (1840). Upon his return from the Cape of Good Hope in 1834, he was appointed the first Astronomer Royal of Scotland, professor of astronomy at the University of Edinburgh, and director of Calton Hill Observatory.

JAMES LICK
(b. Aug. 25, 1796, Stumpstown [now Fredericksburg], Pa., U.S.—d. Oct. 1, 1876, San Francisco, Calif.)

James Lick was a U.S. philanthropist who endowed the Lick Observatory, Mount Hamilton, near San Jose, Calif.

After an incomplete elementary education and an apprenticeship as a carpenter, Lick worked for a year as a piano maker in Baltimore, a trade he resumed after spending 17 years in South America. In 1848 he arrived in San Francisco and at once commenced purchasing real estate, acquiring holdings not only in Santa Clara Valley but also at Lake Tahoe, on Santa Catalina Island, and in Nevada.

Lick never married and at his death disposed of the bulk of his fortune in philanthropic endowments. He provided $700,000 for a telescope more powerful than any other in the world. The ultimate result was the Lick Observatory, equipped with a 91-cm (36-inch) Clark refractor. Upon completion in 1888, the facility was turned over to the University of California.

CLAUDE-LOUIS MATHIEU
(b. Nov. 25, 1783, Macon, France— d. March 5, 1875, Paris)

The French astronomer and mathematician Claude-Louis Mathieu worked on the determination of the distances of the stars.

After a brief period as an engineer, Mathieu became an astronomer at the Observatoire de Paris and at the Bureau des Longitudes in 1817. He later served as professor of astronomy at the Collège de France, Paris, and from 1829 was professor of analysis at the École Polytechnique, Paris. He represented Macon in the Chamber of Deputies (1834–48). For many years he edited the work on population statistics, *L'Annuaire du Bureau des Longitudes*, and published *L'Histoire de l'astronomie au XVIIIᵉ siècle* (1827; "The History of Astronomy of the 18th Century").

JOHANN PALISA
(b. Dec. 6, 1848, Troppau, Silesia [now Opava, Czech Republic]—d. May 2, 1925, Vienna, Austria)

Johann Palisa was a Silesian astronomer best known for his discovery of 120 asteroids. He also prepared two catalogs containing the positions of almost 4,700 stars.

Palisa briefly was an assistant astronomer at the observatories in Vienna and Geneva before being appointed director (1872–80) of the Austro-Hungarian naval observatory at Pola (now Pula, Croatia), a position that carried with it the rank of commander. From 1880 to 1919 he was a member of the staff at the Vienna Observatory. By 1891, when the photographic plate was first used in astronomy, he had found 83 of the 120 asteroids he eventually identified by visual observation alone. His star catalogs were published in 1899, 1902, and 1908.

GIUSEPPE PIAZZI
(b. July 16, 1746, Ponte di Valtellina, Lombardy, Habsburg crown land [Italy]—d. July 22, 1826, Naples)

Italian astronomer Giuseppe Piazzi discovered (Jan. 1, 1801) and named the first asteroid, or "minor planet," Ceres.

Piazzi became a Theatine monk in about 1764 and a professor of theology in Rome in 1779, and in 1780 he was appointed professor of higher mathematics at the Academy of Palermo. Later, with the aid of the viceroy of Sicily, he founded the Observatory of Palermo. There he produced his great catalog of the positions of 7,646 stars and demonstrated that most stars are in motion relative to the Sun. There he also discovered Ceres and the high proper motion of the important double star 61 Cygni.

JOHN POND
(b. 1767, London, Eng.—d. Sept. 7, 1836, Blackheath, Kent)

John Pond was the sixth astronomer royal of England and organized the Royal Greenwich Observatory to an efficiency that made possible a degree of observational precision never before achieved.

Pond was elected a fellow of the Royal Society in 1807 and served from 1811 to 1835 as astronomer royal. During Pond's term, obsolete and worn-out instruments at Greenwich were replaced and the staff increased from one to six, enabling him to complete in 1833 a catalog of positions of 1,112 stars with an accuracy previously unknown. He was a member of the Royal Astronomical Society from the time of its founding in 1820.

ISAAC ROBERTS
(b. Jan. 27, 1829, Groes, Clwyd [now in Conwy], Wales—d. July 17, 1904, Crowborough, Sussex, Eng.)

The British astronomer Isaac Roberts was a pioneer in photography of nebulae.

In 1883 Roberts began experimenting with astronomical photography, taking pictures of stars, the Orion and Andromeda nebulae, and the Pleiades cluster. Although the photographs proved difficult to interpret, they were revealing. His three-hour exposure of the Pleiades showed the nebulosity surrounding these stars, and his photographs of Andromeda showed its spiral structure. Roberts's photographs were exhibited regularly at the Royal Astronomical Society and earned him the Society's Gold Medal in 1895.

WILLIAM PARSONS, 3RD EARL OF ROSSE
(b. June 17, 1800, York, Eng.—d. Oct. 31, 1867, Monkstown, County Cork, Ire.)

The Irish astronomer William Parsons, 3rd earl of Rosse, built the largest reflecting telescope, the "Leviathan," of the 19th century.

In 1821 Parsons was elected to the House of Commons. He resigned his seat in 1834 but in 1841 inherited his father's title, becoming the 3rd earl of Rosse, and served as one of the Irish peers in the House of Lords.

Lord Rosse was obsessed with the idea of constructing a truly large telescope and worked for five years to find an alloy suitable for the mirror. His mirrors were made of speculum metal, an alloy of approximately two parts copper to one part tin by weight. (Some makers added traces of other metals.) Adding more copper makes the mirror less brittle and therefore less likely to break, but the mirror is more susceptible to the development of small surface fissures in the cooling process, tarnishes faster, and has a less white colour. Because he was at first unable to cast large pieces without using too much copper, his first 91-cm (36-inch) diameter mirror was composed of 16 thin plates soldered to a brass framework.

The moderate success of this telescope encouraged Lord Rosse to try to cast a solid 91-cm mirror. After much experimentation he succeeded in casting and cooling the mirror without cracking it, a serious problem in the construction of all large telescopic mirrors. In 1842 he began work on a mirror of 183-cm (72-inch) diameter. Three years later the four-ton disk was mounted, and the installation was completed at his Birr Castle estate in Ireland. Sixteen metres (54 feet) in length, Lord Rosse's telescope was used primarily to observe nebulae on those rare occasions when weather conditions permitted.

With his telescope, however, he discovered the remarkable spiral shape of many objects then classed as "nebulae," which are now recognized as individual galaxies. His drawing of the spiral galaxy M51 is a classic work of mid-19th-century astronomy. He studied and named the Crab Nebula. He also made detailed observations of the Orion Nebula. Though his telescope was dismantled in 1908, it was not until the 254-cm (100-inch) reflector was installed in 1917 at the Mount Wilson Observatory in California that a larger telescope was used. The telescope was later reconstructed and the original masonry mounting restored; these can be seen in the castle grounds at Birr, Ire.

SAMUEL SCHWABE
(b. Oct. 25, 1789, Dessau, Anhalt, Ger.—d. April 11, 1875, Dessau)

The amateur German astronomer Samuel Heinrich Schwabe discovered that sunspots vary in number in a cycle of about 10 years; he announced his findings in 1843, after 17 years of almost daily observations. Schwabe also made (1831) the first known detailed drawing of the Great Red Spot on Jupiter. He was awarded the Gold Medal of the Royal Astronomical Society in 1857 and was elected a foreign member of the Royal Society in 1868—a singular honour for an amateur scientist at that time.

FÉLIX TISSERAND
(b. Jan. 13, 1845, Nuits-St.-Georges, Côte-d'Or, France—d. Oct. 20, 1896, Paris)

French astronomer François-Félix Tisserand was noted for his textbook *Traité de mécanique céleste*, 4 vol. (1889–96; "Treatise on Celestial Mechanics"). This work, an update of Pierre-Simon Laplace's work on the same subject, is still used as a sourcebook by authors writing on celestial mechanics.

Before publishing his work, Tisserand had already established his brilliance in his doctoral dissertation (1868), analyzing Charles-Eugène Delaunay's lunar theory, and in his work as director of the Toulouse Observatory (1873–78). In 1874 he was elected to the Academy of Sciences as a corresponding member and was elevated to full membership in 1878. In 1892 Tisserand was appointed director of the Paris Observatory, and while there he contributed to the production of a still-unfinished international photographic star catalog, the *Catalogue photographique de la carte du ciel* ("Photographic Catalog of the Map of the Sky").

CHARLES YOUNG
(b. Dec. 15, 1834, Hanover, N.H., U.S.— d. Jan. 3, 1908, Hanover)

American astronomer Charles Young made the first observations of the flash spectrum of the Sun, during the solar eclipses of 1869 and 1870.

He studied the Sun extensively, particularly with the spectroscope, and wrote several important books on astronomy, of which the best known was *General Astronomy* (1888). In 1879 he made accurate measurements of the diameter of Mars. He was professor of astronomy at Princeton University from 1877 to 1905.

FRANZ XAVER VON ZACH
(b. June 4, 1754, Pest or Bratislava, Hung.—d. Sept. 2, 1832, Paris, France)

The German-Hungarian astronomer Franz Xaver, Freiherr (baron) von Zach, was patronized by Duke Ernst of Saxe-Gotha-Altenburg.

Zach built an observatory on the Seeberg near Gotha and directed the observatory—one of the most important of the time—from 1791, when it was completed, until 1806. During this period Zach enlisted 24 astronomers throughout Europe in making a systematic search for new comets and for the planet between Mars and Saturn expected on the basis of Bode's law (the Titius–Bode law). The principal result was the discovery of several asteroids. Zach's most lasting achievement was the editing of three scientific journals during the interval 1798–1826, including the *Monatliche Correspondenz* ("Monthly Correspondence"), which was designed to facilitate the rapid dissemination of scientific news.

20TH CENTURY

WALTER ADAMS
(b. Dec. 20, 1876, Syria—d. May 11, 1956, Pasadena, Calif., U.S.)

The American astronomer Walter Sydney Adams is best known for his spectroscopic studies. Using the spectroscope, he investigated sunspots and the rotation of the Sun, the velocities and distances of thousands of stars, and planetary atmospheres.

Born of missionary parents who returned to the United States when he was 8 years old, Adams studied astronomy at Dartmouth College (Hanover, N.H.), the University of Chicago, and the University of Munich. In 1904 he became a member of the original staff of Mount Wilson Observatory in California, where he served as director from 1923 to 1946. Adams took an important part in planning the 5,080-millimetre (200-inch) telescope for the Palomar Mountain Observatory.

ROBERT AITKEN
(b. Dec. 31, 1864, Jackson, Calif., U.S.—d. Oct. 29, 1951, Berkeley, Calif.)

Robert Grant Aitken specialized in the study of double stars, of which he discovered more than 3,000.

From 1891 to 1895, Aitken was professor of mathematics and astronomy at the University of the Pacific, Stockton, Calif. In 1895 he joined the staff of Lick Observatory, Mt. Hamilton, Calif., as assistant astronomer, becoming associate director in 1923 and director in 1930; he retired in 1935. He published *The Binary Stars* (1918) and *New General Catalogue of Double Stars Within 120° of the North Pole* (1932).

HAROLD AND HORACE BABCOCK
Respectively, (b. Jan. 24, 1882, Edgerton, Wis., U.S.—d. April 8, 1968, Pasadena, Calif.) and (b. Sept. 13, 1912, Pasadena, Calif., U.S.—d. Aug. 29, 2003, Santa Barbara, Calif.)

With his son, Horace Welcome Babcock, Harold Delos Babcock invented the solar magnetograph, an instrument allowing detailed observation of the Sun's magnetic field, in 1951. With their magnetograph the Babcocks demonstrated the existence of the Sun's general field and discovered magnetically variable stars. In 1959 Harold Babcock announced that the Sun reverses its magnetic polarity periodically.

Harold Babcock was on the staff of Mount Wilson Observatory, California, from 1909, being semiretired from 1948.

Horace Babcock attended the California Institute of Technology in Pasadena and the University of California. He worked at the Massachusetts Institute of Technology and at the California Institute of Technology before joining the staff of Mount Wilson and Palomar Mountain observatories in 1946; he served as director of the observatories from 1964 to 1978. In the 1950s, working with his father, he developed the solar magnetograph; using the device, the two men demonstrated the existence of the Sun's general field and discovered magnetically variable stars. Babcock's other work included studies of the glow of the night sky, the rotation of galaxies, and telescope design. In the early 1970s he helped establish the Las Campanas Observatory in the Chilean Andes.

I.S. BOWEN
(b. Dec. 21, 1898, Seneca Falls, N.Y., U.S.—d. Feb. 6, 1973, Los Angeles, Calif.)

Ira Sprague Bowen was an American astrophysicist whose explanation of the strong green emission from nebulae (clouds of rarefied gas) led to major advances in the study of celestial composition. This emission, which was unlike that characteristic of any known element, had previously been attributed to a hypothetical element, "nebulium." Bowen showed, however, that the emission was identical with that calculated to be produced by ionized oxygen and nitrogen under extremely low pressure.

Bowen in 1926 joined the faculty of the California Institute of Technology, Pasadena, where he became a full professor in 1931. In 1946 he became director of the Mount Wilson Observatory and served as director of the Hale Observatories, which comprise Mt. Wilson and Palomar observatories, from 1948 until 1964. In 1938 Bowen invented the image slicer, a device that improves the efficiency of the slit spectrograph, which is used to break up light into its component colours for study. Bowen retired as observatory director in 1964, becoming a distinguished-service staff member.

ERNEST BROWN
(b. Nov. 29, 1866, Hull, Yorkshire, Eng.—d. July 22, 1938, New Haven, Conn., U.S.)

British-born American mathematician and astronomer Ernest William Brown was known for his theory of the motion of the Moon.

Educated at the University of Cambridge in England, Brown began there to study the motion of the Moon by a method devised by G.W. Hill of the United States. Hill had carried the process far enough to show its suitability for solving the problem, and Brown completed the theory. In 1919, after 30 years of work, Brown published his lunar tables, thereby making obsolescent those that had been in use for more than 60 years.

Brown returned to Cambridge almost every summer, but he worked chiefly in the United States. He accepted an appointment at Haverford College, Pennsylvania, in 1891, and was professor of mathematics at Yale University from 1907 until his retirement in 1932.

ROBERT HANBURY BROWN
(b. Aug. 31, 1916, Aruvankadu, India—d. Jan. 16, 2002, Andover, Hampshire, Eng.)

British astronomer and writer Robert Hanbury Brown was noted for his design, development, and use of the intensity interferometer.

Brown graduated from the University of London in 1935. During and after World War II he worked with Robert Alexander Watson-Watt and then E.G. Bowen to develop radar and its uses in aerial combat. In the 1950s he applied his experience with radar to radio astronomy, developing radio telescope technology at Jodrell Bank Observatory and mapping radio sources in the sky. This work led him to design a radio interferometer capable of resolving radio stars while eliminating atmospheric distortion from the image (1952).

With Richard Q. Twiss, Brown applied the principles of radio interferometry to measuring the angular size of bright visible stars, thus developing the technique of intensity interferometry. Brown and Twiss set up an intensity interferometer at Narrabri in New South Wales, Australia, for the measuring of hot stars. From 1964 to 1981 Brown was a professor of physics and astronomy at the University of Sydney. He later served as president (1982–85) of the International Astronomical Union. His major books include *The Exploration of Space by Radio* (1957; with A.C.B. Lovell), *The Intensity Interferometer* (1974), and *Man and the Stars* (1978). His autobiography, *Boffin*, was published in 1991.

WILLIAM W. COBLENTZ
(b. Nov. 20, 1873, North Lima, Ohio, U.S.—d. Sept. 15, 1962, Washington, D.C.)

William Weber Coblentz was an American physicist and astronomer whose work lay primarily in infrared spectroscopy. Coblentz developed more accurate infrared spectrometers and extended their measurements to longer wavelengths. In 1905 he published a lengthy study of the infrared emission and absorption spectra of numerous elements and compounds. In 1914–16 he published improved values for the Stefan-Boltzmann constant of blackbody radiation and helped to confirm Planck's radiation law. He turned then to astrophysics and measured the infrared radiation from stars, planets, and nebulae. From 1905 until 1945 Coblentz was chief of the Radiometry Section of the U.S. National Bureau of Standards and is considered responsible for the adoption of radiometric standards. In 1937 he was awarded the Rumford Gold Medal by the American Academy of Arts and Sciences.

ANDRÉ-LOUIS DANJON
(b. April 6, 1890, Caen, France—d. April 21, 1967, Paris)

The French astronomer André-Louis Danjon was noted for his important developments in astronomical instruments and for his studies of Earth's rotation.

Danjon served in the French army (1914–19) and then became an astronomer at the University Observatory at Strasbourg. In 1930 he became its director, and the following year he was appointed professor of astronomy at the University of Strasbourg. In 1945 he became director of the Paris Observatory and in 1946 attained the post of professor of astronomy at the Sorbonne. He became director of the Institute of Astrophysics of Paris in 1954.

While studying the methods of positional astronomy, Danjon concluded that the transit had reached its ultimate in precision and began looking for a fundamentally new instrument. The result of his work was the prismatic 60° astrolabe, now known as the Danjon astrolabe. Within four years of its introduction (1956), the Danjon astrolabe was being used in more than 30 major observatories.

Danjon developed other precise instruments for positional and magnitude determinations and used them to investigate the irregularities in the rotational period of Earth. In 1958 he concluded that certain sudden increases in Earth's rotational period coincided with exceptionally intense solar activity.

He served as president of the International Astronomical Union (1955–58) and retired from academic life in 1963.

Audouin Dollfus
(b. Nov. 12, 1924, Paris, France)

The French astronomer Audouin-Charles Dollfus was the successor to Bernard Lyot as the principal French authority on the solar system.

Dollfus made several balloon flights for high-altitude observations, including the first stratospheric ascension in France. On the basis of comparative light-polarizing qualities, he concluded that the surface material of Mars consists of pulverized limonite (an iron oxide, Fe_2O_3) and prepared a map of Venus showing what he believed to be permanent features. On Dec. 15, 1966, he discovered Saturn's 10th known satellite, Janus.

Robert Emden
(b. March 4, 1862, St. Gallen, Switz.— d. Oct. 8, 1940, Zürich)

The Swiss physicist and astrophysicist Robert Emden developed a theory of expansion and compression of gas spheres and applied it to stellar structure.

In 1889 Emden was appointed to the Technical University of Munich, where he became professor of physics and meteorology in 1907. His famous book *Gaskugeln* (1907; "Gas Spheres") was a very important early work on the theory of stellar structure; it develops the physical theory of a gas sphere acted upon by its own gravity. He also devised a hypothesis, no longer taken seriously, to explain sunspots.

In 1924 Emden became honorary professor of astrophysics at the University of Munich, where he remained until his retirement in 1934. He took a leading role in founding the *Zeitschrift für Astrophysik* ("Journal of Astrophysics") in 1930 and edited it for six years.

John Evershed
(b. Feb. 26, 1864, Gomshall, Surrey, Eng.—d. Nov. 17, 1956, Ewhurst, Surrey)

In 1909 English astronomer John Evershed discovered the horizontal motion of gases outward from the centres of sunspots, a phenomenon sometimes called the Evershed effect.

In 1906 Evershed became assistant director of the Kodaikānal and Madras observatories in India, later becoming director. On an expedition to Kashmir in 1915, he made the first measurements supporting Albert Einstein's prediction that the wavelength of light emitted by a massive body (in this case the Sun) should be increased by an amount proportional to the intensity of the local gravitational field. Evershed retired in 1923, returning to England; in 1925 he built his own solar observatory at Ewhurst. He went on six expeditions to observe total solar eclipses from Norway (1896), India (1898), Algeria (1900), Spain (1905), Australia (1922), and Yorkshire (1927).

George Ellery Hale
(b. June 29, 1868, Chicago, Ill., U.S.—d. Feb. 21, 1938, Pasadena, Calif.)

American astronomer George Ellery Hale was known for his development of important astronomical instruments, including the Hale Telescope, a 200-inch (508-cm) reflector at the Palomar Observatory, near San Diego. The most effective entrepreneur in 20th-century American astronomy, Hale built four observatories and helped create the new discipline of astrophysics. He is known also for his research in solar physics, particularly his discovery of magnetic fields in sunspots.

Hale was born into a wealthy Chicago family and from an early age was enraptured by science. He built his first observatory at age 20 at the Hale home and acquired a professional long-focus refractor and spectroscopic apparatus that were competitive with the equipment of most colleges. Graduating from the Massachusetts Institute of Technology with a bachelor's degree in physics in 1890, Hale elucidated in his senior thesis his design for a spectroheliograph, an instrument for photographing the Sun in a very narrow range of visible wavelengths (that is, monochromatic light).

Hale's work and his observatory came to the attention of William Rainey Harper, the first president of the new University of Chicago, which was funded by millionaire John D. Rockefeller. Harper attracted Hale and his observatory to the university in 1892. In October of that year, Harper and Hale secured support from the transportation magnate Charles T. Yerkes to build a great observatory with a 40-inch (102-cm) refractor, which would be the largest in the world. Hale broke with traditional observatory planning, in which observatories were merely buildings that housed telescopes, and designed the new facility, Yerkes Observatory, with space for "laboratories for optical, spectroscopic, and chemical work."

In 1894 Hale founded *The Astrophysical Journal*, which helped professionalize astrophysics by defining standards by which astrophysical phenomena were to be described and discussed. Since its founding, *The Astrophysical Journal* has become the premier publication of research in astronomy.

At its opening in 1897, the Yerkes Observatory engaged in a full program of solar and stellar astrophysics, but Hale was always planning larger telescopes. Soon his staff was fabricating a 60-inch

The 200-inch Hale Telescope, housed at the Palomar (Calif.) Observatory, is the culmination of namesake George Ellery Hale's lifetime quest to build ever bigger and more powerful telescopes. Peter Stackpole/Time & Life Pictures/ Getty Images

(152-cm) reflector. In 1904 Hale established an observing station, the Mount Wilson Solar Observatory, at the summit of Wilson's Peak in southern California. The 60-inch reflector was installed at Mount Wilson four years later at an independent facility supported by the newly established Carnegie Institution of Washington in Washington, D.C.

Hale was a major driver in the establishment of the American Astronomical Society in 1899. Hale was also very active in international science. In 1904 he founded the International Union for Cooperation in Solar Research, which after World War I (1914–18) was transformed into the International Astronomical Union.

Hale's rationale for building observatories centred on the problem of stellar evolution, or how stars change as they age. However, he was also interested in a wide variety of solar phenomena. Fascinated with the structure of sunspots, Hale was able to show by 1908 that they were magnetically active storms of swirling gas in the solar photosphere. This discovery, made possible by Hale's application of the Zeeman effect to solar spectroscopy, confirmed his conviction that the key to astronomical progress lay in the application of modern physics.

Well before his 60-inch reflector was in operation on Mount Wilson, Hale had set his sights on a 100-inch (254-cm) reflector. As he had with Yerkes, Hale pursued a local philanthropist, hardware magnate John D. Hooker, for support. Delayed by the imposing challenge of producing the mirror and then by World War I, the 100-inch reflector finally became operational at Mount Wilson in 1918. Hale had for a third time built the largest telescope in the world.

In the interim, more of his energies focused on the national organization of scientific activities through his creation in July 1916 of the National Research Council (NRC), which marshaled scientific expertise for national needs, specifically to ready the country for war. Hale spent most of the war years chairing the NRC in Washington, D.C., and as a result became a central figure in the postwar reorganization of international science.

In 1920 a 20-foot (6-metre) stellar interferometer mounted by American physicist A.A. Michelson on Hale's 100-inch reflector made the first measurement of a star's diameter. Since the diameters of even more stars could be measured with a larger telescope, Hale was convinced of the scientific necessity for large telescopes. Throughout the 1920s he wrote a series of popular articles on the possibilities of large telescopes, waxing romantic about the many compelling rationales underpinning astronomy's insatiable need for light-gathering power. In 1928 he attracted some $6 million from the Rockefeller Foundation's International Education Board for the construction of a 200-inch (508-cm) reflector; this was a major coup at a time when overall support for science in the United States was hardly robust. Over the next two decades there would be many technical and social obstacles to the completion of the telescope. Hale died in 1938; construction of the telescope was halted during World War II (1939–45), but eventually, in 1948, the 200-inch Hale Telescope at the Palomar Observatory saw first light. It was the largest telescope in the world until 1976.

HENDRIK VAN DE HULST
(b. Nov. 19, 1918, Utrecht, Neth.— d. July 31, 2000, Leiden)

Dutch astronomer Hendrik Christoffel van de Hulst predicted theoretically the 21-cm (8.2-inch) radio waves produced by interstellar hydrogen atoms. His calculations later proved valuable in mapping the Milky Way Galaxy and were the basis for radio astronomy during its early development.

In 1944, while still a student, van de Hulst made theoretical studies of hydrogen atoms in space. The magnetic fields of the proton and electron in the hydrogen atom can align in either the same or opposite directions. Once every 10 million years or so a hydrogen atom will realign itself and, van de Hulst calculated, emit a radio wave with a 21-cm wavelength.

Van de Hulst was appointed a lecturer in astronomy at the University of Leiden in 1948 and four years later was made a professor there. He retired in 1984. In addition to his work in radio astronomy, he made valuable contributions to the understanding of light scattering by small particles, the solar corona, and interstellar clouds. Beginning in the 1960s van de Hulst became a leader in international and European space research and development efforts. His numerous awards include the Bruce Medal of the Astronomical Society of the Pacific (1978).

KARL JANSKY
(b. Oct. 22, 1905, Norman, Okla., U.S.— d. Feb. 14, 1950, Red Bank, N.J.)

Karl Jansky was an American engineer whose discovery of radio waves from an extraterrestrial source inaugurated the development of radio astronomy, a new science that from the mid-20th century greatly extended the range of astronomical observations.

In 1928 Jansky joined the Bell Telephone Laboratories in New Jersey, where his assignment was to track down and identify the various forms of interference that were plaguing telephone communications. He built a linear, directional antenna by which he was able to identify all the sources of interference except one. After months of study he discovered in 1931 that the source of the unidentified radio interference came from the stars. By the following spring he concluded that the source lay in the direction of the constellation Sagittarius, which Harlow Shapley and Jan H. Oort had established as the direction of the centre of the Milky Way Galaxy.

Jansky published his findings in late 1932 but did not pursue the further development of radio astronomy, a task performed by the American engineer and amateur astronomer Grote Reber. In honour of Jansky's epoch-making discovery, the unit of radio-wave emission strength was named the jansky.

SIR BERNARD LOVELL
(b. Aug. 31, 1913, Oldland Common, Gloucestershire, Eng.)

The English radio astronomer Sir Alfred Charles Bernard Lovell was founder and director (1951–81) of England's Jodrell Bank Experimental Station.

Lovell attended the University of Bristol, from which he received a Ph.D. degree in 1936. After a year as an assistant lecturer in physics at the University of Manchester, he became a member of the cosmic-ray research team at that institution, working in this capacity until the outbreak of World War II in 1939, when he published his first book, *Science and Civilization*. During World War II, Lovell worked for the Air Ministry, doing valuable research in the use of radar for detection and navigation purposes for which he was awarded the Order of the British Empire in 1946.

On returning to the University of Manchester in 1945 as a lecturer in physics, Lovell acquired a surplus army radar set for use in his research on cosmic rays. Because interference from the surrounding city hampered his efforts, he moved the equipment, which included a searchlight base, to Jodrell Bank, an open field

Lovell Telescope, a fully steerable radio telescope at Jodrell Bank, Macclesfield, Cheshire, Eng. Jodrell Bank Science Centre

located about 20 miles south of Manchester. Shortly thereafter, authorities at the university agreed to provide him with a permanent establishment at the site, which already belonged to the university's botany department, and to sponsor the construction of his first radio telescope, for which he used the searchlight base as a mounting.

Lovell's initial investigations with the instrument involved the study of meteors. About 15 years earlier, when radio waves had been bounced off meteors during certain meteor showers, some astronomers had noted that the number

of meteors observed visually was much smaller than the number of radio echoes received, an indication that the showers actually consisted of more meteors than could be seen. To determine if the echoes were meteoric in origin, Lovell used his new radio telescope to observe a particularly intense meteor shower on the night of Oct. 9–10, 1946. As the shower first increased and later decreased in intensity, radio signals from the instrument's transmitter were directed toward the shower. Throughout the evening, not only did the number of optical sightings coincide with the number of radio echoes being received, but the timing of the two rates was also as predicted, conclusively proving that the echoes were caused by the meteors.

Having established this fact, Lovell could now apply radio techniques to meteor showers previously unknown because they occurred during daylight hours. Further experiments showed that orbits of meteors are elliptical, confirming the belief that these bodies are members of the solar system and are not of interstellar origin.

In recognition of his work and growing reputation, Lovell was appointed by the University of Manchester to the position of senior lecturer in 1947 and reader in 1949; from 1951 to 1980 he was professor of radio astronomy at the university. During this time, he had already begun planning and building a bigger and more sophisticated radio telescope, which, when it was completed in 1957, was the world's largest of its kind, with a diameter of 250 feet. The structure rotates horizontally at 20° per minute, and the reflector itself moves vertically at 24° per minute. While work on the telescope was in progress, Lovell published *Radio Astronomy* (1952), *Meteor Astronomy* (1954), and *The Exploration of Space by Radio* (1957).

Lovell frankly admitted that it was mainly the prospect of using the new radio telescope to track the first Sputnik, scheduled for launch by the Soviet Union on Oct. 4, 1957, that spurred his efforts to complete the instrument by that time. By supplying a much-needed boost to the prestige of the project at a time when it was being seriously threatened by rapidly rising costs, this application of the instrument guaranteed its success and Lovell's personal fame. Ever since, the giant radio telescope at Jodrell Bank has been a vital tool for pinpointing the exact locations of Earth satellites, space probes, and manned space flights, as well as for collecting data transmitted by instruments in some of these vehicles.

Because of the widespread publicity given to Jodrell Bank and its director, coupled with the latter's reputation as a popularizer of science, the British Broadcasting Corporation in 1958 invited Lovell to give a series of radio talks, known as the Reith Lectures, which were published in 1959 as *The Individual and the Universe*. When Lovell was knighted (1961) for his pioneering work in radio astronomy, 20 investigations—mostly on radio emissions originating thousands of millions of light years away—were in progress at Jodrell Bank. Some of this work is discussed in his book *The Exploration of Outer Space* (1962). His research has since been concerned mainly with cosmology; radio emissions from outer space, including those from pulsars (discovered in 1968); the measurement of the angular diameters of distant quasars; and flare stars.

Lovell received a number of honorary degrees from various academic institutions as well as honorary membership in several academies and organizations. He was elected a fellow of the Royal Society in 1955, receiving its Royal Medal in 1960. From 1969 to 1971 he was president of the Royal Astronomical Society, and he received the Society's Gold Medal in 1981.

Bernard Lyot
(b. Feb. 27, 1897, Paris, France—d. April 2, 1952, Cairo, Egypt)

French astronomer Bernard-Ferdinand Lyot invented the coronagraph (1930), an instrument that allows the observation of the solar corona when the Sun is not in eclipse.

Before Lyot's coronagraph, observing the corona had been possible only during a solar eclipse, but this was unsatisfactory because total eclipses occur only rarely and the duration of such eclipses is too short (no more than seven minutes) to allow prolonged scientific observation of the corona. Merely blocking out the Sun's radiant disk was insufficient to view the comparatively dim corona because of the diffusion of the Sun's light by the atmosphere, whose brightness rendered the delicate corona invisible. But by going to the Pic du Midi Observatory high in the French Pyrenees, where the high altitude resulted in less atmospheric diffusion, and by equipping his coronagraph with an improved lens and a monochromatic filter that he had developed, Lyot succeeded in making daily photographs of the Sun's corona. In 1939, using his coronagraph and filters, he shot the first motion pictures of the solar prominences.

Lyot was elected to the Academy of Sciences in 1939, and was also awarded the Gold Medal of the Royal Astronomical Society in that year.

Seth Nicholson
(b. Nov. 12, 1891, Springfield, Ill., U.S.—d. July 2, 1963, Los Angeles, Calif.)

The American astronomer Seth Barnes Nicholson was best known for discovering four satellites of Jupiter: the 9th in 1914 (at Lick Observatory, Mount Hamilton, Calif.), the 10th and 11th in 1938, and the 12th in 1951 (all at Mount Wilson Observatory, Calif.).

Educated at Drake University, Des Moines, Iowa, and at the University of California (Ph.D., 1915), Nicholson was on the Mount Wilson Observatory staff from 1915 to 1957. Of greater astrophysical significance than his satellite discoveries was his investigation of sunspots, especially their magnetic properties and terrestrial effects. With the American astronomer Edison Pettit, he made many thermocouple measurements of stellar and planetary radiation.

Charles Perrine
(b. July 28, 1867, Steubenville, Ohio, U.S.—d. June 21, 1951, Villa General Mitre, Arg.)

The American astronomer Charles Dillon Perrine discovered the sixth and seventh moons of Jupiter in 1904 and 1905, respectively. In 1904 he published a calculation of the solar parallax (a measure of the Earth–Sun distance) based on observations of the minor planet Eros during one of its close approaches to Earth.

Perrine worked at the Lick Observatory in California from 1893 to 1909 and then until his retirement in 1936 was director of the Argentine National Observatory in Córdoba. His work included counts of extragalactic nebulae and the discovery of 13 comets.

JOHN PLASKETT
(b. Nov. 17, 1865, Woodstock, Ont., Can.—d. Oct. 17, 1941, Victoria, B.C.)

John Stanley Plaskett was a Canadian astronomer remembered for his expert design of instruments and his extensive spectroscopic observations.

Plaskett, a skilled mechanic and photographer, graduated from the University of Toronto in 1899. In 1903 he joined the staff of the Dominion Observatory at Ottawa, where he initiated astrophysical research and devised a spectrograph that made the telescope at Ottawa equivalent to much larger instruments.

In 1913 Plaskett persuaded the Canadian government to finance the construction of a 183-cm (72-inch) reflector. That instrument, largely designed by Plaskett, was placed in operation near Victoria, B.C., in 1918. He was appointed director of the observatory at Victoria in 1917. He used the new telescope to study binary stars and the distribution of calcium in interstellar space. In 1922 he

resolved a very massive binary star (Plaskett's star), and in 1930 he deduced the distance and direction of the centre of gravity of the Milky Way Galaxy and the pattern of rotation about it. After his retirement in 1935 he supervised the grinding and polishing of the 2-metre (82-inch) mirror for the telescope of the McDonald Observatory, Fort Davis, Texas.

GROTE REBER
(b. Dec. 22, 1911, Chicago, Ill., U.S.— d. Dec. 20, 2002, Tasmania, Austl.)

The American astronomer and radio engineer Grote Reber built the first radio telescope and was largely responsible for the early development of radio astronomy, which opened an entirely new research front in the study of the universe.

When radio engineer Karl Jansky announced his discovery of radio signals from the stars in 1932, Reber tried to adapt his shortwave radio receiver to pick up interstellar radio waves. He failed, but in 1937 he built a bowl-shaped antenna 9.4 metres (31 feet) in diameter that served as the only radio telescope in the world until after World War II. By 1942 he had completed the first preliminary radio maps of the sky, concentrating on high-frequency shortwave signals, and discovered that in certain regions radio signals are particularly strong but apparently unrelated to any visible celestial object.

In 1947 Reber moved his radio telescope to Sterling, Va., and in Washington, D.C., he served as chief of the Experimental

Microwave Research Section. In 1951 in Hawaii he built a new radio telescope and concentrated on mapping celestial sources of low-frequency long-wave signals 5.5 to 14 metres (18 to 46 feet) in wavelength. In 1954 he joined the Commonwealth Scientific and Industrial Research Organization in Tasmania, Austl., one of the few places on the surface of Earth at which the atmosphere is occasionally transparent to electromagnetic radiation more than 30 metres (98 feet) in wavelength. Although he accepted a position in 1957 at the National Radio Astronomy Observatory in Green Bank, W.Va., where a radio telescope 43 metres (140 feet) across had just been completed, he returned to Bothwell, Tasmania, in 1961 to help complete the mapping of sources of radio waves with a 270-metre (886-foot) wavelength.

An energetic and entertaining speaker, in his later years Reber spoke out on what he perceived to be problems with relativity theory and big-bang cosmology. He believed that much of the redshift observed in the spectra of distant galaxies was due to the forward scattering of light as it traversed the cosmos.

HERBERT TURNER
(b. Aug. 13, 1861, Leeds, Yorkshire, Eng.—d. Aug. 20, 1930, Stockholm, Swed.)

English astronomer Herbert Hall Turner pioneered many of the procedures now universally employed in determining stellar positions from astronomical photographs.

In 1884 Turner was appointed chief assistant at the Royal Observatory, Green-wich, and in 1893 he became Savilian professor of astronomy and director of the University Observatory at Oxford. A plan for international cooperation in compiling an astrographic chart and catalog had been formulated in 1887 at Paris. Turner worked unceasingly on Oxford's share of the project and made innovations in astronomical photography that contributed to the success of the project. Through his efforts, Oxford was the second observatory to finish its share of the catalog, and he then turned to helping others finish their zones. After the formation of the International Astronomical Union in 1919, he was appointed president of the committee in charge of the project. He also contributed much to worldwide seismological studies and established Oxford as an international centre of seismological research.

A prolific writer as well as an exceptional speaker, Turner produced four popular expositions of astronomy: *Modern Astronomy* (1901); *Astronomical Discovery* (1904); *The Great Star Map* (1912); and *A Voyage in Space* (1915). At his suggestion the distant solar system object discovered by the American astronomer Clyde W. Tombaugh in 1930 was named Pluto.

YRJÖ VÄISÄLÄ
(b. Sept. 6, 1891, Kontiolahti, Russia—d. July 21, 1971, Rymättylä, Fin.)

The Finnish meteorologist and astronomer Yrjö Väisälä was noted for developing meteorological measuring methods and instruments.

After receiving his Ph.D. in 1922, Väisälä joined the faculty of the Geodetic Institute of Turku University (1925) and worked as an astronomer and surveyor, completing a magnetic survey of Earth and inventing the light-interference system for measuring long paths (on the order of 100 metres [328 feet]) for use as baselines in geodetic surveys (1927).

Later in his career, Väisälä turned to meteorology and developed, among other things, a new method of radio direction finding (1951). In 1952 he helped found the Turku University Astronomical Observatory and was its director until his death. Väisälä received the Honorary Award of the Finnish Academy of Sciences and Letters in 1954.

CHAPTER 6

THE IMPACT OF ASTRONOMY

No area of science is totally self-contained. Discoveries in one area find applications in others, often unpredictably. Various notable examples of this statement involve astronomical studies.

Newton's laws of motion and gravity emerged from the analysis of planetary and lunar orbits. Observations during the 1919 solar eclipse provided dramatic confirmation of Albert Einstein's general theory of relativity, which gained further support with the discovery and tracking of the binary pulsar designated PSR 1913+16. The behaviour of nuclear matter and of some elementary particles is now better understood as a result of measurements of neutron stars and the cosmological helium abundance, respectively. Study of the theory of synchrotron radiation was greatly stimulated by the detection of polarized visible radiation emitted by high-energy electrons in the supernova remnant known as the Crab Nebula. Dedicated particle accelerators are now being used to produce synchrotron radiation to probe the structure of solid materials and make detailed X-ray images of tiny samples, including biological structures.

IMPACT OF TECHNOLOGICAL DEVELOPMENTS

Astronomy has not been immune from technological change. Computers allow astronomers to obtain much more data than was possible just mere decades ago. With the coming

INTERNATIONAL ASTRONOMICAL UNION (IAU)

The International Astronomical Union (IAU) is the senior body governing international professional astronomical activities worldwide, with headquarters in Paris. It was established in 1919 as the first of a series of international unions for the advancement of specific branches of science. Its professed mission is to promote and safeguard the science of astronomy in all its aspects through international cooperation.

The IAU is made up of various divisions, commissions, and working groups representing the various areas of astronomical research, teaching, and other endeavours. In the early 21st century it had a membership of some 8,000 professional astronomers from about 60 adhering countries. It is the only organization recognized professionally for the naming of astronomical bodies, which it does solely on the basis of merit, history, or discoverer's privilege. The IAU holds a general assembly every three years in varying parts of the world at which professional astronomers meet to discuss research, new cooperative ventures, and similar matters of professional interest.

of the space age, satellite observatories now study the entire electromagnetic spectrum.

COMPUTERS

Besides the telescope itself, the electronic computer has become the astronomer's most important tool. Indeed, the computer has revolutionized the use of the telescope to the point where the collection of observational data is now completely automated. The astronomer need only identify the object to be observed, and the rest is carried out by the computer and auxiliary electronic equipment.

A telescope can be set to observe automatically by means of electronic sensors appropriately placed on the telescope axis. Precise quartz or atomic clocks send signals to the computer, which in turn activates the telescope sensors to collect data at the proper time. The computer not only

makes possible more efficient use of telescope time but also permits a more detailed analysis of the data collected than could have been done manually. Data analysis that would have taken a lifetime or longer to complete with a mechanical calculator can now be done within hours or even minutes with a high-speed computer.

Improved means of recording and storing computer data have also contributed to astronomical research. Optical disc data storage technology, such as the CD-ROM (compact disc read-only memory) or the DVD-ROM (digital video disc read-only memory) disc, has provided astronomers with the ability to store and retrieve vast amounts of telescopic and other astronomical data.

ROCKETS AND SPACECRAFT

The quest for new knowledge about the universe has led astronomers to study electromagnetic radiation other than just visible light. Such forms of radiation, however, are blocked for the most part by Earth's atmosphere, and so their detection and analysis can only be achieved from above this gaseous envelope.

During the late 1940s, single-stage sounding rockets were sent up to 160 km (100 miles) or more to explore the upper layers of the atmosphere. From 1957, more sophisticated multistage rockets were launched as part of the International Geophysical Year, a scientific endeavor designed to gather information in 11 Earth science categories. These rockets carried artificial satellites equipped with a variety of scientific instruments.

Beginning in 1959, the Soviet Union and the United States, engaged in a "space race," intensified their efforts and launched a series of unmanned probes to explore the Moon. Lunar exploration culminated with the first manned landing on the Moon by the U.S. Apollo 11 astronauts on July 20, 1969. Numerous other U.S. and Soviet spacecraft were sent to further study the lunar environment until the mid-1970s.

Starting in the early 1960s both the United States and the Soviet Union launched a multitude of unmanned deep-space probes to learn more about the other planets and satellites of the solar system. Carrying television cameras, detectors, and an assortment of other instruments, these probes sent back impressive amounts of scientific data

and close-up pictures. Among the most successful missions were those involving the Soviet Venera probes to Venus and the U.S. Viking 1 and 2 landings on Mars and Voyager 2 flybys of Jupiter, Saturn, Uranus, and Neptune. When the Voyager 2 probe flew past Neptune and its moons in August 1989, every known major planet had been explored by spacecraft. Many long-held views, particularly those about the outer planets, were altered by the findings of the Voyager probe. These findings included the discovery of several rings and six additional satellites around Neptune, all of which are undetectable to ground-based telescopes.

Specially instrumented spacecraft have enabled astronomers to investigate other celestial phenomena as well. The Orbiting Solar Observatories (OSOs) and Solar Maximum Mission, Earth-orbiting U.S. satellites equipped with ultraviolet detector systems, have provided a means for studying solar activity. Another example is the Giotto probe of the European Space Agency, which enabled astronomers to obtain detailed photographs of the nucleus of Comet Halley during the 1986 passage of the comet.

WIDE IMPACT

Astronomical knowledge has also had a broad impact beyond science. The earliest calendars were based on astronomical observations of the cycles of repeated solar and lunar positions. Also, for centuries, familiarity with the positions and apparent motions of the stars through the seasons enabled sea voyagers to navigate with moderate accuracy.

Perhaps the single greatest effect that astronomical studies have had on our modern society has been in molding its perceptions and opinions. Our conceptions of the cosmos and our place in it, our perceptions of space and time, and the development of the systematic pursuit of knowledge known as the scientific method have been profoundly influenced by astronomical observations. In addition, the power of science to provide the basis for accurate predictions of such phenomena as eclipses and the positions of the planets and later, so dramatically, of comets has shaped an attitude toward science that remains an important social force today.

Appendix A: Beyond Telescopes Other Astronomical Instrumentation

Telescopes are not the only tools used to investigate astronomical objects. Other astronomical instruments are often helpful.

ALMUCANTAR

The almucantar is an instrument invented by American astronomer Seth Carlo Chandler for determining latitude or time by observing the times of transit of stars across a fixed almucantar. The term also refers to any circle of the celestial sphere parallel to the horizon. When two objects are on the same almucantar, they have the same altitude.

ARMILLARY SPHERE

The armillary sphere was an early astronomical device for representing the great circles of the heavens, including in the most elaborate instruments the horizon, meridian, Equator, tropics, polar circles, and an ecliptic hoop. The sphere was a skeleton celestial globe, with circles divided into degrees for angular measurement. In the 17th and 18th centuries such models—either suspended, rested on a stand, or affixed to a handle—were used to show the difference between the Ptolemaic theory of a central Earth and the Copernican theory of a central Sun.

The earliest known complete armillary sphere with nine circles is believed to have been the *meteōroskopion* of the Alexandrine Greeks (*c.* 140 CE), but earlier and simpler types of ring instruments were also in general use. Ptolemy, in the *Almagest*, enumerates at least three, and it has been stated that Hipparchus (146–127 BCE) used a sphere of four rings. The Arabs employed similar instruments with diametric sight rules, or alidades, and it is likely that those made and used in the 12th century by Moors in Spain were the prototypes of all later European armillary spheres.

ASTROLABE

An astrolabe was an early scientific instrument used for reckoning time and for observational purposes. One widely employed variety, the planispheric astrolabe, enabled astronomers to calculate the position of the Sun and prominent stars with respect to both the horizon and the meridian. It provided them with a plane image of the celestial sphere and the principal circles—namely, those representing the ecliptic, celestial equator, and tropics of Cancer and Capricorn. Because of such features, the planispheric astrolabe can be regarded as a kind of rudimentary analogue computer.

Although astrolabes have been traced to the 6th century, they appear to have come into wide use from the early Middle Ages in Europe and the Islamic world. By about the mid-15th century, astrolabes were adopted by mariners and used in celestial navigation. The so-called mariner's astrolabe was later supplanted by sextants.

The typical planispheric astrolabe employed by medieval astronomers measured from 8 to 46 cm (3 to 18 inches) and was made of metal—usually brass or iron. It had several principal parts: a base plate (the mater) with a network of lines representing celestial coordinates; an open-pattern disk (the rete) with a "map" of the stars, including the aforementioned circles, that rotated on the mater around a centre pin corresponding to the north celestial pole; and a straight rule (the alidade), used for sighting objects in the sky. The alidade made it possible to use the astrolabe for surveying applications—e.g., determining the height of a mountain. Most astrolabes also had one or more plates (called climates) that were engraved with coordinate lines for different latitudes and were placed between the mater and the rete.

BINOCULARS

Binoculars are an optical instrument, usually handheld, for providing a magnified stereoscopic view of distant objects, consisting of two similar telescopes, one for each eye, mounted on a single frame. A single thumbwheel may control the focus of both telescopes simultaneously, and provision may be made for adjusting the focus of each separately to allow for varying characteristics in the two eyes. Binoculars are designed to give an upright view that is correctly oriented left-to-right. Because they allow use of both eyes in a natural way, they are more comfortable than single telescopes, provide depth perception, and improve visual acuity by giving the human visual system two sets of data to process and combine.

In most binoculars, each telescope is provided with two reflecting prisms. The prisms reinvert, or erect, the inverted image supplied by the objective of each telescope. They prescribe a folded path for the light rays, allowing a shorter overall length for the instrument. When the prisms used are of the Porro type, they also provide better depth perception at greater distances by allowing the two objectives to be set farther apart than the eyepieces.

Binoculars' primary optical characteristics are commonly described by two numbers, the first of which is followed by a multiplication sign—for instance, 7×50. The first number indicates the magnification (e.g., 7×, meaning "7 times") and the second the diameter of the objective in millimetres (1 inch is about 25 millimetres). This latter figure is a measure of the light-gathering power of the instrument. For a given magnification, larger objectives produce a brighter image in dim light but also create a more massive binocular. Handheld binoculars designed for typical uses such as hunting, sports watching, nature study, or amateur astronomy range from about 6×30 to 10×50. Instruments having greater magnifications and light-gathering power are too heavy to hold steady, especially for long periods, but they can be fixed to a tripod or other mount.

In applications in which depth perception is not important, a single telescope, called a monocular, may be employed. It is essentially one-half of a binocular and usually incorporates prisms in the light path.

Opera glasses and field glasses are binoculars with simple, often inexpensive lens systems and narrow fields of view and are usually made with magnifications of 2.5× to 5×. The lenses used in most binoculars are coated on some or all of their air-to-glass surfaces to reduce reflections.

CELESTIAL GLOBE

The celestial globe is a representation of stars and constellations as they are located on the apparent sphere of the sky. Celestial globes are used for some astronomical or astrological calculations or as ornaments.

Some globes were made in ancient Greece; Thales of Miletus (fl. 6th century BCE) is generally credited with having constructed the first. Some Arabic globes made as early as the 11th century are extant. Among the seafaring peoples of the Pacific islands, globes were used to teach celestial navigation.

COELOSTAT

The coelostat is a device consisting of a flat mirror that is turned slowly by a motor to reflect the Sun continuously into a fixed telescope. The mirror is mounted to rotate about an axis through its front surface that points to a celestial pole and is driven at the rate of one revolution in 48 hours. The telescope image is then stationary and nonrotating. The coelostat is particularly useful in eclipse expeditions when elaborate equatorial mounting of telescopes is impossible. Other instruments applying the principle of the coelostat for similar observations are the heliostat, which produces a rotating image of the Sun, and the siderostat, which is like a heliostat but is used to observe stars.

CORONAGRAPH

A telescope that blocks the light of a star inside the instrument so that objects close to the star can be observed is called a coronagraph. It was invented in 1930 by the French astronomer Bernard Lyot and was used to observe the Sun's corona and prominences.

When a coronagraph is used to observe the Sun, a round metal screen blocks the overwhelming brightness of the Sun's central disk, or photosphere. Other screens and diaphragms block reflections of the photospheric image. The coronagraph must be used at high altitudes and on very clear days, when the atmospheric diffusion of light is at a minimum; imperfect lenses or dust inside the instrument will scatter enough photospheric light to obscure the dim solar corona.

HELIOSTAT

The heliostat is used in solar telescopes to orient and focus sunlight along a fixed direction. A typical heliostat consists of a flat plane mirror and a curved parabolic mirror. The plane mirror is mounted along an axis parallel (i.e., equatorial) to Earth's axis and rotated slowly by a motor to reflect light from the Sun. The parabolic mirror focuses the reflected rays into the telescope along a fixed direction while the Sun traverses the sky. Therefore, as the telescope's field of view rotates, different celestial objects move quickly into view.

Portable heliostats are useful in studying solar eclipses because they eliminate the need to mount telescopes equatorially. Larger models, installed at permanent positions around the world, have also been employed to track both the Sun and the stars.

MILLS CROSS

First demonstrated in the 1950s by the Australian astronomer Bernard Yarnton Mills, the Mills Cross type of radio telescope is based on the interferometer. It consists of two interferometers erected in two straight rows intersecting at right angles. Up to a mile long, the rows may be composed of hundreds of antennas of several possible types. Electronic comparison of differences in the way the two perpendicular rows receive a signal allows exact determination of the position in the sky of the signal's source. For this purpose, the cross works practically as well as a single huge antenna with the same overall diameter; such a single antenna would be vastly more difficult, if not impossible, to build.

ORRERY

An orrery is a mechanical model of the solar system used to demonstrate the motions of the planets around the Sun, probably invented by George Graham (d. 1751) under the patronage of Charles Boyle, 4th Earl of Orrery. In use for several centuries, the device was formerly called a planetarium. The orrery presents the planets as viewed from outside the solar system in an accurate scale model of periods of revolution (with Earth completing a year's rotation in about 10 minutes). The planets' sizes and distances, however, are necessarily inaccurate.

RADIO INTERFEROMETER

A radio interferometer is an apparatus consisting of two or more separate antennas that receive radio waves from the same astronomical object and are joined to the same receiver. The antennas may be placed close together or thousands of kilometres apart.

The principle of a radio interferometer's operation is the same as for an optical interferometer, but, because radio waves are much longer than light waves, the scale of the instrument is generally correspondingly greater. Parts of a radio wave reach the spaced antennas at different times. This time difference is compensated for by a variable-delay mechanism, and the waves can be made to interfere, much as in the optical interferometer. In another version, the spacing of the antennas can be changed in an attempt to make the waves interfere; the distance between them for interference depends on the wavelength and on the diameter of the source of the waves. The diameter can be calculated when the other quantities are known. If the diameter of the radio-wave source is not too small to be resolved by the interferometer, the radio signals will alternately reinforce and cancel each other in a manner analogous to the way fringes are produced in the optical interferometer.

SIDEROSTAT

The siderostat is any of a class of astronomical instruments consisting of a flat mirror that is turned slowly by a motor to reflect a given region of the sky continuously into a fixed telescope. In the traditional siderostat, the mirror is rotated by a lever arm connected to a motor that turns at a rate of one revolution every 24 hours. This so-called Foucault siderostat provides a fixed but rotating image. In recent years the Foucault siderostat has been largely supplanted by the heliostat, which is a polar siderostat, and by the coelostat.

Appendix B: Notable Observatories and Telescopes

The observatories and telescopes that astronomers use are often as awe-inspiring as the objects that are studied with them. From the vast radio dish of Arecibo to the brooding stones of Stonehenge, these sites and instruments stand out from the others because of their size, capabilities, or discoveries.

ARECIBO OBSERVATORY

The Arecibo Observatory is located 16 km (10 miles) south of the town of Arecibo in Puerto Rico. It is the site of the world's largest single-unit radio telescope. This instrument, built in the early 1960s, employs a 305-metre (1,000-foot) spherical reflector consisting of perforated aluminum panels that focus incoming radio waves on movable antenna structures positioned about 168 metres (550 feet) above the reflector surface. The antenna structures can be moved in any direction, making it possible to track a celestial object in different regions of the sky. The observatory also has an auxiliary 30-metre (100-foot) telescope that serves as a radio interferometer and a high-power transmitting facility used to study Earth's atmosphere.

Scientists using the Arecibo Observatory discovered the first extrasolar planets around the pulsar B1257+12 in 1992. The observatory also produced detailed radar maps of the surface of Venus and Mercury and discovered that Mercury rotated every 59 days instead of 88 days and so did not always show the same face to the Sun. American astronomers Russell Hulse and Joseph H. Taylor, Jr., used Arecibo to discover the first binary pulsar. They showed that it was losing energy through gravitational radiation at the rate predicted by physicist Albert Einstein's theory of general relativity, and they won the Nobel Prize for Physics in 1993 for their discovery.

CERRO TOLOLO INTER-AMERICAN OBSERVATORY (CTIO)

Cerro Tololo Inter-American Observatory (CTIO) was founded in 1965 in Chile as the southern branch of the Kitt Peak National Observatory. It is located on top of two mountains, Cerro Tololo, which is 2,200 metres (7,200 feet) high, and Cerro Pachon, which is 2,700 metres (8,800 feet) high; both mountains are about 460 km (285 miles) north of Santiago and 80 km (50 miles) inland from the coastal city of La Serena. It is operated by the Association of Universities for Research in Astronomy and funded by the U.S. National Science Foundation.

The CTIO houses several telescopes and auxiliary instruments, the most significant of which are the 8-metre (26-foot) Gemini South, the 4-metre (13-foot) Southern Observatory for Astrophysical Research Telescope, and the 4-metre Victor M. Blanco Telescope. The observatory is best noted for its research on the central region of the Milky Way Galaxy, the Magellanic Clouds, and high-energy cosmic radio and X-ray sources.

CRIMEAN ASTROPHYSICAL OBSERVATORY

The Crimean Astrophysical Observatory is a major astronomical observatory, located at Nauchny and Simeiz in Crimea, Ukraine. It was established in 1908 as a branch of the Pulkovo Observatory (near St. Petersburg) and houses modern optical reflecting telescopes with diameters of 1.20 and 2.65 metres (3.94 and 8.69 feet). It also operates several small radio telescopes, the most important of which is a high-precision, steerable paraboloid, 22 metres (72 feet) in diameter.

EUROPEAN SOUTHERN OBSERVATORY (ESO)

The astrophysical organization European Southern Observatory (ESO) was founded in 1962. Its activities are financially supported and administered by a consortium of 13 European nations—Belgium, the Czech Republic, Denmark, Finland, France, Germany, Great Britain, Italy, the Netherlands, Portugal, Spain, Sweden,

and Switzerland. ESO's scientific, technical, and administrative headquarters are in Garching, Germany, near Munich.

ESO operates at three sites in Chile—the La Silla Observatory, located about 600 km (370 miles) north of Santiago at an altitude of 2,400 metres (7,900 feet), the Very Large Telescope (Paranal Observatory) on Paranal, a 2,600-metre-high (8,500-foot) mountain about 130 km (80 miles) south of Antofagasta, and the Atacama Large Millimeter/submillimeter Array (ALMA) located about 50 km (30 miles) east of San Pedro de Atacama on the Chajnantor plateau at an altitude of 5,000 metres (16,000 feet). The La Silla site has six optical telescopes with diameters as large as 3.6 metres (142 inches). The Very Large Telescope facility consists of four 8.2-metre (323-inch) and four 1.8-metre (71-inch) supplementary telescopes, which were designed to be used individually or in combination as a giant interferometer. Completion of ALMA, an array of 66 12-metre (39-foot) radio telescopes, is scheduled for 2012.

HALE OBSERVATORIES

The Hale Observatories is an astronomical research unit that included the Palomar Observatory of the California Institute of Technology and the Mount Wilson Observatory of the Carnegie Institution of Washington, Washington, D.C. Both observatories were established under the guidance of the American astronomer George Ellery Hale.

The Palomar and Wilson observatories were operated jointly by the two institutions as the Hale Observatories from 1948 until 1980, when their administration was separated.

GEORGE ELLERY HALE TELESCOPE

The George Ellery Hale Telescope is one of the world's largest and most powerful reflecting telescopes and is located at the Palomar Observatory, Mount Palomar, Calif. Financed by the Rockefeller Foundation, the telescope at Palomar was completed in 1948 and named in honour of the noted American astronomer George Ellery Hale, who supervised the designing of the instrument.

The main mirror of the Hale Telescope measures 5 metres (200 inches) across and weighs 14.5 tons. It is made of Pyrex (a borosilicate glass with a lower coefficient of expansion), carefully ground and polished to the correct curvature and coated with aluminum to give a durable, highly reflective surface. The entire movable part of the telescope weighs more than 500 tons, yet it is so smoothly supported and delicately balanced on hydrostatic bearings that a $1/12$-horsepower motor can turn it to follow the apparent rotation of the sky. The tube, of open-girder construction, is 18 metres (60 feet) long. Near its upper end, at the prime focus of the great mirror, is a capsule-type cage in which an astronomer may ride while observing. Alternatively, secondary mirrors allow the use of other viewing arrangements.

JODRELL BANK OBSERVATORY

The Jodrell Bank Observatory (formerly the Nuffield Radio Astronomy Laboratories) is the location of one of the world's largest fully steerable radio telescopes, which has a reflector that measures 76 metres (250 feet) in diameter. The telescope is located with other smaller radio telescopes at Jodrellbank (formerly Jodrell Bank), about 32 kilometres (20 miles) south of Manchester in the county of Cheshire, Eng.

Immediately after World War II the British astronomer Alfred Charles Bernard Lovell, working at the University of Manchester's botanical site at Jodrell Bank with war-surplus radar equipment, began research in radio and radar astronomy. Construction of the telescope began in 1952. Operation began shortly before the launching, on Oct. 4, 1957, by the Soviet Union of the first artificial Earth satellite (Sputnik I); and the satellite's carrier rocket was tracked at Jodrell Bank by radar.

Most of the operational time at Jodrell Bank is devoted to astronomy rather than to tracking and communication, but the telescope has been part of the tracking network for the United States program of space exploration and monitored most of the Soviet accomplishments. The Jodrell Bank telescope transmitted the first photographs from the surface of the Moon, received Feb. 6, 1966, by the Soviet Luna 9 probe. In 1987 the 76-metre telescope was renamed the Lovell Telescope. It and another telescope at Jodrell Bank are two elements of a seven-telescope array, the Multi-Element Radio Linked Interferometer Network (MERLIN), which uses microwave links to connect the individual telescopes into a radio interferometer 217 kilometres (135 miles) in diameter.

KITT PEAK NATIONAL OBSERVATORY (KPNO)

The Kitt Peak National Observatory (KPNO) is located on the Papago Indian Reservation 80 km (50 miles) southwest of Tucson, Ariz., U.S., at an elevation of 2,100 metres (6,888 feet). It was established in 1958 by the National Science Foundation (NSF) in response to a long-felt need by astronomers in the eastern half of the United States for access to excellent optical observing facilities in a favourable climate. Operated by the Association of Universities for Research in Astronomy under contract with the NSF, the observatory houses a collection of two radio and 21 optical telescopes, the largest of which is the 4-metre (13-foot) Mayall Telescope. The observatory also features the largest telescope ever designed for solar observation and a smaller vacuum tower telescope, which is also used for studying the Sun.

KUIPER AIRBORNE OBSERVATORY

The Kuiper Airborne Observatory was a Lockheed C-141 jet transport aircraft specially instrumented for astronomical observations at high altitudes. Named for the American astronomer Gerard P. Kuiper, it was operated (1971–95) by the U.S. National Aeronautics and Space Administration.

The observatory, equipped with a 0.9-metre (36-inch) Cassegrain reflecting telescope, was typically flown at an altitude of 12,500 metres (41,000 feet) to measure infrared radiation emitted by planets, stars, galaxies, and other celestial objects. Much of the infrared radiation in certain spectral regions is absorbed by water vapour and carbon dioxide in Earth's lower atmosphere and so cannot be detected by ground-based telescopes. The major discoveries of the Kuiper Airborne Observatory include the rings of the planet Uranus, stars in the process of formation, and molecules in interstellar space and in planetary atmospheres. A more sophisticated airborne observatory, a modified Boeing 747 named the Stratospheric Observatory for Infrared Astronomy (SOFIA) and developed by the United States and Germany, is scheduled to begin observations in 2010.

LICK OBSERVATORY

Lick Observatory was the first major mountaintop observatory built in the United States and the world's first permanently occupied mountaintop observatory. It is located about 21 km (13 miles) east of San Jose, Calif., U.S., atop Mount Hamilton.

Building on Mount Hamilton began in 1880 with funds bequeathed four years earlier by a wealthy Californian, James Lick. The observatory's first major telescope, a 91-cm (36-inch) refractor with optics by Alvan Clark & Sons, went into use in 1888 and remained the largest in the world until the completion of the 102-cm (40-inch) refractor at Yerkes Observatory in 1897. (At James Lick's request, his remains were interred under the support pier of the refractor when it was installed.) In 1895 the observatory acquired a 91-cm reflecting telescope built by Andrew Common in England and owned by Edward Crossley. In the 1930s its mirror was one of the first large mirrors to be aluminized, providing photographic access to the near-ultraviolet region of the spectrum; in the 1960s the Crossley reflector served as a valuable test bed for developing new techniques in spectrophotometry.

Although associated since the beginning of its operation with the University of California, the Lick Observatory was at first an autonomous facility. Between 1886 and 1891, through the efforts of James Keeler, then head of the observatory's spectroscopy program, Lick became the most powerful spectroscopic observatory in the world. After Keeler became its director in 1898, the observatory established a graduate fellowship program and strengthened academic ties with the University of California's Berkeley campus by arranging to have its staff teach there. Since that time Lick has been a major source of astronomers trained in spectroscopy.

In the first two decades of the 20th century, Lick excelled in the collection of spectroscopic data on stellar velocities and visual data on binary stars. Nevertheless, its original 91-cm refractor had been built as a visual instrument and was not suited for photography. Moreover, its Crossley reflector, although at the forefront of deep-sky photography and spectroscopy at the turn of the century, was by the 1920s overshadowed by the more powerful 152-cm (60-inch) and 254-cm (100-inch) reflectors at Lick's southerly California neighbour, Mount Wilson Observatory, and the 183-cm (72-inch) reflector at the Dominion Astrophysical Observatory in Victoria, British Columbia, Canada.

Between the 1920s and World War II, Lick was directed by a series of competent but unremarkable astronomers and, as a result, became seriously compromised by a weak senior staff and outdated equipment. Although it benefited from the presence of several young and highly promising instrumental and observational astronomers, it also experienced continued pressure from the Berkeley campus to disband the resident staff and turn the facility into an observing station for the growing university system. After the war, as American astronomy became more campus-based, Lick was one of the last major observatories to lose its autonomy, coming under full university control in the mid-1960s. By then, however, under a pair of strong directorships and with the addition of a 305-cm (120-inch) reflector in 1959 and the institution of a vigorous program to modernize its instrumentation, Lick had regained much of its earlier prominence as a leader in observational astronomy. As the result of improvements in the speed and efficiency of spectrographs and photoelectric spectrum scanners on the 305-cm reflector, Lick was the first observatory to compete with the Palomar Observatory's 5-metre (200-inch) Hale Telescope in the field of extragalactic astronomy.

Lick Observatory astronomers currently are headquartered at the Santa Cruz campus of the University of California, but the facility's instrumentation is available to all campuses of the university system.

MAUNA KEA OBSERVATORY

The Mauna Kea Observatory in Hawaii, U.S., has become one of the most important in the world owing to its outstanding observational conditions. It is operated by the University of Hawaii and lies at an elevation of 4,205 metres (13,796 feet) atop the peak of Mauna Kea, a dormant volcano on north-central Hawaii island.

The observatory was founded in 1964 at the urging of the influential American astronomer Gerard Kuiper, and a 2.2-metre (88-inch) reflector used for planetary studies went into service there in 1970. Mauna Kea subsequently became the site of the world's most important collection of telescopes designed for observations in the infrared range. Three large reflectors—the 3.8-metre (150-inch) United Kingdom Infrared Telescope, the 3.6-metre (142-inch) Canada-France-Hawaii Telescope, and the 3-metre (118-inch) NASA Infrared Telescope Facility—went into service there in 1979. In addition, a 15-metre

(49-foot) British-Dutch submillimetre- and millimetre-wavelength telescope, the James Clerk Maxwell Telescope, was completed in the late 1980s, and a similar 10.4-metre (34-foot) millimetre wave telescope, the Caltech Submillimeter Observatory, owned by the California Institute of Technology (Caltech), was completed early in the '90s. Another radio astronomy facility, the Submillimeter Array, a group of eight 6-metre (20-foot) diameter antennas owned by the Smithsonian Astrophysical Observatory and the Academia Sinica Institute of Astronomy and Astrophysics of Taiwan, was added in 2003.

The Keck telescope, a 10-metre (33-foot) multimirror telescope operated jointly by Caltech and the University of California, was completed at Mauna Kea in 1992. It is the largest reflector in the world and is used for both optical and infrared observations. Another Keck telescope went into operation on Mauna Kea in 1996. Two other large optical telescopes, the Japanese 8.2-metre (27-foot) Subaru and the multinational 8-metre (26-foot) Gemini North, began observations in 1999.

Mauna Kea is the site of many major telescopes because its viewing conditions are the finest of any Earth-based observatory. The site lies at an elevation almost twice that of any other major observatory and above 40 percent of Earth's atmosphere; there is thus less intervening atmosphere to obscure the light from distant stellar objects. A high proportion of nights at Mauna Kea are clear, calm, and cloudless owing to local weather peculiarities and the fact that the mountaintop lies above cloud cover most of the time. The high elevation and extremely dry, clear air make the site ideal for observing astronomical objects that emit radiation at far-infrared wavelengths, which are easily blocked by atmospheric water vapour.

MCDONALD OBSERVATORY

McDonald Observatory was founded in 1939 by the University of Texas, on the legacy of the Texas financier William J. McDonald, on Mount Locke near Fort Davis, Texas. The observatory includes the original 208-cm (82-inch) reflector, for many years the world's second largest telescope; a 272-cm (107-inch) reflector, dedicated in 1968; two smaller reflectors; and the 920-cm (362-inch) Hobby-Eberly Telescope, a telescope that only moves in azimuth.

The observatory, which until 1963 was operated under a joint agreement with the University of Chicago, has been directed by such noted astronomers as Otto Struve, Gerard Kuiper, Bengt Strömgren, W.W. Morgan, and Harlan J. Smith. Discoveries credited to the observatory include those of Nereid, a satellite of Neptune, and Miranda, a satellite of Uranus. Principal research has emphasized stellar composition and evolution and the properties of external galaxies. Other research specialties include high-speed photometry and lunar laser and satellite ranging.

MMT OBSERVATORY

The MMT Observatory has one of the world's largest astronomical telescopes, located on top of 2,600-metre-high (8,530-foot) Mount Hopkins, 60 km (37 miles) south of Tucson, Ariz. When it was built in 1979, it was originally called the Multiple Mirror Telescope (MMT) because it combined the light collected by six 180-cm-diameter (70-inch) telescopes into a single image. It thus had the light-gathering power of a single 450-cm (176-inch) telescope.

Because of many technical innovations, the construction of the MMT cost substantially less than that of a conventional telescope of comparable size. At the time of the MMT's construction, making one giant mirror would have been very expensive. However, subsequent innovations in mirror fabrication made the production of large mirrors more affordable. Therefore, from 1998 to 2000, the six mirrors of the MMT were replaced by a single 650-cm (255-inch) mirror. The MMT was renamed the MMT Observatory. The MMT Observatory is jointly owned and operated by the Smithsonian Institution and the University of Arizona.

MOUNT STROMLO AND SIDING SPRING OBSERVATORIES

The Mount Stromlo and Siding Spring observatories in southeast Australia are operated by the Australian National University.

Mount Stromlo Observatory is situated at an elevation of 768 metres (2,520 feet) on Mount Stromlo, 10 km (6 miles) west of Canberra. It was founded in 1924 as a centre for solar studies but shifted its emphasis in the 1940s to stellar astronomy. Its main telescope is a 1.9-metre (74-inch) reflector. The Mount Stromlo Observatory's viewing capability was threatened in the 1950s by the lights of the growing city of Canberra, and so a new site was established at an elevation of 1,165 metres (3,822 feet) on Siding Spring Mountain, about 31 km (19 miles) from Coonabarabran, New South Wales. On Jan. 18, 2003, a bushfire destroyed all five telescopes at Mount Stromlo. Rebuilding of some of the facilities began shortly thereafter.

The Siding Spring Observatory was originally a field station for the Mount Stromlo site, but it has become in itself one of the most important optical observatories in the world. Its main telescope is the Anglo-Australian Telescope, which was jointly built by Australia and Great Britain and has been operated by them since 1975. The instrument is a 3.9-metre (153-inch) reflector that has notably distortion-free optics and an extremely precise computer-controlled system for pinpointing and tracking celestial objects. The telescope is most useful for viewing distant cosmic objects of extremely faint luminosity. The Siding Spring Observatory also has the 2.3-metre (91-inch) Advanced Technology Telescope, which was built in 1984 and was designed to use new telescope technology. There are six other telescopes at Siding Spring, including the 1.2-metre (48-inch) Schmidt telescope, which is owned and operated by the United Kingdom Science Research Council. It has been used to extend the sky survey conducted by its sister instrument, the 1.2-metre (48-inch) Schmidt telescope at the Palomar Observatory, to the southern skies.

MOUNT WILSON OBSERVATORY

The Mount Wilson Observatory is located atop Mount Wilson, about 16 km (10 miles) northeast of Pasadena, Calif.

It was established in 1904 by American astronomer George Ellery Hale as a solar-observing station for the Yerkes Observatory, but it soon became an independent observatory funded by the Carnegie Institution of Washington. Hale built a series of ever-larger solar telescopes at the summit of Mount Wilson. In 1908 a 152-cm (60-inch) reflector, then the largest in the world, was added for observations of stars and galaxies. In the same year, Hale used both his solar telescopes and his laboratory experiments to demonstrate that sunspots were magnetically active regions in the Sun's photosphere. A complementary physics laboratory and suite of administrative and maintenance offices were also built in nearby Pasadena, making Mount Wilson the first stratified observatory complex in the world.

In 1918 a 254-cm (100-inch) reflecting telescope was put into service. It was not only the most powerful telescope in the world but also a versatile astronomical test bed for new observational techniques. In 1920 the angular diameter of a star was first measured with an interferometer mounted on this telescope, and soon the telescope was being used for astronomical spectroscopy that exploited not only the enormous light-gathering power of the 100-inch mirror but also the innovative subterranean Coudé focus that accommodated a wide range of spectroscopic devices.

The 100-inch telescope's most important discovery was American astronomer Edwin Hubble's determination of the distance to the Andromeda Nebula in 1924. He showed that the nebula lay beyond the bounds of the Milky Way Galaxy and hence was a galaxy in its own right. Then in 1929, building on the work of American astronomer Vesto Slipher, Hubble and his assistant, Milton Humason, demonstrated that galaxies were moving away from one another. This movement is the expansion of the universe. Throughout the 1930s and '40s, Hubble and his associates used the 100-inch reflector to refine the extragalactic distance scale and to probe the large-scale structure of the universe.

In 1944 the German-born American astronomer Walter Baade successfully resolved the inner regions of the Andromeda Galaxy with the 100-inch reflector and performed photometric studies that showed two populations of stars of different ages and compositions. The difference between the two populations, called Populations I and II, was a critical clue to the evolution of galaxies.

The 100-inch telescope remained the largest telescope in the world until 1948, when it was surpassed by the Palomar Observatory's 504-cm (200-inch) Hale Telescope, which was designed largely by Mount Wilson staff. Palomar was initially operated jointly by Mount Wilson and the California Institute of Technology, and eventually the two observatories were combined as the Hale Observatories. They are now separate entities, and, although Mount Wilson is still owned by the Carnegie Institution of Washington, it is operated by a consortium known as the Mount Wilson Institute (MWI). MWI has updated the instrumentation, including the 60- and 100-inch reflectors and the solar telescopes. These updates took advantage of the seeing conditions, which are still excellent, and successfully applied adaptive optics and interferometric techniques to problems in solar and stellar astrophysics.

NATIONAL RADIO ASTRONOMY OBSERVATORY (NRAO)

The National Radio Astronomy Observatory (NRAO) is the national radio observatory of the United States. It is funded by the National Science Foundation and is managed by Associated Universities, Inc., a consortium of nine leading private universities. Its headquarters are in Charlottesville, Va.

The NRAO was established in the mid-1950s and acquired its first operational radio telescope in 1959. It now has four principal observing facilities: at Green Bank, W.Va.; at Kitt Peak, near Tucson, Ariz.; at a site 80 km (50 miles) west of Socorro, N.M; and at a site 50 km (30 miles) east of San Pedro de Atacama in Chile. The NRAO was originally headquartered at the Green Bank site, whose chief instrument was a 91-metre (300-foot) partially steerable radio telescope that was completed in 1962 but which inexplicably collapsed in 1988. Its replacement, the Green Bank Telescope, which entered operation in 2000, has an aperture of 100 metres (330 feet) and is one of the world's largest fully steerable radio telescopes.

The NRAO has several other important radio telescopes. The Very Large Array, near Socorro, is one of the most powerful radio telescopes in the world. The Very Long Baseline Array (VLBA) is an array of 10 identical 25-metre (82-foot) radio telescopes spread across the United States that are used for very long baseline interferometry. The Atacama Large Millimeter Array (ALMA), an array of 66 12-metre (39-foot) radio telescopes near San Pedro de Atacama on the Chajnantor plateau in Chile at an altitude of 5,000 metres (16,000 feet), is planned for completion in 2012.

PALOMAR OBSERVATORY

Palomar Observatory is located on Mount Palomar, about 65 km (40 miles) north-east of San Diego, Calif. The observatory is the site of the famous Hale Telescope, a reflector with a 508-cm (200-inch) aperture that has proved instrumental in cosmological research. The telescope, built in 1948 and named in honour of the American astronomer George Ellery Hale, was the largest instrument of its kind until 1976.

In 1928 the Rockefeller Foundation's International Education Board awarded a $6 million grant to the California Institute of Technology (Caltech) for the construction of a 200-inch telescope to complement and extend the capabilities of Hale's Mount Wilson Observatory. In 1934, after several years of searching, the 1,867-metre-high (6,126-foot) Mount Palomar was selected as the site for the new instrument. In the next year the Corning Glass Works succeeded in the difficult task of producing a fully acceptable 200-inch Pyrex mirror blank. The 20-ton blank was shipped by rail to Caltech for grinding and polishing.

Construction of the 1,000-ton rotating dome, the split-ring equatorial mounting, and a complex mirror-support system began in 1936 and was managed by a team of Caltech and Mount Wilson astronomers, physicists, and engineers. Some of the nation's largest manufacturing firms, such as the Westinghouse Electric Company, were also involved. World War II delayed the telescope's completion until 1948. It had four times the light-collecting power of the next-largest telescope, the 254-cm (100-inch) reflector at Mount Wilson.

To take full advantage of a telescope of this unprecedented size, Caltech built two powerful Schmidt cameras, one 122 cm (48 inches) and the other 46 cm (18 inches), that surveyed the sky deeper than it had ever been before. The larger Schmidt camera produced the National Geographic Society–Palomar Observatory Sky Survey in the 1950s, which was a collection of 935 pairs of 36-cm (14-inch) square glass photographic plates that recorded, down to the 20th magnitude, all objects that were visible from Mount Palomar.

The 200-inch telescope operates in three optical configurations: at prime focus for wide-field deep-sky operations and for spectroscopy of the faintest and most distant galaxies; at an intermediate Cassegrain focus for detailed study of brighter objects; and at a subterranean Coudé focus for high-dispersion spectroscopy. By 1950 an extremely fast prime-focus spectrograph with solid Schmidt optics had become available; for decades this instrument made the Palomar telescope the most powerful for probing the dynamics of the universe. The 200-inch telescope was the first in the world to have an observing cage for the astronomer inside the telescope tube at prime focus; in the 1960s observations made from this cage determined that quasars were the most distant objects in the universe.

The observatory has been constantly upgraded with new technologies, mainly high-speed computers, servo-feedback systems, position sensors, and electronic detectors, such as charge-coupled devices (CCDs), that vastly improved both the efficiency and the sensitivity of the instrument.

From its inception the Palomar Observatory was administered jointly with Mount Wilson Observatory as the Hale Observatories by a consortium created by Caltech and the Carnegie Institution of Washington. Since 1980, Mount Wilson Observatory and Palomar Observatory have been separate entities. Mount Palomar also contains 152-cm (60-inch) and 61-cm (24-inch) reflectors and an experimental interferometer.

ROYAL GREENWICH OBSERVATORY

The Royal Greenwich Observatory was, until its closure in 1998, the oldest scientific research institution in Great Britain. It was founded for navigational purposes in 1675 by King Charles II of England at Greenwich, and the astronomer in charge was given the title of astronomer royal. Its primary contributions were in practical astronomy—navigation, timekeeping, determination of star positions, and almanac publication. The observatory began publishing *The Nautical Almanac* (1766, with data for 1767), which established the longitude of Greenwich as a baseline for time calculations. The almanac's popularity among navigators led in part to the adoption in 1884 of the Greenwich meridian as Earth's prime meridian (0° longitude) and the starting point for the international time zones.

The observatory was gradually transferred from Greenwich to Herstmonceux in Sussex from 1948 to 1957, in a search for clearer skies, and it was moved to the Institute of Astronomy of the University of Cambridge in 1990. A controversial cost-cutting measure, announced by the Particle Physics and Astronomy Research Council in 1997, brought about the shutdown of the observatory in October 1998. The institution's equipment and operations, including the William Herschel Telescope and other instruments located on La Palma in the Canary Islands, were consolidated under the UK Astronomy Technology Centre, headquartered at the Royal Observatory Edinburgh. Some historic instruments and resources at Cambridge were returned to the Old Royal Observatory, which was renamed the Royal Observatory Greenwich. The old observatory is open to the public and is administered by the nearby National Maritime Museum.

STONEHENGE

The archaeological site of Stonehenge is located about 30 km (18.5 miles) south of the circular monument of Avebury and 13 km (8 miles) northwest of Salisbury, in Wiltshire, England. Built in prehistoric times—the digging of ditches began about 3100 BCE—it is a monumental circular setting of large standing stones surrounded by an earthwork. Although their claim has been discredited, some have theorized that Stonehenge at one time may have served as an ancient observatory.

The Stonehenge that visitors see today is considerably ruined, many of its stones having been pilfered by medieval and early modern builders (there is no natural building stone within 21 km [13 miles] of Stonehenge); its general architecture has also been subjected to centuries of weathering. The monument consists of a number of structural elements, mostly circular in plan. On the outside is a circular ditch, with a bank immediately within it, all interrupted by an entrance gap on the northeast, leading to a straight path called the Avenue. At the centre of the circle is a stone setting consisting of a horseshoe of tall uprights of sarsen (Tertiary sandstone) encircled by a ring of tall sarsen uprights, all originally capped by horizontal sarsen stones in a post-and-lintel arrangement. Within the sarsen stone circle were also configurations of smaller and lighter bluestones (igneous rock of diabase, rhyolite, and volcanic ash), but most of these bluestones have disappeared. Additional stones include the so-called Altar Stone, the Slaughter Stone, two Station stones, and the Heel Stone, the last standing on the Avenue outside the entrance. Small circular ditches enclose two flat areas on the inner edge of the bank, known as the North and South barrows, with empty stone holes at their centres.

The modern interpretation of the monument is based chiefly on excavations carried out since 1919 and especially since 1950. Archaeological excavations in the latter part of the 20th century suggest three main periods of building—Stonehenge I, II, and III, the last divided into phases.

In Stonehenge I, about 3100 BCE, the native Neolithic people, using deer antlers for picks (the carbon-14 dating of which has helped to date the monument), excavated a roughly circular ditch about 98 metres (320 feet) in diameter; the ditch was about 6 metres (20 feet) wide and 1.4 to 2 metres (4.5 to 7 feet) deep, and the excavated chalky rubble was used to build the high bank within the circular ditch. Two parallel entry stones on the northeast of the circle were also erected (one of which, the Slaughter Stone, still survives). Just inside the circular bank they also dug—and seemingly almost immediately refilled—a circle of 56 shallow holes, named the Aubrey Holes (for their discoverer, the 17th-century antiquarian John Aubrey). The Station stones also probably belong to this period, but the evidence is inconclusive. In addition, a timber henge (circle) may have been erected at the site.

Stonehenge I was used for about 500 years and then reverted to scrubland.

During Stonehenge II, about 2300 BCE, the complex was radically remodeled. About 80 bluestone pillars, weighing up to 4 tons each, were erected in the centre of the site to form what was to be two concentric circles, though the circles were never completed. (The bluestones came from the Preseli Mountains in southwestern Wales and were either transported directly by sea, river, and overland—a distance of some 385 km [240 miles]—or were brought in two stages widely separated in time.) The entranceway of this setting of bluestones was aligned approximately upon the sunrise at the summer solstice, the alignment being continued by a newly built and widened approach (the Avenue), together with a pair of Heel stones. The double circle of bluestones was dismantled in the following period.

The initial phase of Stonehenge III, starting about 2000 BCE, was when the linteled circle and horseshoe of large sarsen stones were erected, the remains of which can still be seen today. The sarsen stones were transported from the Marlborough Downs 30 km (20 miles) to the north and were erected in a circle of 30 uprights (only 17 of which are still standing) capped by a continuous ring of stone lintels. Within this ring was erected a horseshoe formation of five trilithons, each of which consisted of a pair of large stone uprights supporting a stone lintel. The sarsen stones are of exceptional size, up to 9 metres (30 feet) long and 4,860 kg (50 tons) in weight. Their visible surfaces were laboriously dressed smooth by pounding with stone hammers. The same technique was used to form the mortise-and-tenon (dovetail) joints by which the lintels are held on their uprights, and it was used to form the tongue-and-groove joints by which the lintels of the circle fit together. The lintels are not rectangular, being curved to produce all together a circle. The pillars are tapered upward. The jointing of the stones is probably an imitation of contemporary woodworking.

In the second phase of Stonehenge III, which probably followed within a century, about 20 bluestones from Stonehenge II were dressed and erected in an approximate oval setting within the sarsen horseshoe. Sometime later, about 1550 BCE, two concentric rings of holes (the Y and Z Holes, today not visible) were dug outside the sarsen circle; the apparent intention was to plant upright in these holes the 60 other leftover bluestones from Stonehenge II, but the plan was never carried out. The holes in both circles were left open to silt up over the succeeding centuries. The oval setting in the centre was also removed.

The final phase of building in Stonehenge III probably followed almost immediately. Within the sarsen horseshoe the builders erected a horseshoe of dressed bluestones set close together, alternately a pillar followed by an obelisk followed by a pillar and so on. The remaining unshaped 60-odd bluestones were set as a circle of pillars within the sarsen circle (but outside the sarsen horseshoe). The largest bluestone of all, traditionally misnamed the Altar Stone, probably stood as a tall pillar on the axial line.

About 1100 BCE the Avenue was extended from Stonehenge eastward and then southeastward to the River Avon, a distance of about 2,780 metres (9,120 feet). This suggests that Stonehenge was still in use at the time.

Why Stonehenge was built is unknown, though it probably was constructed as a place of worship of some kind. Notions that it was built as a temple for Druids or Romans are unsound, because neither was in the area until long after Stonehenge was last constructed. Early in the 20th century, the English astronomer Sir Joseph Norman Lockyer demonstrated that the northeast axis aligned with the sunrise at the summer solstice, leading other scholars to speculate that the builders were sun worshipers. In 1963 an American astronomer, Gerald Hawkins, purported that Stonehenge was a complicated computer for predicting lunar and solar eclipses. These speculations, however, have been rejected by most Stonehenge archaeologists. "Most of what has been written about Stonehenge is nonsense or speculation," said R.J.C. Atkinson, archaeologist from University College, Cardiff. "No one will ever have a clue what its significance was."

Stonehenge and the nearby circular monument of Avebury were collectively added to UNESCO's World Heritage List in 1986.

UNITED STATES NAVAL OBSERVATORY (USNO)

The United States Naval Observatory (USNO) in Washington, D.C., is an official source, with the U.S. National Institute of Standards and Technology (NIST; formerly the National Bureau of Standards), for standard time in the United States. The positional measurement of celestial objects for purposes of timekeeping and navigation has been the main work of the observatory since its beginning. In 1833 the first small observatory building was constructed near the Capitol. Time signals for the public were first given (1844) by the dropping of a ball from a staff on an observatory building. In 1904 the observatory broadcast the world's first radio time signals.

The observatory has been enlarged and moved several times. A 102-cm (40-inch) reflecting telescope acquired in 1934 was moved in 1955 to Flagstaff, Ariz., to obtain better atmospheric conditions, and a 155-cm (61-inch) reflector has been in use at Flagstaff since 1964. An optical interferometer of three 50-cm (20-inch) telescopes was built at the Flagstaff station in 1996; three more telescopes were added to the interferometer in 2002. Other stations are maintained in Florida and in Argentina.

Statutory responsibility for "standard time" (i.e., establishment of time zones in the United States) is currently lodged with the Department of Transportation. The Naval Observatory is specifically responsible for standard time, time interval, and radio-frequency standards for use by the U.S. Department of Defense and its contractors. Both the USNO and the NIST maintain independent time standards, but since October 1968 they have been coordinated to maintain synchronization to approximately one microsecond. USNO broadcasts time and frequency information at intervals (as the NIST does on a 24-hour basis). Both agencies cooperate with the Bureau International de l'Heure in Paris.

URANIBORG

The Uraniborg observatory was established in 1576 by the Danish astronomer Tycho Brahe. It was the last of the primitive observatories in that it antedated the invention of the telescope (c. 1608); and it was the first of the modern observatories in that it was completely supported by the state and produced the first organized, extensive array of dependable data in astronomical history, including a catalog of more than 1,000 stars.

In 1576 Frederick II of Denmark granted the island of Ven (off the coast of southern Sweden, then under Danish hegemony) in fief to Tycho. A palatial three-story building was constructed in which student astronomers and staff were quartered and royalty was sometimes entertained. Instruments included quadrants, parallactic rulers, and armillary spheres, built to Tycho's demanding standards of accuracy. Johannes Kepler based his laws of planetary motion on computations with the precise data accumulated at Uraniborg. The observatory was abandoned when Tycho's fief was withdrawn in 1597.

VERY LARGE ARRAY (VLA)

The Very Large Array (VLA) is a radio telescope system situated on the plains of San Agustin near Socorro, N.M. The VLA went into operation in 1980 and is the most powerful radio telescope in the world. It is operated by the National Radio Astronomy Observatory.

The VLA consists of 27 parabolic dishes that are each 25 metres (82 feet) in diameter. Each dish can be moved independently by transporter along rails laid out in an enormous Y pattern. (The arms of this pattern extend about 21 km [13 miles] each.) The resolution of the VLA is altered by changing the positions of the dishes. The radio signals recorded by the component dishes are integrated by computer to give a resolving power equal to that of a single dish as large as 36 km (22 miles) in diameter, depending on the configuration of the array and the wavelength being observed. The VLA's maximum angular resolution is better than a tenth of an arc second, comparable to that of the Hubble Space Telescope at optical wavelengths.

YERKES OBSERVATORY

Yerkes Observatory is located at Williams Bay on Lake Geneva in southeastern Wisconsin. The Yerkes Observatory of the University of Chicago was named for its benefactor, transportation magnate Charles T. Yerkes, and was opened in 1897. It contains the largest refracting telescope (40 inches [1 metre]) in the world. The refractor has been used for solar and stellar spectroscopy, photographic parallaxes, and double-star observations, while other more modern telescopes at the site have been equipped for photoelectric, polarimetric, and spectroscopic applications.

Yerkes Observatory epitomized American astronomer George Ellery Hale's passion for building observatories with laboratories to link physics to the stars. When Hale left Yerkes in 1904 to establish Mount Wilson Observatory, his second in command and successor, stellar spectroscopist Edwin B. Frost, managed to keep the observatory open. Frost initiated formal graduate training at Yerkes, awarding the first Ph.D. in 1912.

Yerkes enjoyed a windfall when in 1926 Texas banker William J. McDonald left a bequest to the University of Texas to build an observatory. Texas, which did not have an astronomy program, approached Frost for advice, and this opened the door in 1932 to a cooperative agreement between the Universities of Chicago and Texas whereby an 82-inch (208-cm) reflector would be built in western Texas and be operated by Yerkes until Texas could build a viable program in astronomy, at which time the observatory would be used jointly. The site of the 82-inch reflector, the second largest telescope in the world at its dedication in 1939, became McDonald Observatory, near Fort Davis, Texas. McDonald, built and guided by the third Yerkes director, Russian American astronomer Otto Struve, was devoted to a wide range of astrophysical research, including stellar and planetary atmospheres and the nature of the interstellar medium. For Struve, McDonald Observatory symbolized the need in modern astrophysics for institutions to collaborate.

In his 15-year tenure as director, Struve built one of the world's strongest and most well-balanced observatory staffs, which included theorists such as Subrahmanyan Chandrasekhar and observationalists such as William Wilson

Morgan. He pushed his staff to execute observational programs that centred on the application of modern physical theory. In so doing, he was probably the first truly modern director of a major American observatory.

Because of light pollution from nearby Chicago, the research that can be conducted at the Yerkes Observatory site is limited, so the present observatory staff conducts observations worldwide. Yerkes engineers and astronomers have also built instruments for other observatories, such as the airborne Stratospheric Observatory for Infrared Astronomy and the Apache Point Observatory in Sunspot, N.M.

APPENDIX C: CONSTELLATIONS

NAME	GENITIVE FORM	MEANING	REMARKS*
Constellations Described by Ptolemy: the Zodiac			
Aries	*Arietis*	Ram	
Taurus	*Tauri*	Bull	*Aldebaran*; Pleiades, M1 (Crab Nebula)
Gemini	*Geminorum*	Twins	Castor, *Pollux*
Cancer	*Cancri*	Crab	Praesepe (star cluster)
Leo	*Leonis*	Lion	*Regulus*
Virgo	*Virginis*	Virgin	*Spica*; Virgo cluster of galaxies
Libra	*Librae*	Balance	
Scorpius	*Scorpii*	Scorpion	*Antares*; many star clusters
Sagittarius	*Sagittarii*	Archer	Galactic centre; many star clusters
Capricornus	*Capricorni*	Sea-goat	
Aquarius	*Aquarii*	Water-bearer	
Pisces	*Piscium*	Fishes	
Other Ptolemaic Constellations			
Andromeda	*Andromedae*	Andromeda (Princess)	M31 (Andromeda Galaxy)
Aquila	*Aquilae*	Eagle	*Altair*
Ara	*Arae*	Altar	
Argo Navis	*Argus Navis*	Ship Argo	now divided into Carina, Puppis, Pyxis, and Vela
Auriga	*Aurigae*	Charioteer	*Capella*; M36, M37, M38 (open star clusters)
Boötes	*Boötis*	Herdsman	*Arcturus*

NAME	GENITIVE FORM	MEANING	REMARKS*
Canis Major	*Canis Majoris*	Greater Dog	*Sirius* (brightest star)
Canis Minor	*Canis Minoris*	Smaller Dog	*Procyon*
Cassiopeia	*Cassiopeiae*	Cassiopeia (Queen)	Tycho's nova, 1572 (visible in daytime)
Centaurus	*Centauri*	Centaur	*Alpha Centauri* (nearest star to Sun), Beta
Cepheus	*Cephei*	Cepheus (King)	Delta Cephei (prototype for Cepheid variables)
Cetus	*Ceti*	Whale	Mira (first recognized variable star)
Corona Austrina	*Coronae Austrinae*	Southern Crown	
Corona Borealis	*Coronae Borealis*	Northern Crown	
Corvus	*Corvi*	Raven	
Crater	*Crateris*	Cup	
Cygnus	*Cygni*	Swan	"Northern Cross"; *Deneb*
Delphinus	*Delphini*	Dolphin	"Job's Coffin"
Draco	*Draconis*	Dragon	Thuban (polestar in 3000 BC)
Equuleus	*Equulei*	Little Horse	
Eridanus	*Eridani*	River Eridanus or river god	*Achernar*
Hercules	*Herculis*	Hercules (Greek hero)	M13 (globular star cluster)
Hydra	*Hydrae*	Water Snake	
Lepus	*Leporis*	Hare	
Lupus	*Lupi*	Wolf	
Lyra	*Lyrae*	Lyre	*Vega*; M57 (Ring Nebula)
Ophiuchus	*Ophiuchi*	Serpent-bearer	

NAME	GENITIVE FORM	MEANING	REMARKS*
Orion	*Orionis*	Hunter	*Rigel, Betelgeuse*; M42 (Orion Nebula)
Pegasus	*Pegasi*	Pegasus (winged horse)	"Great Square"
Perseus	*Persei*	Perseus (Greek hero)	
Piscis Austrinus	*Piscis Austrini*	Southern Fish	*Fomalhaut*
Sagitta	*Sagittae*	Arrow	
Serpens	*Serpentis*	Serpent	
Triangulum	*Trianguli*	Triangle	M33 (nearby spiral galaxy)
Ursa Major	*Ursae Majoris*	Great Bear	seven brightest stars are Big Dipper or Plough
Ursa Minor	*Ursae Minoris*	Lesser Bear	Polaris (the north polestar)
Southern Constellations, added *c.* 1600			
Apus	*Apodis*	Bird of Paradise	
Chamaeleon	*Chamaeleontis*	Chameleon	
Dorado	*Doradus*	Swordfish	Large Magellanic Cloud
Grus	*Gruis*	Crane	
Hydrus	*Hydri*	Water Snake	
Indus	*Indi*	Indian	
Musca	*Muscae*	Fly	
Pavo	*Pavonis*	Peacock	
Phoenix	*Phoenicis*	Phoenix (mythical bird)	
Triangulum Australe	*Trianguli Australis*	Southern Triangle	
Tucana	*Tucanae*	Toucan	Small Magellanic Cloud
Volans	*Volantis*	Flying Fish	

NAME	GENITIVE FORM	MEANING	REMARKS*
Constellations of Bartsch, 1624			
Camelopardalis	*Camelopardalis*	Giraffe	
Columba	*Columbae*	Dove	constellation formed by Plancius, 1605
Monoceros	*Monocerotis*	Unicorn	
Constellations of Hevelius, 1687			
Canes Venatici	*Canum Venaticorum*	Hunting Dogs	M51 (Whirlpool Galaxy)
Lacerta	*Lacertae*	Lizard	
Leo Minor	*Leonis Minoris*	Lesser Lion	
Lynx	*Lyncis*	Lynx	
Scutum	*Scuti*	Shield	
Sextans	*Sextantis*	Sextant	
Vulpecula	*Vulpeculae*	Fox	M27 (Dumbbell Nebula)
Ancient Asterisms Now Separate Constellations			
Carina	*Carinae*	Keel [of Argo]	*Canopus*
Coma Berenices	*Comae Berenices*	Berenice's Hair	Coma (star cluster); north galactic pole
Crux	*Crucis*	[Southern] Cross	*Acrux, Becrux*
Puppis	*Puppis*	Stern [of Argo]	
Pyxis	*Pyxidis*	Compass [of Argo]	
Vela	*Velorum*	Sails [of Argo]	
Southern Constellations of Lacaille, c. 1750			
Antlia	*Antliae*	Pump	
Caelum	*Caeli*	[Sculptor's] Chisel	
Circinus	*Circini*	Drawing Compasses	
Fornax	*Fornacis*	[Chemical] Furnace	
Horologium	*Horologii*	Clock	
Mensa	*Mensae*	Table [Mountain]	

NAME	GENITIVE FORM	MEANING	REMARKS*
Microscopium	*Microscopii*	Microscope	
Norma	*Normae*	Square	
Octans	*Octantis*	Octant	south celestial pole
Pictor	*Pictoris*	Painter's [Easel]	
Reticulum	*Reticuli*	Reticle	
Sculptor	*Sculptoris*	Sculptor's [Workshop]	south galactic pole
Telescopium	*Telescopii*	Telescope	

*First-magnitude stars are given in italics.

APPENDIX D: SELECT GROUND-BASED OPTICAL TELESCOPES

NAME	APERTURE (METRES)	TYPE	OBSERVATORY	LOCATION	DATE OBSERVATIONS BEGAN
Gran Telescopio Canarias	10.4	reflector	Roque de los Muchachos Observatory	La Palma, Canary Islands, Spain	2007
Keck I, Keck II	10, 10	reflector	Keck Observatory	Mauna Kea, Hawaii	1993, 1996
Southern African Large Telescope	11.1 × 9.8	reflector		Sutherland, South Africa	2005
Hobby-Eberly Telescope	11.1 × 9.8	reflector	McDonald Observatory	Fort Davis, Texas	1999
Large Binocular Telescope	2 mirrors, each 8.4	reflector		Mount Graham, Arizona	2008
Subaru	8.3	reflector		Mauna Kea, Hawaii	1999
Antu, Kueyen, Melipal, Yepun	8.2, 8.2, 8.2, 8.2	reflector	Very Large Telescope	Cerro Paranal, Chile	1998, 1999, 2000, 2000
Frederick C. Gillett Gemini North Telescope	8.1	reflector	International Gemini Observatory	Mauna Kea, Hawaii	2000
Gemini South Telescope	8.1	reflector	International Gemini Observatory	Cerro Pachon, Chile	2000
MMT	6.5	reflector	MMT Observatory	Mount Hopkins, Arizona	2000

NAME	APERTURE (METRES)	TYPE	OBSERVATORY	LOCATION	DATE OBSERVATION BEGAN
Walter Baade, Landon Clay	6.5, 6.5	reflector	Magellan Telescopes	Cerro Las Campanas, Chile	2000, 2002
Bolshoi Teleskop	6	reflector	Special Astrophysical Observatory	Zelenchukskaya, Russia	1976
Hale Telescope	5	reflector	Palomar Observatory	Mount Palomar, California	1948
William Herschel Telescope	4.2	reflector	Roque de los Muchachos Observatory	La Palma, Canary Islands, Spain	1987
Victor M. Blanco Telescope	4	reflector	Cerro Tololo Inter-American Observatory	Cerro Tololo, Chile	1974
Anglo-Australian Telescope	3.9	reflector	Siding Spring Observatory	Siding Spring Mountain, New South Wales, Austl.	1974
Nicholas U. Mayall Telescope	3.8	reflector	Kitt Peak National Observatory	Kitt Peak, Arizona	1970
Canada-France-Hawaii Telescope	3.6	reflector		Mauna Kea, Hawaii	1979
	3.6	reflector	La Silla Observatory	La Silla, Chile	1977
Hooker Telescope	2.5	reflector	Mount Wilson Observatory	Mount Wilson, California	1918
Samuel Oschin Telescope	1.2	reflector	Palomar Observatory	Mount Palomar, California	1948
	1	refractor	Yerkes Observatory	Williams Bay, Wisconsin	1897
Lick Refractor	0.9	refractor	Lick Observatory	Mount Hamilton, California	1888

APPENDIX E: SELECT RADIO TELESCOPES

FILLED-APERTURE TELESCOPES			
NAME	DIAMETER OF DISH (METRES)	SHORT WAVELENGTH LIMIT (CM)	LOCATION
Arecibo Observatory	305	6	Arecibo, P.R.
Green Bank Telescope	110 x 100	0.3	Green Bank, W.Va., U.S.
Effelsberg Radio Telescope	100	1	Effelsberg, Ger.
Lovell Telescope	76	6	Jodrell Bank, Cheshire, Eng.
Parkes Observatory	64	1	Parkes, N.S.W., Austl.
IRAM Pico Veleta Observatory	30	0.1	Pico Veleta, Spain
Haystack Radio Telescope	37	0.3	Westford, Mass., U.S.
RATAN-600	576	1	Zelenchukskaya, Russia
Nobeyama Radio Observatory 45-m Telescope	45	0.1	Nobeyama, Japan
Caltech Submillimeter Observatory	10	0.05	Mauna Kea, Hawaii, U.S.
James Clerk Maxwell Telescope	15	0.04	Mauna Kea, Hawaii, U.S.
Heinrich Hertz Submillimeter Telescope	10	0.06	Mount Graham, Ariz., U.S.

ARRAYS				
NAME	SIZE OF ARRAY (KM)	NUMBER OF DISHES	DIAMETER OF DISH (METRES)	SHORT WAVELENGTH LIMIT (CM)	LOCATION
Very Large Array	36	27	25	0.7	Socorro, N.M., U.S.
Westerbork Synthesis Radio Telescope	3.2	14	25	6	Westerbork, Neth.
Australia Telescope Compact Array	3	6	22	0.3	Narrabari, N.S.W., Austl.
Very Long Baseline Array	8,000	10	25	0.3	U.S. Virgin Islands to Hawaii
Combined Array for Research in Millimeter-wave Astronomy	2	16	6 x 10 m, 10 x 6 m	0.1	Big Pine, Calif., U.S.
Submillimeter Array	0.5	8	6	0.03	Mauna Kea, Hawaii, U.S.
Giant Metrewave Wavelength Telescope	25	30	45	21	Pune, India
Multi-Element Radio Linked Interferometer Network	217	7	1 x 76 m, 1 x 32 m, 1 x (32 x 25) m, 4 x 25 m	1.3	southern England
IRAM Plateau de Bure Interferometer	0.4	6	15	0.1	Plateau de Bure, France
Nobeyama Millimeter Array	0.6	6*	10	0.1	Nobeyama, Japan

*Sometimes the Nobeyama 45-metre filled-aperture telescope is used as a seventh dish of this array.

almucantars Lines of equal altitude around the sky.

aperture The maximum diameter of a light beam that can pass through an optical system, such as a telescope.

ascendency The condition of being dominant.

astrolabe Instrument used for making precise determinations of the positions of stars and planets, for reckoning time and observational purposes.

astrophysics Using physical and chemical knowledge to understand the nature of celestial objects and their physical processes.

azimuth The angle clockwise around the horizon, usually starting from the north.

biota Organisms that reside in a specific region or period, considered as a group.

calendrical Pertaining to the calendar.

collimator An optical device that produces parallel rays of light from a focal plane source, giving the appearance that the source is located at an infinite distance.

cosmology The scientific study of the universe as a unified whole.

cuneiform System of writing that originated in the ancient Middle East.

dark matter A component of the universe whose presence is discerned from its gravitational attraction rather than its luminosity.

the decans Thirty-six star configurations circling the sky somewhat to the south of the ecliptic.

diurnal Occurring daily or in the daytime.

ecliptic The great circle of the zodiac traced out by the Sun on its annual circuit.

ephemeris A table giving the positions of one or more celestial bodies, often published with supplementary information.

equinox Either of the two moments in the year when the Sun is exactly above the equator and day and night are of equal length; also, either of the two points in the sky where the ecliptic (the Sun's annual pathway) and the celestial equator intersect.

extrasolar planet Any planetary body that orbits a star other than the Sun.

interferometry The distribution of a common reference signal to an antenna that returns the received signal to a central laboratory, where it is correlated with the signals from other antennas.

isotropic Identical in direction and with regard to physical properties.

luminosity The quality of emitting light.

magnitude Unit of measurement for star luminosity.

nebula Any of the various tenuous clouds of gas and dust that occur in interstellar space.

nomenclature System of naming organisms.

parabolic Having the shape of a parabola, which is a conic section produced by the intersection of a right circular cone and a plane parallel to an element of the cone.

parallax The difference in direction of a celestial object as seen by an observer from two widely separated points, used to measure the distance of said objects from Earth and the Sun.

photometry The measurement of the brightness of stars and other celestial objects.

planispheres Representations of the celestial sphere on a flat surface.

precession Phenomenon associated with the action of a spinning body, consisting of a comparatively slow rotation of the axis of rotation about a line intersecting the spin axis.

quasars Any of a class of rare cosmic objects of high luminosity that often have strong radio emission that is observed at great distances.

rectilinear Moving in, or consisting of, straight lines.

redshifts An increase in the wavelength of electromagnetic radiation toward the red end of the electromagnetic spectrum.

scintillation The "twinkling" of stars as seen by the unaided eye.

spectrograph A device that enables astronomers to analyze the chemical composition of planetary atmospheres, stars, nebulas, and other celestial objects.

zenith The point on the celestial sphere directly above an observer on Earth.

ziggurats Terraced towers from which ancient astronomers tracked the movement of the Sun, Moon, and visible planets.

FOR FURTHER READING

Andersen, Geoff. *The Telescope: Its History, Technology, and Future.* Princeton, NJ: Princeton University Press, 2007.

Bely, Pierre. *The Design and Construction of Large Optical Telescopes.* Berlin, Germany: Springer, 2003.

Brunier, Serge, and Anne-Marie Lagrange. *Great Observatories of the World.* Richmond Hill, Ontario: Firefly Books, 2005.

Ferguson, Kitty. *Tycho & Kepler.* New York, NY: Walker Publishing Company Inc., 2002.

Gates, Evalyn. *Einstein's Telescope: The Hunt for Dark Matter and Dark Energy.* New York, NY: W. W. Norton & Company, 2009.

Hanel, R.A. *Exploration of the Solar System by Infrared Remote Sensing.* New York, NY: Cambridge University Press, 2003.

Harrington, Philip S. *Star Watch: The Amateur Astronomer's Guide to Finding, Observing, and Learning About Over 125 Celestial Objects.* Hoboken, NJ: John Wiley & Sons, 2003.

Heifetz, Milton D., and Wil Tirion. *A Walk Through the Heavens: A Guide to Stars and Constellations and Their Ledgends.* Cambridge, England: University of Cambridge Press, 2004.

Hirshfeld, Alan W. *Parallax: The Race to Measure the Cosmos.* New York, NY: Henry Holt and Company, 2002.

Jones, Kenneth Glyn. *Messier's Nebulae and Star Clusters.* Cambridge, England: Cambridge University Press, 2008.

Kanas, Nick. *Star Maps: History, Artistry, and Cartography.* Berlin, Germany: Springer Praxis, 2009.

Marriott, Leo. *Universe: Images from the Hubble Telescope.* New York, NY: Chartwell Books, 2007.

Mix, Dr. Lucas John. *Life in Space: Astrobiology for Everyone.* Cambridge, MA: Harvard University Press, 2009.

Moche, Dinah L. *Astronomy: A Self-Teaching Guide.* Hoboken, NJ: John Wiley & Sons, 2009.

North, John. *Cosmos: An Illustrated History of Astronomy and Cosmology.* Chicago, IL: University of Chicago Press, 2008.

Schulz, Norbert. *From Dust to Stars: Studies of the Formation and Early Evolution of Stars.* Berlin, Germany: Springer Praxis, 2005.

Seeds, Michael A., and Dana Backman. *Astronomy: The Solar System and Beyond.* Belmont, CA: Brooks/ Cole, 2009.

Tyson, Neil deGrasse. *The Sky Is Not the Limit: Adventures of*

an Urban Astrophysicist.
Amherst, NY: Prometheus
Books, 2004.

Wilson, R.N. *Reflecting Telescope
Optics I: Basic Design
Theory and Its Historical
Development.* Berlin, Germany:
Springer, 2007.

Wilson, Thomas L., et. al. *Tools of Radio
Astronomy.* Berlin, Germany:
Springer, 2009.

Wright, Helen. *James Lick's Monument:
The Saga of Captain Richard Floyd
and the Building of the Lick
Observatory.* Cambridge, England:
Cambridge University Press, 2003.

INDEX